Sir Ale

A Biographical Study

written by

Peter Darvill

Peter Darvill

Able Publishing

Sir Alec Clegg - A Biographical Study

Copyright © Peter Darvill 2000

ISBN 0 907616 67 4

Published by:

Able Publishing
13 Station Road
Knebworth
Herts SG3 6AP

Tel: (01438) 812320 / 814316 Fax: (01438) 815232
Email: fp@ablepublishing.co.uk
Website: http://www.ablepublishing.co.uk

Contents

PREFACE
by Sir David Attenborough

I had a number of uncles. Two were married to my mother's sisters. One, Alec, was her young brother. He was so much younger, in fact, that he was only a few years older than my elder brother Richard. And when I first remember him, he was unmarried. So he was different and special.

He was also very funny. A great practical joker. Once, when we were on holiday in Anglesea, playing on the beach, we saw a swimmer on the horizon, clearly heading towards the shore. We watched, astounded. When we stood up and waded ashore we saw it was Uncle Alec. 'Where have you come from?' we asked, our jaws sagging. 'Oh I swam across from the mainland,' he said. He had, of course, arrived to spend a few days with the family and instead of coming straight down to join us on the beach had swum round from the next bay up the coast. But my brothers and I had no doubt that he had swum the Menai Strait. Uncle Alec could do anything.

A car journey with him was full of interest and laughs. Humps in the road or bridges he called 'oo-ers', because of what they did to your stomach. But what qualified one to be an oo-er? Did it depend on how steeply it rose? Or did speed have something to do with it? If so, could you predict whether one, as you approached it, would be an oo-er or not? And how was it that a church spire in the distance was continually hopping from one side of the road to another? Uncle Alec, you see, was a marvellous uncle.

In later years when he was Chief Education Officer in the West Riding, and I was newly married, he stayed with us when he came to London for meetings. He still had a supply of jokes. They were nearly all based on the doings of children - sometimes his own, more often culled from his encounters with some of the thousands of Yorkshire children for whose education he had responsibility. His insight into childhood, his affection for children was deep and profound; and his concern that the talents and potential of every child should have every opportunity to flower was intense and unshakeable. He was, as I have said, an ideal uncle. And not just for me.

SIR ALEC CLEGG

INTRODUCTION

When I saw the tea chests full of tape recordings and the shelves of metal cabinets packed with films and files of private papers, I realised that for a budding biographer such sights could be a promised land, or a prison. The massive store of information had been brought to Woolley Hall and put in one of the cellars when the West Riding ended in 1974. It had remained there, undisturbed, for nearly two decades and it is fair to describe this collection as one of the most comprehensive on any twentieth century educationalist. It is a promised land, not a prison.

The collection is testimony to the thorough research, discussion and the use of administrative skill which can turn policy into practice in schools. Moreover time and time again one is reminded that a good public service depends on the quality of personal relationships within the service, and between the staff and the elected members. The collection is punctuated, often in unlikely places and in unexpected form, by personal letters which reflect the wide range of contacts acquired by Alec Clegg. These range from Ministers of Education, academics and artists to men and women from all walks of life. They wrote in many cases because he had touched a chord in their lives by what he had done or said. Looking at the title of one group of files, 'Strictly Personal', some sceptics might assume they contained sensitive items beyond the boundaries of a public servants' normal collection of correspondence. Others could anticipate attractive insights into the recesses of public life, potentially the sources of a champagne biography. Yet a thorough survey of routine corres-pondence illustrates many of the same characteristics of honest, uninhibited, personal expression. These common features underline the fact that the respect and affection for Sir Alec was rooted in personal qualities rather than office or title.

Harry Rée's study of 'The Life and Achievements of Henry Morris' illustrates how even in a time of deep economic depression in the 1930's imagination, stamina and personal energy could bring about long term advances in education. Many of the qualities Harry Rée identified in Morris's work were echoed in Sir Alec's achievements in the West Riding after 1945. These two outstanding educationalists saw schools as a source of social progress which could improve the lives of individuals and communities. Neither saw their departments as part of a framework of local government devoted solely to the efficient realisation of the policy decisions of elected members. Both realised their positions enabled them to influence policy and to accelerate, or slow down, those aspects of change which could improve or threaten the quality of education in schools or colleges. They lived in, and wrestled with, the ambivalence of their jobs. Their ideas had an impact far beyond their own authorities for both charted new routes for educational progress. Harry Rée ended his study with the words -

'...I hope that this book has gone some way to show, that the most maverick individual can work within the system, can bend it to constructive ends and can yet retain humanity, integrity and sensitivity.'

Alec Clegg was born into a family of teachers. His grandfather was a village schoolmaster and his father was headmaster of a secondary school in Long Eaton in Derbyshire. Alec Clegg went to his father's school and then to Bootham School in York. From there he went to Clare College in Cambridge where he took a degree in Modern Languages. After he completed his degree he went to the London Day Training College, which he describes as '... perhaps the luckiest thing that ever happened to me,' for there he listened to '... probably the most distinguished trio of educationalists lecturing together at any one time - Cyril Burt, John Dover Wilson and Percy Nunn.'

Alec Clegg got a job at St Clement Danes' Holborn Estate Grammar School and in an article in the Times Educational Supplement just after he retired he remarked in typical fashion that he was one of the few who got a job in the London area-

'... for which incidentally at that time there were more applicants than there were £'s a year offered for it.'

SIR ALEC CLEGG
THE MAN, HIS IDEAS AND HIS SCHOOLS

YEARS AT ST. CLEMENT DANES

St. Clement Danes' Holborn Estate Grammar School was originally in central London, in the Holborn Estate, before a new school was built on Du Cane Road Hammersmith. Sir Edward Du Cane, Surveyor General of Prisons, was renowned for his financial ability and emphasis on economy. The public buildings of Du Cane Road school, hospital and prison with the immense flat field of Wormwood Scrubs behind prompted Ian Nairn, 'Nairn's London', to ask the question, 'Could it be a marvellous place to grow up in?'

For a schoolboy who walked from East Acton each morning past the grim blocks of warders apartments, the prison itself, the Hammersmith Hospital and who finally reached school the answer was 'Yes'. But it was not this close and unusual juxtaposition of buildings which commanded attention but the smaller things such as the magpie moth caterpillars which swarmed in the hedges in front of the warders' flats in early summer. A matchbox full collected on the way to school could provide endless amusement after they were set free in boring lessons. Music and Geography were the best areas for such games. Mr. Johnson, the Music teacher, played and conducted with his back to the class whilst Geography lessons took place in the dark - comprising a sequence of slides plus commentary. In both cases the risk of detection was significantly reduced. The lampposts were another attraction for they were systematically covered with yellow fascist stickers readily available from Mosley supporters in the senior parts of the school. Once the Burlington School for Girls was built nearby clandestine links between the pupils of the two schools were soon established. Regular correspondence and meetings between Connie Cook and her attractive but slim companion 'Streaky' Bacon took place beneath the walls of Wormwood Scrubs Prison. As John Raimbach put it in his 'report' on the young Mr. Clegg, who taught French and Games at the school between 1932 and 1937:-

'Whilst Hitler and his Brownshirts were preparing to devour Europe, a young man called Mr. Clegg was busying himself teaching us restless young teenagers French in all its aspects and outside the classroom - coaching field events and football.'

By the 1930's the school was a two form entry direct grant Boys' Grammar School. Most of the fee payers were in one form for they had been in the school since the age of eight with the only female member of staff, Miss Smith. The other form was largely filled with scholarship boys. The fee payers tended to get the pick of the staff and some of the teachers who took the other form looked upon the scholarship boys, who came from Ladbroke Grove, Notting Hill and the rougher districts, as a lower order of society. The school could boast at least three senior staff who worked for examination boards. Each of them reminded us of this fact making regular appeals to the 'God' of examinations and how exam success would ensure a bright future. Other staff, especially in art and games, cultivated an easier, friendly relationship with pupils and it is significant that Alec Clegg is remembered more as a teacher of games than a teacher of modern languages. Rex Barrett remembers Alec Clegg reacted 'favourably' in connection with my efforts at long jump' and remarked that 'he was too fat to get anywhere near a five minute mile'. Similarly John Raimbach still recalls vivid snapshots of Alec Clegg as a person rather than for his teaching skills. His description of Alec Clegg in the classroom is worth quoting in full -

"His demeanour was gentle but firm, whilst his delivery was measured, articulate and unmistakably clear. He would pace up and down the rows of desks his hands behind his back and slid twixt his belt and hips, with his coat open. He had a liking for ungarish sports coats, flannel trousers and - as I remember - a penchant for hand knitted woollen ties in plain colours. A comforting and reassuring appearance.

He had a penetrating wit, and in a few well chosen words, which obviously came easily to him, he would paint a character vignette of a personality or situation, as the occasion arose. As often as not the victim would be some idiot (the class was full of them) who chose to initiate inordinate distractions from class procedure.

He was respected and liked by most of us schoolboys, but he really came into his own on the sports track. His enthusiasm was contagious, his expertise eagerly shared and the successes of the school's competitive performances were clear evidence of his influence."

The school magazine 'The Dane' for January 1937 contains an article by Alec Clegg on athletics divided into "do's" and "don'ts". The first of the don'ts was "Don't specialise too early". One of our greatest performers and teachers of field events, F.M.A. Webster, says, "That there is a time to specialise is undoubtedly true, but that time is not while one is still at school."

The talks he gave after he became Chief Education Officer for the West Riding contain occasional reminiscences of his work as a teacher.

In a talk he gave in 1973 on the changing role of the teacher, he said - 'When I started teaching in the early thirties my role was not very different from that of the teachers on my father's staff except that the curriculum had by then become ossified by external examinations.'

Qualified in French and German he reflected on the shortcomings of the 'Old translation method', geared to examination rather than conversation in a foreign country. He compared the translation method with his experience of learning German during a stay of four months in Germany. He felt a discussion between a language teacher and a psychologist might produce some useful ideas to improve the quality and effectiveness of language teaching, especially for the average pupil. His recollections of teaching French and those of his pupils point to the games field as something of a relief from the necessary routine of the classroom. Temporary relief was turned into permanent relief after four years teaching during which time he felt he had learned ... 'with some success how to fool external examiners.'

BIRMINGHAM, CHESHIRE AND WORCESTERSHIRE

Between 1939 and 1945 Alec Clegg worked in three authorities: Birmingham, Cheshire and Worcestershire. He described their differences as follows -

"The difference between Birmingham and Cheshire was a difference of administration, the difference between Birmingham and Cheshire on the one hand and Worcestershire on the other was a difference in educational purpose and ideal. In the first two their aim was the efficiency of the machine; in the third it was the quality of the product."

In Birmingham the Chairman of Education was Byng Kenrick, a man of great integrity, who established for Alec Clegg his ideal of what a person who opted for public service "... could and should be". One of the Kenrick Chamberlain family compared Byng to his cousin Neville, the Prime Minister, saying "Byng is a much finer man than cousin Neville".

Alec Clegg was the first Administrative Assistant appointed in Birmingham and initially he was given the freedom to devise his own programme of work. He decided to devote a week to each section of the Education Department. He filled two large volumes with his notes along with copies of regulations and forms which he described later as "... One of the best statements now in existence of what went on in an education office in the thirties."

The first volume centres attention on over a hundred issues which were part of the day to day work of an education office, but towards the end the under-lying economic and social problems of Birmingham and the country as a whole become more and more apparent. The second volume is largely a collection of forms and notes which deal with issues such as public assistance, unemployment and health. The predicament of many families at this time was summarised by B.S. Rowntree in 'The Human Needs of Labour', Page 128 -

"We are confronted then by the incontrovertible fact that the incomes of a considerable proportion of unskilled labourers must be substantially increased if their elementary human needs are to be met."

The two volumes deal with matters as wide apart as caretakers' incomes and their style of life and the sorts of questions that might be posed to applicants for teaching posts. For the week ending 17th October, 1936, two caretakers - one at Acocks Green the other at Hastings Road - earned £7-0-7 and £7-2-7 respectively. Added to the detailed analysis of each of these sums is the note that " ... this does not include increment for letting of chairs, card tables, crockery, tea urns, preparation of refreshments ... ". One of the caretakers was reported to have a new car each year whilst in other parts of Birmingham rumour had it that caretakers were able to buy holiday cottages. Rumour or not Alec Clegg was not exaggerating their comparative affluence for in 1936 the average wage for male heads of families was 63 shillings. The list of personal qualities and experience anticipated in applicants for caretaking posts was detailed and those thought to be promising were put on a Reserve List. A similarly careful procedure was used for probationer teachers.

In 1935 115 probationers were appointed to the authority, some went straight to permanent jobs, but the authority sought to adhere to the practice that probationers went to a good school for two or three months so that a reliable assessment of their potential could be made. At the start of the second volume Alec Clegg gathered a substantial list of questions which might be put to candidates for posts in infant, junior or senior schools. Four of those in the collection of forty three for candidates for junior schools were -

- What features of Infant teaching seem to you worth carrying over into Junior classes?
- By what means have you given reality to the teaching of one of the three "R's"?
- Do you think organised visits to places outside school are for Junior children worth the work they involve?
- How would you make your school really attractive to the eye?

It does not seem unreasonable to see in questions such as these the impact of Steward Street School, and to see also the beginnings of some of the developments Alec Clegg fostered in the West Riding.

The attention to detail is very apparent in the collection of forms and comments on the placements of youngsters from Depressed Areas seeking their first jobs under the Juvenile Transference Scheme. Fourteen authorities around Birmingham were taking part and a Clearing House Scheme was set up so that as Alec Clegg wrote

" ... we get in touch with the lads concerned and find jobs for them." Birmingham had its own Juvenile Employment and Welfare Sub-Committee which overlooked a system of vocational guidance. Alec Clegg's interest in young people went well beyond the achievement of qualifications and the acquisition of a satisfactory job. Perhaps the best example of what pleased him most is to be found amongst six detailed sets of notes on care and protection cases which came before the courts in Birmingham. The case concerned a sixteen year old girl who wished to get married. Her father's refusal to give his consent led to the mother leaving home and the girl running away. An Assistant Superintendent sought to get the father's consent as the girl was pregnant. After two adjournments the father gave in and the girl was able to marry. Alec Clegg's indelible stamp can be seen in the comment he added to the tidy typewritten account of the case. The Assistant Superintendent was invited to be best man " ... and is still in communication with the couple who are very happy indeed".

In his travels he visited 'an extraordinary school', Steward Street, which is described in graphic detail by the headteacher, Arthur Stone, in 'Story of a School', Education Pamphlet Number 14 (4). Also Alec Clegg found ' ... a very pretty assistant mistress at Paganel Road Infant School', whom he married.

The description of Steward Street School, situated in the older part of Birmingham, gives an insight into how imaginative teaching can, even in the most depressing circumstances, raise the spirit of youngsters and create confidence and self discipline. These qualities were essential to youngsters who in 1940 faced a world at war and an adult community which was now awake to the price to be paid for the wasted years between 1919 and 1939. As Arthur Stone says-

"The school itself was bounded by factories on three sides. The playground was entirely overlooked by factory windows and nowhere was there the possibility of encouraging a blade of grass to grow. The nearest park was half a mile away and there were no open spaces in near vicinity where children could play in safety ...".

"... These few words give you a glimpse of the stark ugliness of the surroundings in which these children lived."

The high quality of the creative work accomplished by the children in Steward Street School prompted Arthur Stone to stress -

"... what I want to point out here and now is that the beauty which came from these children could not have been superimposed by environment or by specially selected teachers, for we are just an inartistic lot of people, but the desire to create came because we allowed it to live, and because, maybe, in some way we could understand why it was there."

The young administrative assistant fresh from the formal framework of the grammar school found Steward Street 'extraordinary'. He could have treasured the experience as an exceptional memory. In fact he used it as an example to be followed. This is an early example of Alec Clegg's appetite to seek quality so as to create quality and to gain the deep satisfaction which comes to educationalists who can see schools contributing to the quality of life for individuals and communities.

Arthur Stone saw the arts as "... the basis of the education which should pervade this school." His priorities were clear -

'The three "R's" I decided, should become a secondary consideration, for I believed that, if I could get that confidence, that interest, that concentration from each child which arise from creative art, I had the ground well prepared then for the three "R's". It must not be thought that I undervalue in any way the importance of the three "R's". I believe, however, that there are things of much greater importance, the development of the personality of a child, his growth as a whole, demand greater

13

attention than the three "R's.' Arthur Stone's priorities were clear but the hard shell of imposed, repetitive practice still dominated the work of a majority of schools.

The war years 1939-1945 inevitably conjure up the picture of the evacuation of Dunkirk, the Battle of Britain and the change in atmosphere from stark survival to eventual victory. The change in social attitudes which took place under the pressure of war is clear when the appeasement of the Chamberlain years is compared to the defiant courage of Churchill"s premiership. The contrast can be found in the quieter spheres of public life, for instance in education. The war years brought changes which were as important, or more important than, the 1944 Education Act which to many was the high point of educational advance between 1939 and 1945. Richard Titmuss described this quiet revolution in his book 'Problems of Social Policy', Page 510 -

'These developments in the provision of meals and milk at school expressed something very close to a revolution in the attitude of parents, teachers and children to a scheme which, only a few years earlier, had not been regarded with much respect or sympathy. In place of a relief measure, tainted with the poor law, it became a social service, fused into school life, and making its own contribution to the physical nurture of the children and to their social education.'

The British seem at their best fighting against overwhelming odds and there is a tendency to overlook the sources of their resilience and success. Nonconformity in its widest sense is one source of these qualities and the nonconformists range from A.J.P. Taylor's 'Trouble Makers' to Edith Sitwell's 'English Eccentrics'; men and women who have pursued an ideal convinced they had something of profound individual, or social value. Richard Titmuss is one of those who will haunt this book - an example of the men and women who for one reason or another did not get the certificates and degrees which were regarded as the necessary passports to the higher orders of society. Perhaps the absence of a degree and the experience of everyday life is why Richard Titmuss appreciated and recorded the sea changes in public attitude which took

14

place in the Second World War. These years were the seed bed of Alec Clegg's ideas on the future of education.

The positive features of his work is Birmingham were absent in Cheshire where Alec Clegg began work in 1939. The outbreak of war brought evacuees from Merseyside into Cheshire and the districts receiving children soon resounded with graphic descriptions of the ill health and bad habits of the newcomers. The proportion of infested children ranged from 22 to 50 per cent amongst the Merseyside evacuees. Evacuation brought to many parts of Britain their first experience of the scale and character of urban poverty, the human cost of the depression of the 1930's. Neville Chamberlain, like so many others, was shocked at the social cost of the depression. In a private letter written in September 1939 he wrote -

"I never knew that such conditions existed and I feel ashamed of having been so ignorant of my neighbours."

The emergencies of war kept Alec Clegg busy. One of his jobs was to take two bus loads of pregnant women from Runcorn to Lytham away from a store of lethal gas. Another was to deal with the material and human problems of a Wirral grammar school. Not only had the school had its roof dislodged by a landmine but the senior science master had committed suicide and the head had sought sanctuary in Scotland. Alec Clegg reflected that he wanted a replacement with good nerves ... "I replaced him with a head who had previously told me that he never went to bed before 2 a.m. and always drank a pint of black coffee in the bath before doing so ..."

Alec Clegg's sense of humour rarely left him but it is scarcely discernible in his account of his years in Cheshire. He wrote -

"I am bound to admit that I learned less from Cheshire than from any other authority and I also met in that county, for the first time in my life, squalid and petty bureaucratic corruption which has left a bad taste in my mouth ever since."

In 1942 Alec Clegg became the first deputy Worcestershire had ever appointed. The new Chief Officer, Robert Logan, had gained some of his ideas from Henry Morris, Cambridgeshire's outstanding Chief Officer, who started the village colleges in that county. Worcestershire soon had a team of very high quality which included Elizabeth Carter and Diana Jordan. Later they were joined by Arthur Stone, from Steward Street School, and Violet Bruce from Cadbury's. The difference these individuals made to the education service was incalculable as Sir Alec put it

" ... the attitude, aims and intentions, the zest, the spirit and the ideals were very different. In Cheshire I did a technician's job, in Worcestershire I began to realise what professionalism in the running of a great human service really meant."

CHAPTER 2

THE PIONEER YEARS -
POST-WAR IN THE WEST RIDING

When one considers the state of any part of Britain in 1945 after six years of war, it is not enough to attempt a balance sheet of destruction and post war needs. It is crucial to understand how the euphoria of winning and the carry over of wartime hopes and attitudes would dictate peacetime development.

A.J.P. Taylor ends his 'English History 1914 - 1945' with this reflection on the British - P.600. "The British were the only people who went through both world wars from beginning to end. Yet they remained a peaceful and civilised people, tolerant, patient and generous. Traditional values lost much of their force. Other values took their place."

Resources for reconstruction and change were very scarce but the will to achieve major changes in the economy and society in general was very strong. It was much later that another historian, Arthur Marwick, was to reflect on the fifties as the time of the 'incredible shrinking social revolution.' The West Riding Education Service does not conform to this pattern. Political control changed but the momentum for creative development in education was maintained and extended. The compartment approach to history can easily miss this fact for it deals with particular issues, or sectors, of the education service and can overlook the interconnected impact of change.

The title of the book describing the first ten years of the West Riding Education Service after the Second World War is 'Ten Years of Change'. These changes can be presented in statistics such as - 60,000 more pupils in 1952 than in 1939 and 125,000 school meals a day in 1952 compared with 7,200 per day in 1939. These were significant advances but many schools required major capital expenditure even to reach an acceptable standard in teaching space and sanitary provision. Such matters are the material side of educational provision but as Alec Clegg wrote in the introduction to "Ten Years of Change"

"It is far less easy to describe to those not too well acquainted with what goes on inside a school the very significant changes which have occurred in aims, method, discipline, and the relation between child and teacher, yet these are probably more significant than mere factual changes ...".

In 'The Long Revolution' Raymond Williams traces the impact of three changes on the quality of modern life - the industrial revolution, the growth of democracy and what he terms the cultural revolution. The third is in his view the most difficult of all to interpret. It is centred on education and he maintains that it is in the primary schools where "the influence of the public educators has been effective". The term 'the long revolution' is invaluable in considering what Alec Clegg and the West Riding Education Service achieved between 1945 and 1974, for it broadens the span of attention from frameworks and statistics to the quality of relationships - in a word, the intangibles - of a public service.

It is not easy fifty years on to appreciate the nature of everday life in the West Riding after the war. However in 'The Inspector Remembers' one gets Cobbett's 'Rural Rides' repeated in the nineteen forties. Her Majesty's Inspector of Schools, Leonard Clark, moved from Devon and Somerset to the West Riding in 1943 and his diary between that year and the end of the war gives an insight into the state of the schools and the quality of education within them. Like Alec Clegg he remembered the amusing and bizarre aspects of his work - the memory of a charming, inefficient rural headmistress with 29 pupils, an age range from five to fourteen, with very little fluency in reading and deplorable written work; of a town school headmaster who explained the circle of boys wringing their hands in a dimly lit hall by saying "I gave them a spelling test this morning and every one of them left the 'd' out of pigeon. He travelled long distances by car and reflecting on what he found wrote - "I soon discovered that there was more life in the West Riding schools than in those with which I had been previously familiar. There was a real desire for education, even though it was often only centred on proficiency by the children in reading, writing and arithmetic".

Amongst the tape recordings Alec Clegg made of individual

schools, their teachers, children and work, is one of Brodsworth Primary School. Although it was close to the largest colliery in the South Yorkshire coalfield it retained its rural character. The original school consisted of two classrooms with a small school house in the centre. Careful adaptation changed the house into an annexe to the infant classroom. The bedrooms were altered into a staffroom and storage area. When one listens to the headmistress, Mrs. Scott, describing the work and organisation of the school one realises how good educatonal practice evolves. It is words such as 'progressive' and 'reform' which conjure up the image of sudden, widespread change. Mrs. Scott reflected on what to her seemed good sense -

"Family grouping - mixed age groups - the integrated day - non streaming - these are nothing new in the village school. We have been carrying on with it all successfully for years. It is our life. We are confident that young children are encouraged to tackle harder things than they would do in a single age group, just by seeing older ones doing things with success."

Whatever they were like - good, bad or idiosyncratic - Alec Clegg made sure that his work as Chief Education Officer contained a regular schedule of visits to schools. Moreover unlike Her Majesty's Inspector, Leonard Clark, his post gave him the opportunity to be a more powerful influence for weeding out the poor quality work and encouraging the good. As Clark said of these early years - "Alec soon showed himself to be one of the outstanding educatonalists of his day".

These snapshots of West Riding schools in the forties show their isolation and individuality. If they were going to retain this individuality in the face of rapid social and economic change after 1945 they would have to be harnessed to a carefully worked out county policy which fostered quality and innovation, identified poor schools and promoted improvements. The West Riding reflected the national emphasis on planning for the future by setting up the Sub-Committee for Post-War Eduction in 1942. Alec Clegg inherited initiatives from his predecessor A.L. Binns and added his own. Together these set in motion developments which were major strands of policy in the years to come.

The sub-committee structure in 1945 covered particular areas of the education service such as primary, further and agricultural education. A new committee for Policy and Fiance was set up so as to concentrate and simplify the policy making process. This change was one of the joint initiatives put forward by Alec Clegg and the Chairman of the Education Committee, Walter Hyman. Alec Clegg could concentrate his attention on this key committee and delegate regular attendance at the other sub-committees to officers of his department. This gave him the opportunity to invest a significant part of his time in regular visits to schools and colleges giving him a clear picture of an education service in action. These visits, along with regular reports from inspectors, advisers and divisional officers plus confidential reports, such as those from the Warden at Woolley Hall, gave him a regular, detailed supply of first hand information.

Thorough, effective formulation of policy needed to be matched by effective execution and the Chief Education Officer came across examples of potentially disastrous administrative delay and unlikely divisional decisions passed on for consideration by the county committee. An example of how a vital need at a school could, in an atmosphere of economy and bureaucratic delay, be held up for eighteen months was investigated for Alec Clegg in the summer of 1949. Sedbergh School needed a fire escape and an exchange of detailed typed minutes passed between the County Architect, the Fire Officer and the Divisional Education Officer. Each letter was dictated, typed, signed and replied to and all parties seemed to concur in avoiding the original plan to build a second staircase. Eventually a decision was reached - a rope ladder at £195, its justification "less expensive!" Such delay in the interests of economy could have had dire consequences yet all these officers were parties to the circuit of delay.

At the opposite extreme a potentially very expensive bizarre proposal could find an express route through the early stages of the decision making process of the West Riding.

Before 1939 a teacher at Pateley Bridge Secondary School had negotiated a deal with a local farmer to use one of the few relatively flat fields in the area as a football pitch. The teacher served in the war and returned to become the headmaster and reminded the farmer of his promise. The farmer said they could continue to use the field but he denied the boys passage across other fields to get there. In frustration the head requisitioned a helicopter and it got as far as County level before it was questioned and rejected.

This mixture of hard work, innovation, frustration and humour colours many aspects of the work of Alec Clegg during his early years in the West Riding. The creation of the Policy and Finance Sub-Committee could be compared to the development of cabinet government but, as at Westminster, changes in government and the influence of powerful inividuals could result not merely in the acceleration or slow down, but the reversal of policies. In education rapid change and uncertainty could be extremely damaging and it fell to the Chief Education Officer to find ways to safeguard educational progress.

Alec Clegg's predecessor had found Walter Hyman a very energetic chairman who could, if he felt the need, bring heavy pressure on an officer. A letter to Walter Hyman from the Clerk to the West Riding Council dated June 1934 was used by Binns and Clegg to define the boundary lines which lay between officers and councillors. The Clerk wrote that the Chairman has " ... no right of interference with the business of the County Council outside the meetings, nor has he any right or duty to give directions to, or otherwise interfere with officers or servants of the County Council and its Committees."

He added "I need hardly add that it will be a pleasure at all times to give you any information which may properly be required to assist you in the discharge of your duties ...". Clear definition went hand in hand with courtesy and mutual trust for officers sought to inform and help councillors in the performance of their duties. On the other hand they were alert to intentional or accidental trespass and Alec Clegg was prompt to ensure such matters were dealt with effectively.

The way council meetings were chaired and the function of deputations were also the subjects of detailed memoranda which presented details of questionable practice and advised on changes, which if made, could ensure efficiency and good practice. A proposed visit to a comprehensive school at Grange-over-Sands of "....an unnecessarily large deputation", "to undertake this work in the absence of any official" was part of a letter from the Chief Education Officer to the Clerk to the Council in November 1948. Much later, after he had retired, Alec Clegg reflected on councillors such as Ezra Taylor, King of Castleford, who was a dominant character on the Education Committee and who chaired the Staffing Sub-Committee. Ezra Taylor's behaviour on one occassion is described in these words -

Ezra was in the chair. "Three in favour and two plus me against". He said "I give my casting vote against so we'll readvertise."

It is interesting to set this recollection alongside the detailed memorandum on Committee Procedure which the Chief Education Officer produced in July 1948. It deals with the abuse of the Chairman's first vote and cited a variety of instances where such abuse occured in earlier meetings. The steady erosion of sharp practice and the build up of an area of common ground between the officers and councillors of all political parties took place beneath a top layer of sharp and often acrimonious debate.

The period 1949 to 1952 was marked by political instability. With Conservative support W.J. Johns, a Liberal, took over the Chairmanship from Walter Hyman in 1949. In 1951 Fuller-Smith, a Conservative, replaced W. J. Johns and, finally, in 1952 Walter Hyman returned. The choppy political waters of these years could be navigated by experienced councillors in all three parties but others saw these conditions as ideal for insurgent activity against other parties and the officers. The Chief Education Officer was accused of introducing multilateral schools by the back door in the 1949-1950 building programme. Seeing that the councillor who made this charge had received a letter a year earlier from Alec Clegg describing in exact terms the function of a Chief Education Officer in relation to the Education Committee it is surprising such a charge was made.

The significant sentence was - "An Education Officer can

deal with his Committee in two ways - give them the facts and let them decide, or give them the facts and his advice and let them decide. I prefer the latter way."

The Chairmanship of W.J. Johns brought further problems for he was at odds with the Vice Chairman, Walter Hyman. Alec Clegg described his position at the time ".... as between the Devil and the deep blue sea", adding "without specifying which is which". Johns was slow at dealing with correspondence and letters to Alec Clegg requesting answers from his Chairman increased in number in 1950. The Chief Education Officer was anxious to avoid such information reaching the Vice Chairman and had often to negotiate satisfactory compromises to protect the name of the service as a whole. Another aspect of the stressful situation was the increasing habit of committee members unexpectedly bringing up issues of detail at meetings. The established practice of preliminary notification and enquiry to officers or the Chairman was ignored and the absence of immediately detailed and satisfactory answers from the Chairman or officers was taken as a personal victory. Alec Clegg's personal papers reflect a growing concern on issues such as these and it is understandable that when writing to Lady Simon of Wythenshawe on the West Riding Development Plan in December 1949 he says -

"West Riding education, in my relatively short experience of it, has been very much the subject of fairly strident political views."

For Alec Clegg these early years in the West Riding, particularly 1949 to 1952, resemble the situation of a builder putting up foundations in stormy weather. However he was architect as well as the builder of a revitalised and expanded education service and undoubtedly enjoyed the inner satisfaction which accompanies creative change. Moreover his views were shared by Walter Hyman and by the team of officers he was building up after his appointment in 1945.

One of the central tasks in these early years was the production of the West Riding Development Plan for Primary and Secondary Education. The 1944 Education Act obliged authorities to ensure they had enough schools of each kind; to give exact details of schools which would have to be altered or closed; and to indicate where new schools would be needed. The vexed question of County and Voluntary Schools prompted the Committee to take the view that where there was only one school in an area, and if it was a Church school which required major adaptation or extension at public expense, it should become a County school. Cases such as this went to the Minister, and over a span of eight years the Minister ruled "against' rather than 'for' such suggestions.

The other matter of contention was the proposal to create all-purpose Secondary Schools - later called multilaterals. The final document is concise and scarcely reflects the vast amount of work and debate that preceded its completion. The careful presentation of the West Riding viewpoint is punctuated by passages such as this quotation from a report of the Advisory Council on Education in Scotland. One can guess that Alec Clegg and Walter Hyman were very happy to include it in their submission to the Minister -

"In defining their policy towards secondary education they have been unable to accept certain suggestions which have been made or implied in various reports of Ministerial circulars. They cannot, for instance, agree:

> That at the age of 11 children can be classified into three recognised mental types and should be allocated to grammar, modern or technical schools accordingly

or   that the numbers to go to each type of school should be determined by an arbritrary percentage of the age group;

or   that at the age of 11 children show certain aptitudes which can be relied upon to indicate the type of secondary school to which a child should be allocated.

The views which the Committee hold on the tripartite division of secondary schools have been excellently expressed in the report of the Advisory Council of Education in Scotland.

'The whole scheme rests on an assumption which teacher and psychologist alike must challenge - that children of twelve sort themselves out neatly into three categories to which these three types of school correspond. It is difficult enough to asssess general ability at that age; how much harder to determine specific bents and aptitudes with the degree of accuracy that would justify this three-fold classification.

Status does not come with the attaching of a name or by a wave of the administrative wand, and the discussion to date has left the position of the modern school neither defined nor secure. Indeed, it seems clear to many that the modern school will in practice mean little more than what is left, once the grammar and technical types have been housed elsewhere, and that the scheme will end not in tripartite equality but in dualism of academic and technical, plus a permanenty depressed element.

But even if the tripartite scheme were wholly feasible, is it educationally desirable? If education is much more than instruction, is in fact life and preparation for life, can it be wisdom thus to segregate the types from an early age? On the contrary, we hold that school becomes colourful, rich and rewarding just in proportion as the boy who reads Homer, the boy who makes wireless sets, and the boy without marked aptitude for either are within its living unity, a constant stimulus and supplement one to another.' "

The Devlopment Plan included proposals to build 241 nursery schools with 40 places in each. Wartime nurseries were to be taken over as day nurseries and the Education Committee would allow schools to be open during the holidays as nurseries or play centres. Economic recession in the fifties forced a change of policy and nursery provision dropped down the scale of priority. No children under five were to be admitted if admission entailed the formation of extra classes or the appointment of extra staff. Secondary education was the priority, and the pressing shortage of teachers ensured that the nursery school once more became the Cinderella of the Education Service.

A co-ordinated plan to cover the needs of handicapped pupils was worked out in relation to the whole North Eastern region. The commonest handicaps were catered for within the West Riding but children with rarer ailments were dealt with on a regional basis. At the same time as the Development Plan was being drawn up three other areas of education were the subjects of detailed studies;

25

Agricultural Education, Technical Education and Mining Education. The range and detail of these studies and the policy statements which followed made the platform upon which future development was based. As with a good building the foundation is rarely appreciated by a casual visitor, but once aware of its character, its value is unlikely to be underestimated.

The study of Agricultural Education in the West Riding was completed in 1950 and it drew attention to the pre-war acrimony between the three Ridings and Leeds University over the use and government of Askham Bryan College. Before 1939 Walter Hyman was a powerful source of dissent, maintaining that the University had neglected the educational potential of the majority who lived in rural areas by concentrating attention on " ... producing a few B.Sc.'s who have got fat jobs". His view was that "nothing worthwhile could be done for the agricultural education of school children and farm labourers until the Council did it for themselves".

In 1949 an agreement was reached that the college became the property of the West Riding in five years time, or when one of the authorities built a Farm Institute, whichever was the sooner.

The report went on to stress the importance of horticultural or agricultural education in secondary schools, particularly modern schools. It pointed out that expenditure on domestic science, woodwork and metalwork rooms was readily accepted, but that similar sums on practical equipment for horticulture was thought 'unwarrantable'. Yet, as this report went on, "... there is no doubt that the fundamental principles of horticulture and agriculture can do an enormous amount not only in the education of a child in a practical suject, but as a basis for his whole scientific training". The logical conclusion for technical education in any form was that "... the last years at school should be definitely vocational". The Brampton Ellis School was quoted as the example to follow, and the report anticipated similar projects being launched at Dinnington, Ripon, Skipton, Snaith and Tadcaster. Also, it put forward the proposal of a hill sheep farming institute in the Craven area. If satisfactory provision was made in full time education it was imperative that similar provision was made in further education. The projected developments in the five towns were envisaged as the likely bases for further initiatives.

The last section of the report dealt with administrative overlap and problems related to the maintenance of estates and the upkeep of playing fields. A committee had been set up before the report was complete, to address the issues raised in this final section.

Significantly, the section on Rural Studies in 'Ten Years of Change' describes how well-thought-out schemes gave secondary youngsters first hand knowledge in this field of study. It went on -

"This change in the Secondary School has been matched by a similar change in the Junior School, where instead of simple studies of the structure of individual plants children now study a typical area, meadow, hedgerow, pond and discover what grows there and why they grow together there." A case of good practice filtering down rather than up, or of good practice in some schools being copied by other schools. A very important source of such exchanges was Woolley Hall with its demonstration school garden and apiary. It is not out of place to quote a passage from a youngster's nature diary which is included in the Muriel Pyrah collection. It read -

"On Saturday I went to Leeds and on the way I peered through the bus window just in time to catch a glimpse of an extremely dirty, brown rat scamper across the corner of a field and into a hole in a wall. The whole incident took place in only seconds".

Education committee members with particular interests or questions received detailed letters from Alec Clegg, in which he followed his rule of giving the facts and adding his personal comments. In a letter to Alderman Collier in November 1950 he set down his thoughts on technical education. He saw the increase in the number of maintained Grammar Schools as a great advance, but pointed out that their presence was a barrier to attracting able youngsters into technical education. As he put it -

"We cannot direct youngsters into techncial education, and we should certainly no longer be content with accepting into the field of technology the leavings of the Grammar School." Alec

Clegg's vision was of a top quality technical high school with a bias towards mechanical engineering and sited near to firms which would support it and recruit from it. If the majority left at sixteen to go to local firms, those who entered the sixth form would concentrate on applied science and engineering with a view to entering university engineering departments. He continued - "I would strongly advise in the first such school to be built that the Committee erred on the side of generosity, while making the reservation that subsequent schools would be more modestly produced."

Alec Clegg felt that a technical strand grafted on to an existing Grammar School would be a major mistake. Even if started as a Grammar School it would not develop its own identity as a school which concentrated on the practical. To achieve this end he felt the appointment of an Assistant Education Officer who concentrated on technical education was essential.

Provision for mining education had been made at Technical Colleges in the South of the Riding in the thirties, at Dinnington, Whitwood and Mexborough. The main concern expressed after 1945 was that only a small number applied for the scholarships the West Riding offered to those wishing to go into the mining industry. Demand for technical courses in this field was increased by the introduction of the Ladder Plan which laid it down that youngsters going into mining had a three month initiation course during which time they spent half their hours in Technical Colleges and the other half of their training at the mines themselves.

The initiatives taken by the Education Committee depended very much upon an ever increasing supply of teachers and new training colleges were established at Wentworth Woodhouse, Bretton Hall and Ilkley. Two emergency training colleges were established at Harrogate and Wakefield, but Alec Clegg had difficulty with the Committee on the issue of teacher secondment to staff such colleges as temporary lecturers. In May 1946 the Committee refused to second serving teachers for more than a year. The fear of losing permanent staff was eventually overcome by the combined efforts of the Ministry of Education, the previous Chief Education Officer A.L. Binns and Alec Clegg; all determined not to put the future at risk by a fixation on immediate needs. The result was that the Committee rescinded its previous resolution and agreed secondment for the full term of the emergency college scheme.

The provision of high quality courses for student teachers and trained teachers was crucial to the expansion and improvement of Britian's education services. In the West Riding the purchase of properties recently used for wartime services or vacated by lordly owners provided an opportunity to meet this pressing need. Properties such as the Wells House Hotel at Ilkley along with Grantley and Woolley Hall were developed as colleges. The process of purchase, renovation and furnishing was, especially in the case of Ilkley Training College, a modern version of 'Pilgrims Progress' - for Alec Clegg a triumph over torments.

Conflict within the council as to which building should be brought caused stress and delay. The imaginative adaption of aristocratic premises to the needs of college staff and students was not easy within limited budgets and with the post war shortage of building materials and furnishings. The very extensive collection of letters and memoranda dealing with Wells House illustrates not only the stamina needed to get a scheme agreed and funded, but the imagination and forethought that went into the aims and the plans of the college.

Alec Clegg's first hand knowledge of these properties was essential in the committee discussions which preceded and followed their purchase. The decision to purchase Wells House which become Ilkley Training College was carried by 22-18 in autumn 1950 - an indication of the closeness of the debate. After the purchase of these buildings Alec Clegg played an important part in their development an example of which is the furnishing of Woolley Hall. The names associated with the physical changes included Gordon Russell, an outstanding furniture designer, whilst the first course included poets such as Edith Sitwell, Robert Gittings and Edmund Blunden.

The correspondence and papers relating to the purpose, purchase and rehabilitation of Woolley Hall between 1945 and its official opening in 1952 are a fascinating record of an educational project which is entering its fifth decade of life.

Its durability is testimony to the quality of its origins and development. Like a major waterway it could change its course, but it had a continutiy which gave it a durability and character all of its own. After one has read and absorbed the content of a collection of papers the sequence is clear; so too are the significant, or in present day terminology, the key stages. Yet the character of the events is often embedded in the trivial or the unusual. The tale of the Aga cooker or of the wall fittings for display illustrate Alec Clegg at his mercurial best - imaginative, energetic, persistent and able to lubricate the vicissitudes of everyday life with a unique sense of humour.

If one wanted a symbol of post war shortages of household goods then the Aga cooker delivered to Woolley by Molletts of Leeds would be perfect. A substantial part of the cooker comprised one that had spent the war rusting in the open at Mirfield. Parts from a similar cooker were used to patch up the one which was delivered and installed. Alec Clegg pointed out that the cooker was not guaranteed, was not bought from the official Aga agents and that he wanted to see whosoever was responsible for its purchase and installation. The final sentence in the correspondence read -

"When this cooker has been installed I must ask you and your colleagues to cook in it, in order to reassure me before the Hall is opened that the cooker does in fact work."

Display was a feature of many West Riding schools and Woolley Hall played its part in encouraging teachers to make classrooms and corridors attractive places. A detailed set of questions on display areas went to Diana Jordan, the first Warden of Woolley, and to advisers such as Basil Rocke. They were asked about the space required, the manner of fitting to the walls and how best to present children's work. Not long before Woolley was opened Alec Clegg wrote to the County Architect complaining of the charge of £8-15-0 for putting up fifty plastic notices. The letter ended -

"If you have any other jobs of this kind would you be so good as to let me know in order that I might proffer my services. I should think that as piece work this is probably much more remunerative than being the Chief Education Officer of the West Riding."

The final phases of repair and alteration were monitored weekly by Bill Morrell, a long serving member of the Advisory team and later Chief Adviser of North Yorkshire. His succinct comments were matched by his minute, neat writing - a reminder of his infallible way of emptying his 'in tray' by scribing a concise reply on any spare space of the original enquiry.

Perhaps the greatest threat to the establishment of Woolley as a centre for refresher courses came just before Christmas in 1951. Alec Clegg wrote to his friend, Toby Weaver, at the Ministry of Education asking if there was any truth in the rumour that many colleges of further education were to be closed, and that a college such as Woolley would not be allowed to open. The depth of Alec Clegg's attachment to Woolley was expressed in this letter -

"If the ban were to fall on this project it would, I think, depress me more than anything else that I have attempted in this county ...".

As the struggle to complete the refurbishment of Woolley neared its end, the focus of attention turned to the courses which were to be arranged. In October 1945 Alec Clegg had described the sort of refresher course he envisaged -

"One type is obvious, teachers must be acquainted with the latest methods in the teaching of their subjects, arithmetic or dancing, Latin or field games. More important, however, is the need for a direct attack on their general sensibilities and breadth of outlook. This can only be effected by bringing them into contact with the best minds in the country, either in industry or music, commerce or art, agriculture or theatre. These two aims can be combined in one course by the careful selection of speakers and lecturers."

The difference between what Woolley Hall offered in 1952 to what teachers experienced on a residential course in 1947 was vividly described by Alec Clegg to Mrs. Bland, a County Alderman from Settle. Three courses were held in the October week that year. One course took place in a modern school. It closed at four o'clock, was cleaned and by six o'clock a group of thirty young, middle aged and elderly women teachers had arrived. Thirty camp beds were already there but the blankets from County Supplies were damp when they arrived. The teachers lived and worked in the school for a week without a single easy chair at their disposal. Woolley promised to give reality to the term refresher course.

In his speech at the Official Opening of Woolley Hall Sir John Maud described it as "... the headquarters of civilization for the West Riding". An over the top remark, or perhaps one with more significance than the speaker realised. The first brochure to describe Woolley Courses contained a foreword by Edith Sitwell which in its own way explored the same vein of enquiry as Sir John Maud. It was a vein which led to children's writing and poetry and to the intangibles of human development. Edith Sitwell wrote -

"I hope that this will be the first of many such conferences, both in my native county of Yorkshire and elsewhere, for in a world which today is torn asunder by so much cruelty and misunderstanding, there is, perhaps, a greater need than ever to direct our thoughts and feelings towards those things which are eternal and incapable of man's measurement." (Foreword to 'Poetry and Children' a course which ran from 21st to the 27th October, 1952.)

Forty years later Richard Hoggart in an article on the beginnings of the Welfare State, looked back to Alec Clegg's span of office in the West Riding referring to him as one "... of the great proconsuls among chief education officers who was loved because he stood for something, was not afraid to say so and respected your right to argue back". Woolley Hall is still the place where such debate can take place.

In terms of personal effort and stress the cost of laying thorough foundations for widespread progress in the West Riding Educational Services was considerable. Men such as Eric Sharpe at Keighley, which became the solitary excepted district in the West Riding, found divided loyalty, firstly to his employer the West Riding, and, secondly to local councillors pressing for excepted district status, almost unbearable. He wrote of bitterness in relationships and his personal need for peace of mind and refreshment of spirit. The political cross currents in the West Riding played a major part in prompting many staff to apply for jobs elsewhere. Seven from the West Riding applied for the Deputy's post in York and Alec Clegg wrote to Oldman, the Chief Education Officer in York, of "... the general flood of applicants from my staff towards yours".

The letters that passed between Alec Clegg and many of his staff are a searching examination of their work, their ideals and the relationship between the department and the education committee. Eric Sharpe said he could recover peace of mind as an Assistant Master in a Grammar School, another condemned "... the crocodile tears of the benevolent but economically minded powers that be."

When Alec Clegg wrote his reminiscences for the Times Educational Supplement in 1974 he devoted a substantial part of the third instalment to how he faced up to the same situation as caused such unhappiness to people such as Eric Sharpe. The passage deserves quotation in full for it reminds one of the simply expressed but profound final verse of Robert Frost's poem 'The Road not Taken' -

'I shall be telling this with a sigh,
Somewhere ages and ages hence;
Two roads diverged in a wood, and I -
I took the one less travelled by,
And that has made all the difference.'

"... if I exclude officers with whom and under whom I worked, the man who gave me the wisest support was Sir Samuel Gurney Dixon of Hampshire. We rarely met, but for reasons which I now find difficult to explain we kept up a correspondence until the time of his death. I received few letters of such wisdom that they altered the course of my life. Some six years after I became Chief Education Officer of the West Riding, political and other pressures were, I felt, almost more than I could bear and I wrote to Gurney Dixon wondering whether or not I should seek another post. I still find his reply deeply moving. Indeed, I know of no statement of its kind more telling in its wisdom.

'If we can satisfy ourselves as to this, then other lesser ideals, however good and praiseworthy and attractive in themselves may in effect be, for us, siren voices turning us away from the true course of our lives. A man wishes to earn a high salary in order that he can give his wife a good home and his children a sound education and make some provision for his family should he die - all of these things being perfectly legitimate and worthy objects to strive for, but siren voices if they deflect him from using his powers and gifts in the way they ought to be used.

Or a man goes into political life, which is distasteful and irksome to him, from a strong sense of duty and for the satisfaction of feeling that as far as in him lies he is promoting the welfare of the nation. But increasingly as time passes, he comes to hate the insincerity and dishonesty and misrepresentation and self-seeking and time serving which seems inseparable from politics and is tempted to abandon it and seek an easier and more congenial way of life. This is to leave the government of the country to those who are less honest and sincere and less disinterested than he is and without his sense of service to the nation and he feels that he is being tempted to desert his post and must not listen.

Or a highly qualified surgeon has one consuming ideal in his heart which is to preach the gospel in equatorial Africa, and he sacrifices a home in England, perhaps marriage and children of his own, money, health, and prospect of professional status, perhaps a university chair or a title, learned societies, pioneer research and old friendships and associations, all these being laudable ideals which appeal to him no less than to other men but which are for him siren voices to which he knows he must turn a deaf ear.

There are times in every man's life when he must decide what in his inmost heart he wants to make of his life.'

The letter went on to apply this kind of reasoning to my moment of indecision with a sympathy and a wisdom which left me in no doubt as to what I should do. Thereby I incurred a debt which I could never repay.

CHAPTER 3

THE DEVELOPMENT PLAN

The centrepieces of education were the schools, and the very thorough local surveys of primary and secondary provision in each area gave a complete picture of what was already in existence in the West Riding. Formal meetings followed informal ones in each area and discussion was followed by proposals for the future. Priorities in terms of buildings and resources, human, and material, could be calculated but the ends to which these would be directed were another matter. This chapter addresses the evolution of West Riding policy in the early years of Alec Clegg's term as Chief Education Officer. Furthermore it explores how far and how extensively and effectively it was carried out.

The incredible shrinking revolution is reflected in this comment on Page 134 of 'Ten Years of Change' where it states -

"It has become fashionable to ridicule the vast amount of work which the preparation of the Development Plan entailed and to condemn the unreality and idealism of the early post war years."

Yet this work fuelled the steady and increased amount of progress made in the West Riding. The book is punctuated with quotations from the work of Charles Hoole who taught in Yorkshire over 300 years ago. It is difficult to escape the conclusion that these quotations reflect the ideas of Alec Clegg, snapshots of his ideals - pertinent and properly attributed to Charles Hoole !

The first quotation used by Alec Clegg, page 9, is -

"The sweet and orderly behaviour of Children addeth more credit to a school than due and constant Teaching." The emphasis is upon the quality of personality rather than classroom achievement.

SECONDARY SCHOOLS

The crucial issue in relation to secondary schools was the classification of pupils prior to entry into grammar, technical or modern schools. Expert views were sought on whether or not it was possible to detect special aptitudes in eleven year old children. Dr. Fleming felt that there was no reliable evidence as to when particular aptitudes emerge. She added that selection which took account of interests, ambitions and performance in a given situation could be a potentially more reliable method. Furthermore she pointed out that this course of action was taken by Army Selection Boards. Professor Thompson of Edinburgh went a little way towards accepting the view that indications of special aptitudes can be detected at eleven, but he said no great reliance can be placed on them. Sir Fred Clarke felt it was not possible to allocate children to schools according to aptitude and that the only sensible course of action was to maintain the maximum degree of fluidity between secondary schools in a given area. These and other expert pieces of evidence enabled the West Riding to state that it was not possible to divide youngsters into three mental types and fit them into an appropriate place in a tripartite system. Moreover when the extent and character of secondary provision in particular divisions of the West Riding were compared, the glaring inequalities were abundantly clear.

In a memoranum to the Sub-Committee in July 1946 Alec Clegg reduced the problem before the Education Committee to two simple facts -

"... that we must not blindly divide our secondary schools into technical, grammar and modern schools, but must by experiment discover the needs of children of 11+ and differentiate our schools gradually according to our discoveries."

The memorandum continued - ·

"Secondly, that for the moment we cannot allocate children to secondary schools according to their age, ability, aptitude, interests and ambitions, becuase we do not know how to do so. We can only try and improve the cumbersome machinery of calculation which we have and try by experiment to build a more sensitive and discriminating instrument which will enable us to treat each child according to his needs."

Alec Clegg and his staff ranged widely for evidence on secondary organisation, from the United States to New Zealand, from Scotland to Czechoslovakia and within the private sector they considered the size and organisation of schools such as Eton and Winchester. The most detailed of the studies was of Scottish secondary education and it was accompanied by three visits to Scottish schools. A letter from F. Arbuckle of the Scottish Education Department contained this sober reflection on their omnibus schools which took all youngsters in an area from 12 to 18 -

"It must, however, be remembered that most of our omnibus schools are not new creations but are often old established secondary schools, originally with a fairly definite academic bias, which have broadened their scope to provide for a much wider range of pupils."

The West Riding visitors thought that even the school at Kirkcaldy which had an 'extraordinary variety of courses' was essentially academic. One of the conclusions was that the Scottish system was so different that it was very dangerous to draw analogies between Scottish and English secondary schools. Alec Clegg's report pointed out the less intellectual youngster received a better education in a good West Riding modern school. It was better fitted to youngster's needs. The positive conclusion, which was supported by very detailed evidence, was that omnibus schools did not suffer in comparison with Scottish selective grammar schools.

NUMBER OF PLACES GAINED AT GLASGOW, EDINBURGH, ST ANDREWS AND ABERDEEN UNIVERSITIES UNDER THE BURSARY COMPETITION - 1946

	Omnibus Schools Under LEA	Voluntary Omnibus Schools	Selective LEA Schools
ST ANDREWS	6	-	8
EDINBURGH	19	-	7
GLASGOW	13	2	10

	Selective Voluntary Schools	Selective Part LEA
ST ANDREWS	3	2
EDINBURGH	17	7
GLASGOW	15	10

ABERDEEN UNIVERSITY

	Omnibus Schools Under LEA	Voluntary Omnibus Schools	Selective LEA Schools
ARTS	6	-	14
SCIENCE	7	-	14
MEDICINE	8	-	13

	Selective Voluntary Schools	Selective Part LEA
ARTS	5	-
SCIENCE	4	-
MEDICINE	3	1

The reassurance that an omnibus school enabled as many, or more youngsters, to reach traditional destinations was helpful to the West Riding visitors. However they expressed an unease about the formality of the Scottish schools - not merely the secondary but the preparatory ones as well.

The evidence from New Zealand was instructive in how to reduce the influence of the universities on the curriculum, particularly of the ablest pupils. Dr. Beaby, Director of Education in New Zealand wrote -

"... that the School Certificite conducted by the Universities was narrowing the curriculum towards the age of 16. They decided, therefore, to divorce the School certificate from the Universities and to introduce the system of accredited schools by which students are admitted to the Universities on the recommendation of the Heads of the schools and the representatives of the Director of Education."

The price paid for this apparent freedom for the schools was a national curriculum.

The large American secondary schools which were of the multilateral type catered for two thousand pupils and a conference in London in August 1944 which considered their introduction in the capital thought they were 'a hazardous experiment' in English conditions. There were arguments against establishing large schools to avoid selection. Probably the experience of small secondary schools contributed to the view that it would be "...impossible to inculcate into pupils ... a spiritual view of life without which learning and technique are barren." From the point of view of youngsters it was felt that there would be a " ... fear of the general lack of tranquillity and serenity which would result from so large an organisation ... a feeling of loneliness for a certain type of child." The case was closed with the generalisation that "multilateralism aimed at elasticity but in practice worked out as large scale regimentation." Later in 1949 a visiting American Professor at Manchester University wrote in The Journal of Education on the conclusion of Harvard University on 'General Education in a Free Society' it included praise for the comprehensive high school, the exact words, adding the succinct comment "that the high school is too fast for the slow and too slow for the fast." Other information gleaned from one of Alec Clegg's friends in France on the education policy of Vichy France and from the Professor of Education at Prague University's public lecture on 'The Multilateral School in Czechoslavakia' added little to what had already been gathered on secondary education.

Alongside evidence from abroad was that which Alec Clegg got from within the West Riding and from schools such as Eton and Manchester Grammar School. Within the West Riding the interwar period had seen a significant development of technical education.

A careful memorandum to the Sub-Committee dated 20th April 1948 summarised twenty years of alternative courses which were developed in Grammar Schools, courses which in many cases were related to the major industries of an area. Courses related to engineering, textiles and agriculture were established in schools one of the best examples of which was Keighley Grammar School, formerly Keighley Trade and Grammar School. Ten examples are quoted in this memorandum but the sad conclusion at the end is - "There are still remnants of these innovations in the schools but that they failed to mature as was originally intended is accounted for by lack of support by the Board of Education and the weight of grammar school tradition impressed upon the schools by the School Certificate, Higher School Certificate, and State and Major Scholarship Examinations."

The size of Manchester Grammar School and Eton was in part the result of steady growth not experiment. Furthermore the character of these schools was as important as, or more important, than the site. Richard Ollard sought a concise expression of Eton's quality when he concluded - Page 202 'An English Education' - "The leisureliness, the comprehensiveness, the tolerance of the Eton regime of those days deriving from its aristocratic inheritance all favoured individual rather than corporate development. Its tradition of scholarship set a pattern of discipline." Many old Etonians found a place in modern Cabinets others such as George Orwell, Aldous Huxley and John Maynard Keynes are reminders that the school did not just turn out upper class carbon copies. Merely to concentrate on size in relation to large public schools is to miss the point completely for the character of the institution is left out.

Winchester deliberately limited its size to around five hundred despite its popularity. Size was a secondary consideration when set against the qualities which gave a school its individuality as an institution.

The debate within the West Riding on the future of secondary education led to correspondence between Alec Clegg and some of the heads of grammar schools. The exchange between Mr. Hugh Leslie Watkinson of Mexbrough Grammar School and Alec Clegg is of particular interest. Watkinson, aged 55 in 1947, held this headship about as long as Alec Clegg held the post of Chief Education Officer. In February he wrote supporting multilateralism but felt it would face very considerable opposition despite the support of many young teachers. The stumbling block would be "the orthodoxy of the older members".

One problem the large school might face was the teaching of subjects such as the Classics. Watkinson provided such teaching at Mexborough and a letter from Bec School in London which he forwarded to Alec Clegg described how a handful of boys, six, started Greek in the fourth year and later went into the sixth form. Having been head of a small grammar school and then moved to probably one of the largest in the country he was able to reflect on the realities experienced in schools which differed a great deal in size.

As head of a small school he knew a majority of the pupils, at Mexborough with between five hundred and a thousand pupils this was not possible and he reflected that

"I know from my own experience that in my own school I do not know the mediocrities, having dealings only with the very good and the delinquents. Candidly I have accepted this disability and I have inspired my Form Masters and Form Mistresses to take upon themselves many of the things that I used to do as Headmaster of a small Grammar School. For example, enquiry into home circumstances of pupils, visiting the sick."

He felt that the Grammar School at Mexborough which was next door to Adwick Road School, a secondary modern, could be amalgamated for a multilateral experiment. Not the least of the gains he foresaw was the social collusion which might result from the mixing of children from different backgrounds. The letters are sincere and reflect the composure of a man whose skill and independence as a head was widely acknowledged, but as he said "my views are making, and will make, me very unpopular with my colleagues, but I cannot help that."

The prestigious place of Classics in the Grammar School curriculum had been stressed by Eric James, headmaster of Manchester Grammar School, and he argued for bigger and better grammar schools rather than multilaterals which he felt would not be able to support small, uneconomic groups studying Classics or Modern Languages. Hugh Watkinson answered this objection and moved the debate into the field of social policy. As multilateral and bilateral were replaced by comprehensive schools as the alternative to the tripartite system, the issue became political. It is no accident that the Citizens Party was born in Mexborough to defend the Grammar School, and it was no accident that one of its founders was a grammar school teacher.

The place of Classics in the curriculum was not a major issue, but it loomed large in the debate for a while. So too did the prospect of concentrating over a thousand youngsters in one building. The 1939-45 war had prompted large scale evacuation of school children. Why, some asked, were authorities "considering massive schools which could be an invitation to terrible disaster during war?" The debate on the future of secondary education was very wide ranging and it is against this backcloth of evidence that one of the statements of Alec Clegg, made in July 1948, summarises the direction and character of West Riding policy for secondary education.

"At a time of educational renaissance it seems highly desirable to keep the position as fluid as possible so that the Development Plan can be carried out during the coming years in a spirit of experiment and enquiry."

With attention focussed very much on how far a comprehensive could match the academic achievements of a grammar school, the first multilateral or comprehensive schools in the West Riding felt obliged to react to such pressure. By 1955 Alec Clegg could write to Alderman Hyman - "Calder High School as a Comprehensive School has in the last two years had more university awards of high quality than ever it had as a Grammar School."

DETAILS OF SCHOLARSHIP AWARDS

HEBDEN BRIDGE GRAMMAR SCHOOL AND CALDER HIGH SCHOOL

Hebden Bridge Grammar School

1944	2 County Major
1945	1 County Major
1946	Nil
1947	1 County Major
1948	1 County Major
1949	Nil

Calder High School

1950	1 State & 1 County Major
1951	1 County Major
1952	2 County Bursaries
1953	1 Open Exhibition at Oxford
	1 State & 1 County Major
1954	3 State & 3 County Majors
	1 County Exhibition

PRIMARY SCHOOLS

The part Arthur Stone played in bringing about change in primary schools in the West Riding is considerable and he is a fine example of the outstanding men and women Alec Clegg gathered together in his early years as Chief Education Officer. The striking fact is the individual qualities of people such as Arthur Stone. They were much less a collection of men and women of academic prowess who could boast service in a list of prestigious institutions; but much more a group whose individuality had an underlying unity of purpose - the sensitive and imaginative education of children.

Son of a headmaster of a village school in Herefordshire situated near to the Welsh border, Arthur Stone remembers how his father and mother ran what was almost a village precursor of the

Welfare State. Even though the Stone family comprised twelve children, three of whom died, they catered for the educational and welfare needs of the children in the village. Arthur's mother made sure sick children got medical care and medicine; they checked if children were absent; they helped families to solve a variety of problems. Brought up in a natural atmosphere of care, it is not unexpected that Arthur Stone did not find it exceptional to run a caring school when he became a headteacher.

When Arthur Stone left school he became a bank clerk but one day said to himself, "I must teach". He trained as a teacher and his first post was at Edlington, a mining village in South Yorkshire. He established himself as a disciplinarian and an innovator dealing with a strike amongst the boys and using local places of interest, such as Conisbrough Castle, as starters for first hand studies. He moved to Birmingham working in a youth centre and then to Steward Street where he began to build a reputation as an outstanding headteacher. Often the children came to school early, keen to continue the work they had in hand and if they wanted to stay after school they did. Dance, movement, art and drama played important parts in the life of the school and one incident clearly went on the short list for Alec Clegg's 'funny file'. David Thompson, HMI, had taken Diana Jordan and Alec Clegg to see an unusual production with a cast of five boys, two dogs, two cats and a parrot. The source of the production were the pets of the youngsters. Unfortunately the animals were less easily controlled than the boys and the event ended with the dogs chasing the cats and the parrot squawking as an ineffective referee.

Arthur Stone saw his school work as the skilful use of his experience and ability to help youngsters to express themselves. The result was a succession of surprises, unexpected in children from a Birmingham slum. As he says in 'Story of a School', Page 8, "And what I want to point out here and now is that the beauty which came from these children could not have been superimposed by environment or by specially selected teachers, for we were just an ordinary inartistic lot of people, but the desire to create came because we allowed it to live, and because, maybe, in some way we could understand why it was there." The same point was made by Sir Herbert Read in 'Education Through Art' - "Art is not taught by any formal, instructional method; it is communicated by example. But just at this point lies a subtle danger, for what should be communicated is not a style, nor even a technique, but confidence in the child's own uninhibited activity."

Emphasis upon the Arts such as Art, Dance and Drama was reflected in the appointments made by Alec Clegg. Apart from Arthur Stone, who was appointed in 1947, other appointments included Diana Jordan, a former pupil of Rudolph Laban, Basil Rocke who had worked with Cizak, and Ruth Scriver who was linked to Herbert Read.

The annual Bingley Vacation Courses in 1948 and 1952 were organised by Arthur Stone. Both courses dealt with the Junior School which Alec Clegg maintained was "... changing more rapidly than any other section of the service." (Page 15, 'Ten Years of Change).

The organisation in the innovative primary schools changed. No longer were children just to receive instruction in a carefully scheduled framework. The preparation, the follow up, the hour by hour and day by day development of individual work was dictated more by a youngster's interest, capacity and incentive to continue and to complete a study, rather than the achievement of a known result by a given deadline. The programme fitted the pupil rather than the opposite where the pupil was fitted into the programme.

Reflecting on the pace of change the Chief Education Officer reckoned the Bingley Course of 1948 was less than five per cent successful but it prompted significant changes in two schools at Thurnscoe and South Kirkby. Visiting advisers commented on the changes which took place, one stating that "The awakened imagination and freed expression is beginning to produce a flow of language that cannot be stopped, and the requisition of exercise books and other materials is becoming a problem."

There were fewer more depressing mining villages than Denaby in South Yorkshire and one of the collection of tape recordings Alec Clegg made comprises the reflections of the headteacher of Balby Street Junior School. There were no children from professional families in his school, they were almost exclusively from miners' and labourers' families. He felt that the inability of many children to communicate in any way was the fault of the society in which they lived. Moreover he added that one of the curses of education "is that so many words are bandied about that don't mean very much." He believed in certain guidance, clear limits and freedom within those limits and the right relationship between the teacher and the child. Art and Music played a vital part in Balby Street's work, so too did the use of the environment. The sorts of pictures painted by youngsters prompted Harold Massingham, a poet, who spent his first twenty years living in the Mexborough area, which included Denaby, to write this of his childrens' drawings

"Their pages have the oldness
Of Painting or Twig-etching!
Spideroid, goblinoid, humanoid
Cartoons of the enemy.

Who or whatever piqued them
Has educated their depths,
For these poor spreadeagled
Grotesques, semi-anonymous

Ha'penny eyes, stitched mouths
And vehement dwarfs,
The biro-line of limbs
Like the cobweb-excrement of fish -

They are all victims
Of seriously awkward smiles."

Basil Rocke was appointed to advise on Art in 1946. He enjoyed a wide range of experience before joining the West Riding team travelling in New Zealand and Australia before returning to England to go to Reading University to study Art. Two years at Reading was followed by two years in Vienna where he studied Art and saw Professor Franz Cizak's childrens' art classes. He took part in the founding of the Euston Road School of Painters before the outbreak of war. In a tribute to Basil Rocke on his death in

1966 Alec Clegg recounted an experience which remained in his memory for years -

"I so well remember the shock that I had when I went into a school in which he had done much work with a very gifted teacher and some thirty-eight paintings of flowers done by thirty-eight children, most of them children of South Yorkshire miners. They were sensitive individual paintings of a quality which I had never seen before and I remember my unspoken astonishment as for the first time I accepted Basil's conviction "that any thirty-eight children treated as these had been treated would become what they had become and would do as they had done." Alec Clegg described the paintings as " ... the instrument of my education."

The process by which the team of inspectors and advisers encouraged the development of what was already in place or got teachers to adopt new methods was concisely described by Dr.A.G. Hughes in his Presidential Address to the Conference of Inspectors of Schools and Educational Organisers in October 1951. Alec Clegg's copy has been carefully marked in two parts of the final part of the address - confirmation of what a good West Riding adviser should do and a blueprint for Woolley Hall which was to open in the following year. Talking of the work of Marion Richardson, a local inspector, Dr. Hughes said -

"In selected schools she showed by demonstration how her philosophy could be put into practice. Teachers continued the work she began, they found a new zest in their work and their rooms became little centres of action research. From these rooms, into which she had injected a little educational and partnership leaven, her influence spread in ever-widening circles. Her work demonstrates that no greater mistake could be made than to think of local inspectors as unproductive workers."

He continued - "It would be true economy for every large local education authority to establish an education staff college as a headquarters for its inspectorate - a place to which teachers, inspectors and administrators could go for co-operative discussion, for practical work in science, the arts and physical education, a place where they could see good examples of childrens' work."

The view that the skilled teacher was engaged in a never

47

ending quest for undiscovered ability and the joy that accompanied its exercise, was beautifully illustrated by the career of Diana Jordan. In her book 'The Dance in Education' she quotes John Stuart Mill's 'Essay on Liberty', a very pertinent choice, to support the view that "dances ... are the life and spirit of the people." She goes on to describe how the teacher should work to create a harmony between an individual child's mind and body - Page 9, "In order to achieve this aim, two things seem to be necessary, first that the child should reveal her personality to the teacher, and secondly, that the teacher should provide the means for developing the hundred and one personalities before her in a class both separately and by co-operation with each other."

In a personal appreciation of Diana Jordan Alec Clegg wrote -

"It was difficult a quarter of a century ago to acknowledge the debt to an assistant adviser in Physical Education even though she had produced in her own longhand the detailed principles and plans which resulted in the new Teachers Colleges at Wentworth Woodhouse and Bretton Hall, and in 1952 had planned and established and had become the Warden of Woolley Hall which was the first residential in-service training centre for teachers in this country."

The dialogues between Alec Clegg and his team of inspectors and advisors, particularly Arthur Stone, Basil Rocke and Diana Jordan, were some of the most important sources of policy and practical initiatives. Diana Jordan and Arthur Stone had a small group of schools, largely in South Yorkshire, such as Wheldon Lane Infants, Thurnscoe the Hill Junior Girls and Bolton-on-Dearne Secondary Modern for Girls where initiatives in movement and dance took place. The feedback of information from schools such as these had in Diana Jordan's words to be "ordered" to ensure that the right help and encouragement was available at the right moment. She went on to advise that "the right sort of course" should be arranged " ... to best help the needs of those who are experimenting as they reach successive stages". This administrative support would sustain, and could lead to extension, of successful initiatives. This was the root of much of the educational progress in the West Riding in the years ahead.

CHAPTER 4

FOUNDATIONS AND FIRST FRUITS

By the early fifties the hopes raised by the 1944 Education Act were fading and under the title, "Can't we do better than this?" a group of prominent educationalists engaged in a radio discussion in February 1953. Two issues raised in this discussion were to play a major part in the development and implementation of education policy in the West Riding. The first was the attitude of many middle class families to state education, the second the progress made and anticipated in infant and junior schools.

The critical view of state education was put by Roy Lewis, joint author with Angus Maude, of 'The English Middle Classes'. He argued that many children were not being educated according to parental wishes. He maintained that state primary schools were inefficient, that classes were too big, and finally, that classes contained a mixture of dull, average and gifted children. An important issue for Roy Lewis was the likely predicament of the ambitious middle class parent who's son or daughter might fail the eleven plus examination and be unable to take the grammar school route to qualifications at sixteen and eighteen, and to a promising, secure future. Lewis saw the state system as something of an expensive, bureaucratic straight jacket conceived in the interest of equality rather than liberty of choice. The predicament of the middle class parent with children relegated, and this is not too strong a term, to the modern school was set against the working class early leaver from the Grammar school. Add to this blunt comparison the doubts about the accuracy of the eleven plus examination and the importance of parental support in a youngster's progress and you have identified important shortcomings in the tripartite system. These reservations contributed to the view Lewis and Maude expressed on Page 187 of 'The English Middle Classes' -

"But hitherto the availability of free education (even for the brighter children, up to university standards) has not greatly weakened the conviction of large numbers of middle-class parents that private schools are best."

The other participants in the radio discussion, especially Ronald Gould of the National Union of Teachers and Alec Clegg, rebutted many of the inaccuracies and oversimplifications put forward by Roy Lewis but the hard fact of middle class reservations on state education remained. These were very important considerations in the West Riding when the first comprehensive schools were set up.

Alec Clegg's part in the discussion cast him as an administrator who acknowledged the need for more teachers and better buildings, and who understood what was possible with available resources. He stressed the high quality of work in infant schools and forecast this progress would carry through into the junior schools within the next ten years. In 1953 one could comfortably assume that Alec Clegg would have agreed with the proposition that his work in the West Riding was in essence what R.A. Butler termed 'the Art of the Possible'. Twenty years on Alec Clegg would very likely have shared this view of the sole critic of the Butler memoirs who believed one should aim at the impossible.

The intangibles of education were marginal to the radio discussion and to most educational debate. Lewis and Maude referred to T.S.Eliot's views on education as 'refreshing'. No doubt they liked his reference to 'the dogma of equal opportunity' but they do not refer to the careful, detailed assessment of the subtle links between education and culture. Eliot (2) found the views of Dr. C.E.M. Joad simple and intelligible and he uses Joad's threefold division of the ends of education as the main props of a careful analysis of these links.

1.   To enable a boy or girl to earn his or her living.
2.   To equip him to play his part as the citizen of democracy.
3.   To enable him to develop all the latent powers and faculties of his nature and so enjoy a good life.

Moreover he says how moved he was by Joad's description of the character of Winchester School and Oxford university. The qualities are blends, happy combinations which cannot be legislated for and which can only be recognised, appreciated and encouraged. In similar vein Edith Sitwell's foreword to the first Woolley Hall course on 'Poetry and Children' reflected that -

"Much of the finest poetry has been composed by those poets who have retained the clear and innocent eye of childhood. And did not Shakespeare tell us that 'the lunatic, the lover and the poet are of imagination all compact'? He could have added 'children' to this list, for their imagination is a glowing and intense manifestation of what they are thinking and feeling. This imagination is about the greatest power they possess and, therefore it must be nurtured if it is to retain its vitality."

Robert Gittings, Edmund Blunden, Kathleen Raine, Leonard Clark and Edith Sitivell contributed to this course. In the years that followed Woolley Hall could be seen as an institution designed to blend many of the elements identified by T.S. Eliot in his 'Notes towards the Definition of Culture'.

Perhaps Woolley courses could be seen as prompts towards the encouragement of culture. Such courses could sustain and increase the confidence of teachers in the continual discovery of talent amongst children. Teaching could be a succession of surprises. The absence of expectation could reduce education to a dull routine, the necessary feature which some teachers and parents espoused as the recipe for examination success.

The anticipated spread of good practice from infant schools to junior schools was to a large extent in the hands of West Riding inspectors and advisers. In-service courses and regular visits to schools could reduce the isolation felt by teachers and give them encouragement and confidence. In the nineteen fifties there were seven inspectors, a senior inspector, an inspector for special schools and one for technical colleges and institutes. In addition there was a group of advisers who were subject specialists covering art, music, handicraft and physical education. These were the outside staff of the education service and what the Chief Education Officer called 'the most effective limb of the Department'.

This limb had undergone a searching examination in November 1948 at a meeting between the Chief Education Officer, his inspectors and his advisers. Alec Clegg's address concentrated on an area of the education service where the cross-fire of administrative propriety and ideals could be intense and demanding. His address was surgically frank and he began by pointing out that the view he expressed was written down "... in order that I may refer to it in the future if need be."

He began with the reports made by inspectors and advisers pointing out that his decision to ask for them had been fully discussed. The specialist advisers had been asked to report on their own subjects and on any general matters which affected the welfare of a school. At a meeting of the Headmasters' Association the reports took on a different character. It was pointed out that the Chief Education Officer had instructed advisers to prepare confidential reports on schools. Moreover on leaving the meeting one head had pointed out to Alec Clegg that the words "snooper" and "Gestapo" were used by "your own advisers" not the heads. Alec Clegg had stressed the honesty and integrity of his intentions to the heads but he was deeply angry with staff who had caused such a serious loss of goodwill. His final words on this issue were -

"I can only say that I trust that the person or persons responsible for this thing will as soon as possible resign from the staff whose good name they have done so much to damage, if for no other reason than that they are in my view unfitted to associate with them."

He moved on to the reports themselves acknowledging that some could raise a good deal of dust which he added "... needed raising". Other reports quickly cobbled together at the end of term to meet his instructions were described as " ... ill considered, trivial and threadbare". Advisers reports were to go straight to him not through the County Inspectors. He would have this information in its raw, honest state not in modified form. Furthermore he wanted to avoid a procedure which would keep outside staff consulting in offices rather than working in schools. He acknowledged there could be overlap and friction so he instituted the practice that all reports from advisers once scrutinised would be passed from him to County Inspectors for information and, where necessary, action.

Half way through his statement he related administration to principles saying -

'In any important Authority such as this, it is clear that if the work of education is to be healthy the normal day-to-day work must be well founded and solid, but it must also be constantly reinvigorated by enlightened experiment and research."

He stressed that the obsession some people had with status was 'obnoxious', and that 'when folk stand on their dignity they do so generally because that is all they have left to stand on'. To follow this condemnation of the status seekers by the proposition that he could submit a memorandum from his deputy to the office boy for comment without causing offence would seem bizarre, or at least extreme, yet his private correspondence with Mr Haynes, his deputy, over many critical issues, shows a depth of trust and honesty which makes this public statement to his advisers more one of fact than fiction.

He stated the functions of the advisers, 'my representatives', and followed it with his final criticism of the service. One adviser had made a false claim for expenses which Alec Clegg described as 'gross carelessness or straightforward theft'. He ended by stressing that the freedom and opportunities enjoyed by advisers had to be matched by a service whose '... quality and integrity... will give no opportunity for adverse criticism.

The radio debate in 1953 showed the West Riding in a national context and by the sixties the anticipated advances in its primary schools had become an established fact. A major source of Alec Clegg's forecast becoming fact was the advisory service. The rigour of Alec Clegg's statement in November 1948 was a good illustration of how he dealt with difficult issues in many spheres of the education service. This crucial meeting has the indelible stamp of his personal energy and commitment which led most of his staff to perform far beyond what could be expected by any rational calculation.

Alec Clegg made no secret of his great interest in Art, Physical Education and some of the Crafts. These, he maintained, were associated with 'his own personal interests'. The collection of advisers' reports covering the years 1955-1968 reflect this interest, and from the point of view of the major areas of the secondary curriculum could be seen as ill- balanced - too much attention to the Chief Education Officer's personal interests, too little attention to subjects such as Mathematics, Science and the Humanities. On the other hand the emphasis on those aspects of primary education which were directly linked with identifying and stimulating the individual interests and qualities of youngsters was fundamental.

It is worth noting that it is not the excitement of painting, modelling or movement which celebrated the advances made in primary schools but the publication of 'The Excitement of Writing'. There was no specialist adviser in this sphere and perhaps, as Alec Clegg hinted on occasions, the specialist could restrict rather than encourage because the subject was seen as more important than the child.

The teams of men and women advisers in Physical Education seem large and to reflect in their numbers the declared interest of Alec Clegg. Yet the subject was part of every pupil's timetable and successful lessons depended on the presence of teachers with commitment and skill. The small schools and a number of other schools did not have staff with qualifications in this subject, consequently it was vital to have advisory teams who could visit schools and assess needs in training and facilities. Area courses which ran for a span of weeks and intensive courses at Woolley Hall were arranged to train and to encourage the 'movement' view of physical education.

The reports sent to the Chief Education Officer gave abundant evidence of the lack of gymnasia, halls, changing rooms, playing fields and equipment. Furthermore, report after report stressed how these shortages exacerbated the problems of staffing. As Mr. Freeling put it in his overall report of April 1958 - "In addition to the lack of staffing in Secondary Schools previously mentioned, the frequent changes of staff in other schools can be discouraging and frustrating - so much so that the problem of attaining any high standard of work from a 'movement' point of view in any particular school, can be extremely difficult."

In the same month another adviser who spent a considerable time in primary schools reflected that " ... where before we had promising schools, we now have promising little areas." Two years later this adviser, Miss Dawson, returned to the Pontefract, Featherstone and Knottingley area and said how heartwarming it was - " ... to see the improvements made to school buildings. Windows have been enlarged, colours brightened, washing and lavatory facilities improved." The source of these improvements in many respects was Ernest Peet, Supervisor of Caretakers, who emphasised high quality caretaking and maintenance in schools described by Mr.Freeling as "persistent crusading".

Typical of the practice adopted by Physical Training advisers to get teachers to consider the movement approach were the eleven sessions arranged by Mr. and Mrs. Easto in the Spen valley and Gaskell divisions in 1956. Some 70 or 80 teachers took part and Ossett Flushdyke Primary School followed up by giving a demonstration at Woolley Hall. This development from a few promising schools to promising little areas, along with regular courses at Woolley Hall created a steady tide of change. Mr. and Mrs. Easto could record the Secondary Modern Schools as the most disappointing and unrewarding part of their work. They added with an air of progress delayed that "at last a beginning has been made" in introducing new methods at Calder High School, one of the first comprehensives built in the West Riding.*

To move from specialist advisers' reports to those of the Warden of Woolley Hall, Diana Jordan, which were regularly sent to Alec Clegg, is to move from accounts often rich in local detail to an independent, overall view of the issues raised on a carefully designed programme of courses. The 1952 'Poetry and Children' Course prompted Diana Jordan to write - "I feel there is a whole world of education to explore here and one very closely allied to movement and rhythm, to drama, to the development of the imagination through the visual arts and to expression in words and music."

Two years later in 1954 forty-two junior school teachers attended a course on 'Movement, Drama and Physical Education.' The Physical Education advisers had invested a lot of time with teachers prior to the course. It is clear that some differences of opinion existed but Diana Jordan wrote -

"Indeed a split in the team seemed to threaten, but entirely owing to Mr. Stone's challenge to them on educational principles all four became more united and more convinced than ever before." Jump another two years to 1956 to a course which dealt with 'Physical Education and its contribution to the development of children', and the role of Arthur Stone as a source of integration in the advisory service is made very clear. Diana Jordan wrote - "It is of course, true to say that this course was a very great tribute to Mr. Stone. It could not have happened had there not been three years at least of deep discussion amongst the main advisers and himself and partnership in preceding courses. Also through Mr. Stone they had been brought into contact with Mr. Schiller and all that that means."

1956

FACILITIES FOR PHYSICAL EDUCATION IN DIVISIONS 2, 3, 4, 8 AND 9   (P.E. Adviser Mrs Taylor)

13	schools have fully equipped gymnasia
9	schools have showers and changing rooms of a sort
12	schools use halls with portable apparatus
8	schools use rented premises which are a
—	distance from the school
42	

STAFFING: 8 fully trained; 8 have done advanced training in college; 23 have no special training at all.

1964

PLAYING FIELDS - DIVISION 7

Junior Schools

10	have adjacent playing fields
71	make use of central playing fields
81	

Secondary Schools

23   have adequate playing fields
<u> 8</u>   have inadequate playing fields
<u>31</u>

The high ground of educational debate was explored in courses such as these and no doubt the Chief Education Officer drew considerable pleasure from them, either as a participant or as a reader of the Warden's reports. On the other hand courses such as one for the heads of secondary modern schools in South Yorkshire prompted reports which must have made very sorry reading for Alec Clegg. There was a general outcry against limited staffing and the unwillingness of specialist teachers, recently out of college, to teach a broad range of subjects. These issues were grim realities in South Yorkshire but discussion did not rise to deal with aims and how they might be achieved. It dwelt on issues such as corporal punishment for girls and whether or not toilet paper should be kept in lavatories. Strangely the place of the toilet roll in school administration was raised after Alec Clegg spoke on 'Making the best of a bad building', in 1954.

The number of advisers and the effort put into child centred education with movement as its centrepiece was questioned by Councillor Lawton at a meeting of the Policy and Finance Sub-Committee in October 1961. His criticism arose out of a long running debate on new methods of teaching Mathematics. The final part of Councillor Lawton's statement addresses what he saw as the West Riding's lop-sided use of resources -

"I should like to state, in conclusion, that I am strongly in favour of any liberalising element which can be introduced into the school curriculum and I believe that expressive movement - the West Riding variant of physical education may be such a liberalising element. I say this because it is the opinion of many people that I have attacked the teaching of physical education. My point is very simple. It is that we are living in an emergency and that one of the most serious root causes of this is the national weakness in mathematics. That being so I just cannot understand the attitude of an authority which views its exposed weaknesses in mathematics with such complacency and concentrates its major effort into a channel which the majority of people must regard as of relatively minor importance."

The Chief Education Officer gathered a detailed and wide collection of evidence on the teaching of number in primary schools which ranged from a table of standards based on HMI reports on West Riding primary schools to reports by advisers who were sent to schools and colleges to appraise new methods such as Cuisenaire. One of the HMI reports on Earby Springfield School says -

"The Headmistress takes a particular interest in the teaching of number to young children and she has planned the work around common experiences in everyday life. The children soon learn to use and to understand money, various weights and measures and to tell the time. Much practical work is done, there is a close link with written language and the children are able to talk confidently about the simple problems which they are expected to solve."

The atmosphere of a good infant or junior school bred a confidence in children and Earby Springfield earned an 'A'. When children moved to the secondary school they entered a world of specialisation and formal methods. After a few days in a grammar school Pamela Marley wrote down her feelings.

"I like the Grammar School but in a way I don't. It seems very old fashioned the way we have to put our hands in the air every time we want to answer a question. Today we had a double period of art. I felt very peculiar not being able to ask about my drawing. I asked my friend's opinion so that helped me a little bit."

Alec Clegg put emphasis on meeting the needs of individual children rather than concentrating on individual subjects. The debate on Mathematics in 1961 is a good illustration of the complexity of educational debate. Councillor Lawton was a West Riding member who was also Chairman of Woolley Hall governors. He wanted more emphasis on the "3 R's" and was impressed by some of the new methods of teaching mathematics. He felt their introduction into West Riding schools could improve the way Mathematics was taught to children. Councillor Lawton felt too much emphasis on movement and the arts could result in inadequate achievement in the 3 R's particularly in arithmetic. Alec Clegg sought information from a variety of sources and Ben Morris, Director of the Institute of Education at the Bristol University, warned him in a number of ways that children's work in mathematics " ... would be likely to improve much more however if teachers were sufficiently skilled to adapt to their own use all the various devices that exist." (3)

This was an important debate and Walter Hyman saw it as a draw. The scepticism of the Chief Education Officer about the new methods surprised him. He was impressed by Councillor Lawton's report but disappointed with his conclusions. Even if it was a draw, the issue of specialist advisers or inspectors does need to be judged against the blunt fact that only fifty out of one hundred and sixty four Local Education Authorities employed their own inspectors in 1965.

A cross section of reports during the fifties and early sixties illustrates the exchange of ideas which took place between Alec Clegg and his team of advisers and inspectors. These dialogues regularly dug into the fundamentals of education in the schools of the West Riding. The reports of four advisers who covered Art, Music, Housecraft and Needlecraft and Rural Studies explored the width and depth of ideas and practice. Without deliberately addressing the issue these reports show how the ideas which lay behind West Riding policy were refined and updated by the latest details of what was going on in the schools.

Mr. Davis, one of the Art Advisers, ran sessional courses for teachers but felt they came to courses " ...for tips for isolated lessons". The subject matter of their lessons and their use of colour was repetitive and dull. In Spring 1956 he wrote - "The teaching of pattern of the more intelligent and deliberate kind brings about much more concentration and application even in the less gifted child than the accidental and unintelligent exercise of 'Taking a Line for a Walk'. It is interesting to see how even the most backward child quite quickly appreciates the underlying structures and growth in patterns of this type and is able to take an intelligent place in a class, perhaps for the first tine." Mr. Davis reflected in one report on the perfect conditions which would give a good teacher the opportunity to explore in full these ideas and the capabilities of youngsters. This ideal provision could be provided in a large comprehensive school and would comprise a large Art room; a pottery and modelling room; a carving room for wood and stone and a fabric printing, weaving and soft toy making room. In December 1956 he reflected on the teaching of art saying it " ... is not an end in itself so much as a means whereby the child can gather the information which is to be interpreted by him in his own way." He wanted regular exchanges of ideas and children's work between junior and secondary schools and he took up Alec Clegg's suggestion that he should " ... concentrate endeavour on one or two particular key areas where there are goodish Junior schools and reasonably good Modern schools."

By 1960 Mr. Davis had developed his ideas further and set down a number of ways in which imaginative work could be carried out. Two examples of the use of observed elements were a painting based on a recent visit to the seashore recalled from memory. The other was an alteration of scale so that a collection of stones became a mountain-side and a group of shrubs and flowers became a jungle. Many of the ideas in these reports on Art have echoes in those of Mr. Day on Rural Studies, who wrote on the work of secondary schools -

"Whether these courses tend towards the sciences or the crafts, I feel that all should be alive to the aesthetic and cultural value of living things." He added at the end "... some of the best Rural Studies recording is done in Art and English."

Miss Jones, a shrewd and conscientious adviser for housecraft and needlecraft, covered the material needs of housecraft staff with great thoroughness. She added to this basic work a sequence of comments on the atmosphere of schools, the qualities of teachers and youngsters and how other staff like Basil Rocke and his wife helped her in the selection of materials for schools. Alec Clegg would have enjoyed reading this comment on students from Ilkley college who were obtaining posts in West Riding schools in the mid fifties.

She wrote - "I find that the students trained in the college possess a sense of home making and artistry, have a high standard of personal grooming, a really wide, vital outlook, are adaptable and not afraid of work." She contrasted neighbouring schools in Featherstone and Goole which were very similar in facilities and their intakes of children but differed a great deal in tone and atmosphere. The logic of her many observations on the individuality of schools and colleges led her to oppose the idea of a common basic scheme in Housecraft for all schools. She contended - "I feel this would destroy originality and (the) personal character of the different colleges, teachers and schools." She continued "... a good scheme is purely personal and must be inspired by the individual to suit the particular situation." By the time one reaches 1963 Miss Jones is considering the implications of what the efforts of advisers and the schools have produced -

"The more I see of our very good primary schools, the educational possibilities of a 9-13 age group school become more apparent, for these schools are alive with education in its broadest sense, with children alight with interest, searching observation and happiness, their capabilities are overwhelming. The progression of. the children, especially with more deprived backgrounds increases through creative expression, and I am delighted that needlework is no longer isolated but part of this in a growing number of schools." These changes spelt a steady breakdown of the boundaries of specialist teaching, an increase in integration and a more imaginative approach in schools. Her reports on Don Valley High School always refer to the artistic exhibitions which greet any visitor and the combination of these displays with a series of studies on particular countries planned to coincide with talks given by people of those countries.

The damage which could be done by a lack of trust and cooperation was vividly illustrated by the relationships between the Music advisers. They could work independently within their own areas encouraging the development of music but joint initiatives were difficult. Alec Clegg found himself at the centre of these differences and he spent a great deal of time attempting to reduce conflict rather than using it to promote initiatives. In this case the direct line from adviser to Chief Education Officer absorbed effort which might have been invested elsewhere.

Miss Spence's reports on Music drew Alec Clegg's attention to issues which ranged from morning assemblies to the unexpected importance of music to the deaf.

Miss Spence contrasted the assembly in Wheatlands Modern School, Harrogate with that in Wedderburn Infants. The modern school assembly began with a reminder to pupils of the penalties they faced by going potato picking in school time. They listened, watched and sang faced by a "... grim row of staff and a featureless wall." Miss Spence observed this is the loveliest school in Harrogate, with windows opening on to sunny fields". The infant school assembly is simply described.

"The children sat in careless groups and sang sweetly; the piano was sensitively played and the gramophone was used at the beginning and the end of the service."

The gramophone could not be used at Wheatlands because at the crucial moment they found the plug was missing."

At Harewood Bridge School for the Deaf the children got intense pleasure from percussion which they heard as vibrations. Miss Spence wanted to form a brass band as an experiment with these children and her reports often describe the connection between musical rhythms and speech rhythms.

If advisers came across unusual talent they often informed the Chief Education Officer. Miss Spence's reports contain details of Susan Tunnell, an outstanding pianist, and her brother who was a fine violinist. However it was Stella Talbot a grocer's assistant with no musical education, whose success gave Miss Spence greatest satisfaction. Stella had a wonderful contralto voice and Miss Spence was instrumental in getting her a special grant for study. She gained a place in the Covent Garden Opera Chorus. Another Music Adviser, Miss Gill, expressed her view of the contribution of music to education in these words -

" ... a living art providing an inexhaustible source of the deepest satisfaction, and an art in which all can take part and enjoy. In music the finest way to appreciation is through participation."

If one moves from the regional to the national stage then Yehudi Menuin in his Chuter Ede Lecture in 1965 sketched out the social importance of music and the arts to the vast majority who went through the state education system.

"They must have their senses stimulated; our senses were given us to guide us, to delight and to warn us. These children most of all could enjoy stimulation of their senses; yet children in the cities are herded into conditions that are shocking to our five senses, from the foods they are given to the noise they must suffer. They spend most of their day, especially if they spend their free time on the street instead of in your beautiful parks, in an aesthetically repulsive environment. How can they be expected to become self-expressive and creative if their own senses that might lead them are blunted and starved?"(4)

Alec Clegg had a deep interest in disadvantaged youngsters and one might anticipate that it would be difficult to apply the ideas which were spreading in the primary schools to Special schools, yet Mr. Easto's account of a winter visit in 1963 to Netherside Hall Special School belies this assumption. He described how in a heavy snowstorm he watched a dozen boys skiing on a fellside equipped with sticks and skis made at the school by the boys themselves. He went on -

"They could all negotiate a simple 'Slalom' Course; performing at least three different turns and half the group were beginning to master the art of jumping. This skill was acquired during the eleven days the snow lasted."

CHAPTER 5

THE BULGE, BUILDINGS AND
THE SHORTAGE OF TEACHERS

Although the birth rate rose from 14.9 in 1939 to 22.6 in England and Wales for the first quarter of 1947 the anticipated long term trend was for a declining and ageing population. From the standpoint of the West Riding Education Service the rise, or bulge, along with the raising of the school leaving age, would significantly increase the school population. The West Riding anticipated a rise from 176,000 in 1939 to 253,000 in 1957. Moreover some parts of the West Riding, particularly the coal mining areas, faced not only the effects of a high birth rate but that of the arrival of many young families in the colliery villages. The bleak prospect was summarised by Alec Clegg in these words - P.11 'Ten Years of Change'.

"The Committee's ration of money to be spent on new schools will be absorbed almost entirely by the need for new school places. The replacement of bad schools, reorganisation of existing schools, and other pressing demands, will not be undertaken until the nineteen sixties. The gravity of this accommodation problem of the next eight years can hardly be exaggerated and it is doubtful whether the full school life of ten years will be maintained in every area of the County." A solitary sentence which described how many West Riding schools met the requirements of the post-war building regulations gave the scale of the task facing the Authority - P.115 'Ten Years of Change'

"When the schools of the Riding were measured against these new regulations not one single school survived the test, and this was possibly the experience of every Authority in the country."

An example of the disposition of Ministers communicating shortcomings in the most presentable form is this passage from the Minister of Education's Report for 1953. The Minister, Miss Florence Horsburgh, stated that in England and Wales one child in six is in a new post-war building." This is one side of the picture, the other was investigated in detailed correspondence between

Alec Clegg and Dr. Kathleen Ollerenshaw. (1) Dr. Ollerenshaw travelled over 3,000 miles in two months visiting schools of all types in England and Wales. Alec Clegg sent her extensive details on the West Riding some of which were used by Dr. Ollerenshaw in an address she gave at the Annual Conference of the National Council of Women of Great Britain.

The other side, the bleak side, showed 2.5 million children in England and Wales in old schools built before 1903 and half a million of these in very old schools built before 1870. In one county 45% of children under eleven years of age were in schools built before 1870. Authorities which did their best to provide makeshift arrangements were in the words of Dr. Ollerenshaw "... penalised now by having such 'temporary' accommodation which they are unable to replace under present restrictions." With this fact in mind it is understandable why some West Riding councillors felt the best chance of getting a new school in their area was to avoid any makeshift answer to the bulge; better a burst than a grumbling appendix.

Rossington was an example of the rapid growth of colliery villages after 1945. It had two secondary modern schools, one for boys and one for girls, both of which expanded so rapidly that some were transferred to Adwick whilst those who remained were accommodated in temporary classrooms. By the time that a new comprehensive was agreed by the West Riding there were sixteen temporary classrooms, one of the biggest and most varied collections in the whole of the county. Adequate staffing depended very much on supply teachers. The prospect of a new school in material and human terms brought a double attraction.

The exchange of letters prompted Dr. Ollerenshaw to express her gratitude not just for the detailed information on the West Riding but for the way in which it was given, as she put it - "It is so easy to be misunderstood in this suspicious world and complete trust and mutual understanding is the only basis of real friendship."

The detailed surveys of accommodation which arrived in Wakefield contained information such as, roof replacement at Slaithwaite Church of England School and temporary accommodation at the Drill Hall for the children;

extensive dry rot in woodwork and plaster at Meltham Church of England School and the general comment that -

" ...the district round Huddersfield has some poor buildings." (2) However part of this area, the Colne Valley, had a good case for new secondary accommodation which was met by the building of Colne Valley High School. Repairs, ingenious makeshift arrangements and the steady increase in the number of new buildings aimed to cope with the bulge in numbers. The Further Education Adviser, Mr. Oakely Hughes could report on an enthusiastic class (3) who embroidered by the light of an oil lamp in an old building in a remote rural part of the Riding, but it was not easy to maintain the morale of teachers in the face of an unending sequence of makeshift arrangements accompanied in many areas by a shortage of staff.

Today it is commonplace to be critical of the tower blocks built in many English towns to meet the pressing need for housing after 1945. To some extent this criticism is matched in the field of education by that directed at prefabricated schools designed for the Consortium of Local Authorities Special Programme (C.L.A.S.P.). These schools cost much less in time and money than those built with traditional materials, but maintenance costs were likely to be heavy. However in mining areas in particular C.L.A.S.P. construction was a crucial factor in providing accommodation for a rapidly rising school population. Elizabeth Layton, Research Officer for the Royal Institute of Public Administration, praised local authority building in the fifties saying -

" ... the development of school building in this country has been outstandingly successful. In this field of architecture it is Britain's most known and acclaimed achievement."

Alongside this progress went the improvement in caretaking and the furnishing of schools. In 1948 Ernest Peet took up his appointment as Supervisor of Caretakers and soon his manual 'A new approach to clean schools', along with regular training courses launched a steady improvement in caretaking. The like of the high quality furniture which went into the West Riding Teacher Training Colleges was not available for schools so the Education

Committee employed a consultant to advise them on school furniture.

Unless a district in the West Riding had an overwhelming case for a new school the likelihood was that they would have to make the best of existing premises. Good maintenance, attractive redecoration, dedicated caretaking and especially high quality teaching could give children a good education. It is clear from advisers reports that unexpectedly and regularly they found the most enlightened teaching in the most unlikely places. This observation underlines the fact that it is the teachers much more than the buildings and equipment who contribute most to children's progress.

THE SHORTAGE OF TEACHERS

The first sentence in a Report on the Supply and Distribution of Teachers prepared by the Yorkshire Association of Education Committees in 1953 summarised what lay ahead -

"The scarcity of teachers for Primary Schools is likely for the next ten years to be a greater threat to the education service than is the shortage of school buildings, and thereafter unless the situation permanently improves there will be no hope of reducing secondary school classes to the thirty in a class which is the size envisaged by present school building."

The correspondence between Alec Clegg and Dr. W.P. Alexander, Secretary of the Association of Education Committees, illustrates the debate on the shortage of teachers at the national level. It had the same rigorous quality as the exchange with Dr. Ollerenshaw and it prompts the reflection that the West Riding, through its Chief Education Officer, opened up a series of personal links which gave it a direct influence on national policy.

In his letters Alec Clegg expressed the view that on West Riding evidence alone Dr. Alexander had failed to realise the very serious nature of the teacher shortage. It was not just a matter of numbers matching needs., of getting enough teachers to cope with the anticipated additional 25,000 in West Riding secondary schools, it was the impact of the bulge on an existing crisis especially in areas such as South Yorkshire. Initially Alec Clegg pointed out the existing shortages in subjects such as Physical Education, Art and Housecraft and the parts of the county where teacher shortages were at their worst. The reply from Dr. Alexander was general and bland stating -

"I think it would be a fair summary of the position to say that while there will undoubtedly be considerable pressure on the secondary schools it is confidently believed that the number of teachers of general subjects will be sufficient." Alec Clegg replied that this view was - " ... almost wholly mistaken."

He pointed out that at least a quarter of the staff in a secondary school covered the following subjects; Physical Education, Housecraft, Handicraft, Art, Music, Needlecraft, Science and Rural Science. No increase in the output of these teachers was expected by 1957. It was possible that the anticipated rise in the demand for teachers in the secondary schools might be met by the transfer of junior teachers into secondary schools. Such a movement might be possible in urban areas but was scarcely possible in rural areas where numbers might decline from 40 to 30 in a school. Moreover those transferred from junior to secondary schools might contain a high proportion of teachers the junior heads did not want. Lastly as areas of the West Riding reorganised and new schools were built with better facilities the demand for specialist teachers to staff the new laboratories, gyms and craft rooms would rise.

THE IMPACT OF RURAL REORGANISATION ON THE DEMAND FOR SPECIALIST TEACHERS IN THE WEST RIDING

October 1955

SCIENCE AND RURAL SCIENCE 9
ART 7
MUSIC 5
HANDICRAFT 14
HOUSECRAFT AND NEEDLEWORK 14
PHYSICAL EDUCATION 14

Source: Letter to the Ministry of Education 21st October, 1955. Prepared by the Specialist Teachers Sub-Comittee.

VACANCIES AND APPOINTMENTS IN FOUR AREAS OF THE WEST RIDING 1957 AND 1958

	1957		1958	
	Vacancies	Appointments	Vacancies	Appointments
CASTLEFORD				
Secondary	22	9	30	7
Primary	38	16	21	12
PONTEFRACT				
Secondary	18	6	20	8
Primary	16	5	9	12 applications
DONCASTER				
Secondary	39	17	38	7
Junior	33	19	17	13
Infant	12	6	16	4
HEMSWORTH				
Secondary	32	20	30	12
Junior	20	12	32	10
Infant	6	2	3	1
	236	112	216	86

The real predicament of a headteacher in a secondary modern school is clinically illustrated by this confidential letter sent to Alec Clegg in the summer of 1958. It is a personal view which no statistical digest can portray.

The head had not had a Mathematics teacher since 1952 and except for one term due to Alec Clegg's initiative there had not been a teacher of Physical Education. Out of a staff of 14, 3 had been rejected by other heads, one seriously unbalanced, another rejected from any school by the Doncaster authority and the last a mischief maker who enjoyed causing problems amongst staff and pupils. Apart from two emergency trained 'lively bright teachers' the remaining staff had serious shortcomings prompting the head to conclude that by 1938 standards, not more than four of my staff would have been appointed to a Secondary School.

Letters such as this were the source of suggestions from Alec Clegg for emergency measures such as, supplementary courses for teachers and local training schemes funded by money from Further Education grants to be adopted. By autumn Dr Alexander had accepted the West Riding standpoint writing -

"If this situation is as described in your letter, than I am not only mistaken but have been badly misled." He ended -

"I am grateful to you for writing to me so directly. That is the kind of letter I find worth reading". Alec Clegg had gained an ally and their joint effort prompted action by the National Advisory Council and the Ministry of Education.

In the closing years of the nineteen fifties the nature of the teacher shortage in West Riding school was subjected to close scrutiny. The details sent to County Hall by Divisional Education Officers, inspectors, advisers and headteachers, gave Alec Clegg exact up to date numbers along with details of the quality of existing staff and the needs of the future. These reports showed an unexpectedly high wastage of teachers in subjects such as Girls' Physical Education. Many expected new buildings and improved facilities would attract staff and ease the teacher shortage, but they forgot that without increased output from the training colleges the gains of the new schools were the losses of the old. Unless extra teachers were trained in subjects such as Physical Education many schools had to make do year after year thankful enough to put someone in front of each class. In spring 1956 Mrs Taylor, an adviser for Girls' Physical Education, found that out of 41 schools only 8 teachers of Girls' Physical Education were fully trained and that apart from a further 8 who had done advanced training at college the rest had had no specialist training at all. Even in 1966 only 18 teachers of Girls' Physical Education in 41 secondary schools had stayed at their schools for 4 years or more.

The correspondence of these years contains a continuous flow of details and prompts on the scale and character of the teacher shortage. They went to bodies such as the Association of Education Committees; to Members of Parliament and the Ministry of Education; to prominent educationalists in the universities, and to newspapers such as the Yorkshire Post, the Guardian and the Observer.

Even when he was in bed with mumps in October 1956 Alec Clegg kept the flow of correspondence going. He reiterated his view of the gravity of the shortage of teachers which would continue up to 1960 in a letter to J.V. Stephenson at the Ministry of Education. He was not optimistic about its impact in the Ministry for it ended - "I don't expect anything to come of it." Nevertheless he encouraged Walter Hymen to bring the matter of the shortage up at a conference he was to attend "...with your characteristic vehemence." The details of the shortages in many areas of the West Riding regularly arrived in County Hall in 1957 and 1958 confirming the grim forecasts of Alec Clegg. The first draft of a letter to be sent on behalf of the Yorkshire Association of Education Committees smacks of the Clegg style where the Ministry is lambasted for its failure to deal with the teacher shortage -

"I am writing at the behest of the Yorkshire Association of Education Committees, an organisation which includes in its membership representatives of a number of the areas afflicted by the present shortage of teaching staff and which has foreseen during the last years its worst forebodings about teachers supply in turn disputed, ignored, heeded too late, and finally realised by the dismal confusion in Circular 333 of an error of nearly 30% in the forecast of teacher increase for 1957." This draft was toned down and a letter went to the Ministry. In a letter to a fellow Chief Education Officer, George Taylor, Alec Clegg described a meeting with two Ministry officials on the crisis in teacher supply. Their view was that -

"We are in an epoch of over full employment and it is, therefore, always going to be difficult to staff the unattractive areas and our bad areas are, therefore, going to continue to suffer. Anything that we do to try and change this will be interpreted as being direction of labour." Alec Clegg translated this superficial, myopic overall view into the school situation in a South Yorkshire colliery village -

"But the most lamentable thing of all, I think, that these children who come from the drab productive areas and from home backgrounds which help them educationally as little as possible are in fact going to be taught by teachers whom nobody else wants."

Labour or Conservative, the West Riding County Council, kept up the pressure to change the Ministry viewpoint. The Conservative Chairman of the Education Committee, Fuller-Smith, wrote to the Yorkshire Post and to the Guardian in May 1958 on the crisis in teacher supply. The Guardian refused to publish the letter on the grounds it had appeared in the Yorkshire Post. Typical of the Chairman and Chief Officer they complained to the Guardian eliciting the lame reply that they did not print what appeared in other papers for it is "...one of our customs." Another approach to the Ministry on six stricken areas giving exact details of vacancies and appointments brought a lengthy unhelpful reply in June 1958. With the next academic year beginning in September it was clear that emergency measures needed to be discussed and available to meet the worst set of circumstances. The measures included raising the age of admission to six; giving extra responsibility allowances to teachers in deprived areas; the staggering of hours with an extra hour each day paid at Evening Institute rates; higher pay for supply teachers; peripatetic teachers in specialist subjects; and lastly double shifts. It was pointed out at the end of these suggestions that some school establishments of staff were deliberate underestimates of needs because inspectors hesitated to increase them knowing teachers were not available to fill the vacancies. What Alec Clegg did not express in his letter to the Ministry in June which ended it would " ... make it unwise for me to reply seriously at this moment. I hope to do so when I am more composed, ... "was probably expressed to a fellow Chief Education Officer, Oxspring, of Staffordshire (16th June, 1958)

"I think we have got to put every ounce of our energies, however, into fighting for the future. If the three year training course goes through based on the sort of half baked promises and incompetence that we have come to expect from the Teachers'

Branch in the last six or seven years, then you and I will be running some of our schools on a double shift for the rest of our professional lives."

A deputation of South Yorkshire M.P.'s met the Minister of Education in June to underline the staffing crisis in their constituencies, but they got a similar response to the one given to Alec Clegg in August by the Parliamentary Secretary, Sir Edward Boyle. He wrote that the shortage of teachers in areas such as the Don Valley " ... is one of maldistribution within the West Riding as a whole, and for this the remedy is to be found locally."

By concentrating on one subject, the shortage of teachers, the details and cross-currents of the rest of Alec Clegg's work in 1958 have been set to one side. The sustained effort to puncture the oft repeated Ministry view of internal maldistribution is all the more impressive when one takes into account the unusual and unexpected crop of difficulties which characterise this year. Alec Clegg could have found many occasions to quote Harry Truman's phrase "the buck stops here". Headteachers who were courting disaster, or who had suffered it, demanded the attention of the Chief Education Officer. A recently appointed grammar school head saw the reinforcement and extension of his status as a matter of belittling elected members of the Education Committee, keeping visitors waiting and adopting a manner directed solely to personal enhancement. Another elderly lady saw her thirtieth year as a head as one of persecution by education officials which could only be stopped by an immediate Whitehall investigation. Wild and libellous statements flowed to London and it was painfully clear she had to be given her notice. Equally clear was the case of a headmaster who in the circumstances had the sense to resign. All these cases occurred in January to be followed by a damning report by H M Inspectors on Bretton Hall College pointing out Education, Music and Art as the worst departments. Mrs.Fitzpatrick, who later chaired the Education Committee, said it - "was the worst report she had ever seen in her life." The college governors clashed over the report broadly dividing into the laymen and the educationalists. The latter felt that the degree of criticism in the report was unmerited. The report prompted debate through the year until in

August in a letter to Sir Charles Morris, Vice Chancellor of Leeds University, Alec Clegg referred to the very good report given to Bretton by the external examiner, Ben Morris. He went on to ask Sir Charles if, given the opportunity, he would mention the report to Mr Flemming at the Ministry. There was a fear that the Ministry were considering the closure of Bretton earlier in the year, but by the end of the summer the rumour was the extension of Bingley College. Alec Clegg gave details of the two colleges comparing the sites and pointing out the advantage of the Bretton site and the availability of teaching practice schools in the more heavily populated areas surrounding the college.

In May there was suspicion of fraud at Askham Bryan Agricultural College. Before the matter was thoroughly investigated the clerk under suspicion died leaving the Chief Education Officer, the County Treasurer and the Governors with a delicate matter to resolve. There were heated governors meetings but the matter proved a damp squib. However if Askham Bryan did not prove an explosive issue comprehensive reorganisation did after the Labour Party took control of the council in August. They wanted an accelerated programme of change. The crossfire between Labour and Conservative parties on the Education Committee was intense at this time. A confidential memorandum of 18th August pointed out that the Labour Party was demanding "... comprehensive schools here, there and everywhere, and any legitimate reservations on such proposals by officers of the Authority would be regarded as inspired by the Conservative opposition. Alec Clegg was adamant that proposals should be looked at thoroughly and he summed the complex position up in these words - "My instinctive reaction to this claimant pressure was to stave off these demands until we had time to look into them and this staving off has been taken in same quarters as hostility to Comprehensive Schools if not outright disloyalty to the Committee. I am not bothered by these reactions in that I think there is any shred of truth in them; I know there is not, and I know that given the time we shall all do our best. On the other hand, it is not a good thing that we should have created these impressions and we must do our best to obliterate them." Alec Clegg came to an agreement with Councillor Hyman on a procedure for dealing with a request for a comprehensive school in an area. The request had to be taken to the Education committee and, if agreed, a resolution 'That the Education Officer be instructed to set out alternative ways of implementing the proposals of the Divisional Executive and submit them to this Committee as soon as possible' should be passed.

A private letter to the Conservative leader, councillor Fuller-Smith, on 19th August described the difficulties of navigation in early August - "May I say to you again privately that in the last week or two we have had a pretty harassed time. The irony of it all is that your supporters on the Right were convinced that I was in the then Vice-Chairman's pocket and was dragging you half-way in it as well. In other words, that Clegg was sold on Compre-hensive Schools. For the last two months, and increasingly so in recent weeks, it is quite obvious that I have been considered by the Left of the other party as the arch enemy of Comprehensive schools. All of which leads me to the conclusion that I might after all be on the right course on this tricky matter."

One final complication and twist in the abrasive pattern of events in 1958 was the attitude of teachers facing the prospect of reorganisation. Their concern about the impact of the shortage of staff might lead to a rigid defence of the status quo. Alderman Hyman, Chairman of Education, apparently took this view of the teachers in Elland until a letter from Alec Clegg pointed out their standpoint was not against reorganisation on comprehensive lines but that the new school

" ... might not be truly comprehensive."

THE WEST RIDING TEACHER TRAINING COLLEGES

When the former country houses such as Bretton Hall and Wentworth Woodhouse were bought and refurbished as teacher training colleges the cost of the changes prompted considerable criticism. The Sunday Express described Wentworth Woodhouse as

" ... a £250,000 temple" for keep-fit girls. More imaginative criticisms of Bretton Hall's facilities were voiced by Councillor

Sutcliffe who suggested a production of Wagner's Lohengrin in a gondola on Bretton lake with Alderman Hyman as coxswain. The sober answer appeared in the Yorkshire Post in a letter from the Chairman of the Education Committee, Fuller- Smith, who pointed out that the three colleges, Bretton, Ilkley and Lady Mabel would supply 299 teachers a year. The quality of the new building and refurbishment at Bretton by the County Architect, H. Bennett, earned this comment from Nikolaus Pevsner. He said -

"They are lightly and freshly handled - especially the Theatre. Any dependence on the style of the house has been avoided. Yet there is emphatically no clash. The house itself and its accessories are of various styles - the new style of the 20th Century marries happily with them."

Apart from the three teacher training colleges and Woolley Hall emergency colleges were set up at Harrogate and Stanley Miners' Hostel. Between them they trained 590 teachers, many of whom were ex-servicemen, who brought a wealth of personal experience into West Riding schools.

Swinton Day Training College

The pressure for more teachers led the Education Committee to propose that a new secondary school at Swinton should be used as a temporary day training college. A large advertisement was put in South Yorkshire newspapers asking those interested in training as teachers to write to the Chief Education officer. There were over 1,000 enquiries and the college was staffed and opened within eighteen months. 184 mature students were selected for the first course and as the 'Final Ten Years' puts it - page 48

'In a very short time it was clear that they possessed unusual qualities.'

Geoff Edwards, who ran the Carnegie Centre at Minsthorpe High School from its opening until his retirement in 1993, recalled some of the early students who were with him at Swinton. Like him they came from other walks of life and included Roy Clarke, playwriter, known now for 'Last of the Summer Wine', Eric Campbell, a writer and Brian Glover and Brian Blessed two well known actors. As with so many of the West Riding schemes they unearthed talent which until that time had remained undiscovered. An emergency situation prompted this initiative and, like many other excursions from the beaten tracks of the educational framework, it illustrates how emergencies and unexpected discoveries often coincide.

When Alec Clegg collected information from six areas (4) on teacher training and the shortage of teachers for the Central Advisory Council for Education in 1962 a majority of the heads, especially those of modern schools, spoke highly of emergency trained teachers. The heads stressed the importance of personality, a sense of humour and a willingness to take part in out of school activities. One went as far as to write " ... personality is all", another wrote " ... an untrained graduate is a great liability in a modern school."

Alec Clegg regularly drew attention to the repercussions in schools of the teacher shortage, especially the lack of continuity in work caused by a rapid turnover of staff. The situation is succinctly expressed in the question which opens Chapter 24, of the Newsom Report - "Are you going to stay with us, Sir?" The predicament of the Don Valley, the Mexborough and Rother Valley divisions in 1955 is clear not only in the vacancies but in the appointment of 135 probationers and the allocation of 21 county supply teachers. The reports of inspectors and advisers to Alec Clegg give some idea of how some of those trained at the three West Riding training colleges performed in schools. The reports of Miss Jones, a Housecraft adviser, between 1956 and 1963 often refer to Ilkley trained teachers. Her comment on five of them who joined the staffs of West Riding schools in 1956 is significant for what it says about their qualities rather than their qualifications. It follows the same line of appreciation as Alec Clegg found in his survey of advisers' viewpoints in 1962. See page 62 and 63.

On the other hand Miss Pollard, the other Housecraft adviser, referred to the 'short stay' housecraft mistresses. Miss Dawson, a P.E. adviser had a similar comment to make -

"It is very rare on the women's side, to get a teacher to stay long enough to see a group of girls through from the first to the fourth year." She called them 'birds of passage' and cited examples such as " ... the best P.E. student from Bingley Training College last year, an 'A1 teaching mark who married before she took up her appointment and will be leaving in June to have her first baby."

Advisers such as Day and Moyes saw regular links with training colleges such as Bretton Hall and St John's College, York as very important for their subject, Rural Studies, in the West Riding. Similar links between the Advisory Service and universities and training colleges were established in other subject areas whilst throughout the whole of its existence Woolley Hall remained a centre of educational discussion in and beyond the West Riding.

Beyond numbers, or quantity, lay quality and this was the feature which determined the effectiveness of an education service. Alec Clegg said the effectiveness of a teaching service would depend on the number of its teachers that can answer this question -

"Why are you teaching what you are teaching in the way that you are teaching it to these particular children at this moment in their development?" (5)

APPENDIX 1

David Medd drew attention to the need to discuss the design of schools with teachers. The results of such discussion not taking place were dealt with at an R.I.B.A. Conference at Cambridge in 1968 where the Strathclyde Building Performance Research Unit presented a paper entitled 'Research Approach to the Design of a Comprehensive School'.

The report pointed out that -

"The lack of this kind of dialogue has painfully visible results. In a recent sample of comprehensive schools we have examined about 40% of the space is unused at any time in spite of the fact that the school is 'full' and needs extensions to accommodate the extra children resulting from raising the leaving age."

CHAPTER 6

THE COMPREHENSIVE DEBATE - THOROUGH OR PARTISAN?

Comprehensive education did not become a pressing, central political issue until the Labour victory in the council elections of 1958. Labour wished to accelerate the changeover from the tripartite to a comprehensive system and consequently the political temperature at County Hall rose sharply. Previously the early comprehensive schools had been established when the Conservatives held office and Alec Clegg's preference for thorough local discussion followed by locally acceptable decisions had been agreed by both parties. The change in political temperature meant the Chief Education Officer and his staff came under increased pressure, and in such circumstances the quality of personal relationships within and beyond the Education Department played a key part in ensuring that acceleration did not lead to ill conceived schemes of reorganisation.

The first opportunity to launch what Alec Clegg termed 'one school for all normal children over the age of 11' occurred when a new school at Hebden Royd was completed after the Second World War. This school, Calder High School, and another at Tadcaster were established as multilaterals in the early fifties. One of the County Council Inspectors wrote of Calder High School - "It is a pity, however, that the pupils are still rather rigidly thought of as 'selected' and 'non selected'; and are always considered under these headings". Alec Clegg's pencilled comment on this report was - "Tell him not to do it." The labels might irritate the inspectors but the results the pupils of the High School obtained in exams and university places should have pleased staff, governors and parents for they were better than those obtained by the old grammar school.

The first 'made to measure', as Alec Clegg termed it, comprehensive school - Colne Valley High School - was opened in 1956. Planned as an eight form entry school with a four storey classroom block facing down the valley, it dominated the hillside by Linthwaite church. At the time of the bulge its intake had doubled to sixteen forms and it was one of the biggest schools in the West Riding. The main entrance with its bank of steps and twin sets of doors led to an unusual entrance hall, not lofty but with a fishpond outside the enquiries hatch. At the back of the hall was the lift shaft and to the right a floor to ceiling window which threw light on to a bronze cockerel by the sculptor, Elizabeth Frink. Practical and artistic, Colne Valley was another school which earned the praise of Nikolaus Pevsner. The organisation and spirit of the school earned similar praise from Her Majesty's Inspectors in a very detailed report compiled after three visits which took place during the spring, summer and winter terms of 1963. The inspectors looked at every aspect of the school from the general assessment, to individual subjects, outside activities and clubs and lastly school meals. The atmosphere of the school was summarised in the final paragraph of the general assessment -

Paragraph 19 - "Visitors to this school quickly became aware of its general aims and of the methods used to implement them, and, more gradually, they gain a firm impression of its very considerable achievements; to connect the two is not always easy but it is most likely that human relationships, at all levels, play a particularly important part. Despite the size of the school, there is a friendly atmosphere in which intimate relationships are established in a way more frequently encountered in the quite small school. It is significant and appropriate that when the Headmaster is not teaching he is freely accessible in his room to staff and pupils alike whatever engagements he may have; and they visit him. But it is the total impact of the school that impresses. This undoubtedly derives partly, and essentially, from the solid success of much of its work, and from the strengths developed by pupils of diverse abilities and qualities. There are weaknesses also, accepted tolerantly as a part of the human pattern but nevertheless tackled with resolution. The other factor contributing to the total impact the school has upon the visitor is the marked sense of unity among the staff, and between staff and pupils. This is a unity of aim and purpose.

The staff know the pupils matter; the pupils know that they are known and that what they do matters. Both are unmistakably proud of the undoubted success achieved by the school, a success firmly established in a relatively short time and in which the Headmaster as a member and leader of the school, has the right to feel a lively satisfaction.

The workload of teachers in this school was heavy, but like other West Riding schools at the front line of educational development it was purposeful and therefore it was not a burden.

The comprehensive schools could feel secure if they received H.M. Inspectors' reports similar to the one on Colne Valley High School. Furthermore one might assume a Chief Education Officer would share this contentment. No doubt Alec Clegg did but his attention was focussed on the lot of the majority entering and going through the secondary schools of the West Riding. He was worried that the emphasis put upon matching, or surpassing, the examination achievements of grammar schools could lead the comprehensives to neglect the needs of the majority. A very detailed exchange of views between Alec Clegg and Walter Hyman in 1957 illustrates vividly where his apprehensions lay. The exchange was prompted by a Fabian Society questionnaire given to Alec Clegg by Walter Hyman. Alec Clegg said that the history of public education since Forster's 1870 Education Act had not been one of hope, but of disillusionment. Unlike William Morris he did not see universal literacy leading to the 'ultimate wisdom of mankind' but to the popularity of 'The News of the World'. The concentration by the Fabians on the abolition of the eleven plus as the centrepiece of the comprehensive revolution was in Alec Clegg's view risky, for allocation to different types of education could continue. The single act of surgery at eleven could be replaced by internal selection and the social inequalities of youngsters could remain as secondary considerations in the running of a school. Alec Clegg contrasted the position of ...

" ... two identically endowed boys, one is born into a home where he hears good speech, is supplied with good books, hears and views with discrimination, absorbs accepted social conventions, and is exposed to a rich variety of aesthetic

81

experiences, and the other is born into a house from which these things are absent, the former will tend to progress further and more easily than the latter."

One year before this was written a thorough sociological study of Featherstone, termed Ashton in the book 'Coal is our Life', was published. The authors fully confirmed the view of Alec Clegg on parental attitudes in colliery districts. P.235 - "Yet only very few Ashton children actually get a grammar school education and very few develop interests broader than those of their parents whose interests can be satisfied with life in Ashton. One reason for this is that the parents themselves obviously can have no real idea of a child's requirements to advance in the educational system. In the competition for grammar school places the child of well-educated parents has inestimable advantages."

The rich seam of neglected talent in the colliery villages of South Yorkshire and Alec Clegg's part in its discovery is beautifully illustrated by the experiences of one of the early entrants to Oxford University under the Oxbridge scheme. The boy, a miner's son, who lived on one of the N.C.B. estates outside Pontefract, went to the local secondary modern school, until he won a grammar school place in Pontefract. His form master wrote of his exceptional industry and ambition and under the Oxbridge Scheme he gained a place at St. Catherine's College. His family suffered a sequence of misfortunes just before he was due to go on voluntary overseas service in Algeria. His grandfather died and both parents suffered serious ill health. His mother was concerned as newspapers reported the murder of volunteers in Algeria and she wrote directly to V.S.O. and incurred the headmaster's displeasure. The situation was fraught and the boy wrote to Alec Clegg describing his predicament and asking his advice. This request led to a sustained exercise of gritty diplomacy in seeking a course of action which would ensure a year abroad and a successful stay at Oxford. At this crucial point in his years at Oxford this miner's son got prompt advice and practical help from the Chief Education Officer. Alec Clegg made but one request in return for this help "... permission to quote from one of the most moving and helpful letters I have received from anybody who has been through our education system." It is this direct contact with youngsters and teachers in schools which led Alec Clegg time and time again to test ideas in the laboratory of every day experience. Personal interaction could help in the achievement of successes such as this, but it was the fruit of individual initiative not part of a framework devoted to the erosion of social inequality. In his debate with Walter Hyman Alec Clegg said -

"There is not the slightest evidence to suggest that a comprehensive school will be more successful in removing the handicaps from which the working-class boy suffers than are, for instance, the existing Grammar Schools in the industrial areas (Wath, Mexborough, Maltby). Indeed, as their range of social origin is as great and their intellectual range greater, the Comprehensive Schools may be even less successful in this respect than the Grammar Schools. Unless this problem is solved, the country is likely to be divided even more decisively into two social classes than it now is."

To the risk of comprehensive schools concentrating on winning public support largely by good exam results and rising numbers of pupils staying on to 16 and beyond, was added that of the schools 'grammarising' the whole of the curriculum. In a later letter to Walter Hyman dated 12th July, 1957 Alec Clegg drew on a wide range of studies to underline what he saw as the likely result of comprehensive schools taking too narrow a view of their role in society.

He wrote - "The significance of all this is that not only the Public School system but the State system of education is producing a social dichotomy in this country. Every major proposal that has to be made should be measured against this fact. Is it going to aggravate the social dichotomy which is already growing at speed? Unless Comprehensive Schools are given first-rate staffing ratios they won't be able to compete. Unless the Grammar Schools in industrial areas are freed from the pressures which force them to ignore their civilising function and focus 100% of their time on academic attainment their children cannot compete. If Modern Schools introduce third-rate Grammar School academic courses the children who go through them will only stand out as inferior to the Public and great Day School products. And perhaps most important of all, any school containing the whole range of children which bends its energies towards helping the more able academically is likely to neglect the bottom half of the ability range and therefore increase the dichotomy. A strong case could be made out for suggesting that the Conservative Party policy deliberately, and Labour policy blindly, are both contributing towards the aggravation of this dichotomy."

The concern Alec Clegg had about the obsessive nature of some grammar school heads to obtain good exam results, and as many university places as possible, was reinforced by attitudes displayed on courses at Woolley Hall. The Warden, Diana Jordan, remarked that many of the courses for grammar school heads " ... develop into a shooting match and the Authority becomes an Aunt Sally." She followed this remark by saying - "I don't think they have the slightest idea that any of us know or perhaps even care as deeply as we do, about children." Woolley ran course after course which aimed to raise the sights of secondary heads, but time after time the attitude recorded by the Warden was, 'Well this is just Clegg and we have heard it before!'

The gulf between the thoughtful, imaginative adviser and the long serving secondary headteacher could be wide and the difference could easily be described as that between preaching and practice. Nevertheless there was a similar gulf between different grammar school heads and it was not just in attitude, but in how beliefs determined the running of a school and the treatment of youngsters.

The attitudes and actions of head teachers varied a great deal and 1952 contained two instances which illustrate how different they could be. The first prompted newspaper outcry, a typical Hyman intervention and professional association response, and the Chief Education Officer landed with the task of trying to achieve a sensible solution. The second instance comprises no more than a conversation and a quiet exchange of letters which open a door to a personal dialogue of singular quality. Perhaps it is attitudes as much as aims which are illustrated in these two instances. However they serve to underline the fact that informal conversation and correspondence can contribute as much to the quality of education as formal meetings and public statements. The second of these instances began with a conversation at Woolley Hall to be followed by an exchange of letters. Like Westminster's corridors and tearooms it was the place for relaxation that contributed as much to the effectiveness of an institution as the Commons or the lecture room.

The first instance concerned the expulsion of two boys and a girl from Ossett Grammar School. The circumstances surrounding the expulsion seemed to call for consultation and compassion rather than the immediate assertion of authority. Neither the governors nor the Chief Education Officer were consulted and two of the youngsters went missing for two days. The professional association of Headteachers expressed their disapproval of the criticism by Alderman Hyman which received wide press coverage. Their attention was concentrated on the impact of criticism on the status of the headteacher rather than the predicament of the youngsters. The personal situations of the three, especially the girl, called for sensitive handling not expulsion and publicity.

This incident can be compared with the personal dialogue between another grammar school head and Alec Clegg on a girl who came from a very difficult home, who was caught stealing and who had attacked a boy with a dinner fork. The head hoped to get her a place in a home for maladjusted children. She was given a place and on leaving went to the local secondary modern school rarely living at home but sleeping rough in a nearby cricket pavilion. She began stealing and the grammar school head believing that if she was sent to an approved school " ... it would be the end of her", decided to offer her accommodation at his home. The court agreed and the girl moved to the grammar school whilst at his home. He told Alec Clegg "I shall never regret having undertaken the task. I have gambled on my knowledge of children and if I succeed; that is all I want." Alec Clegg asked that he be contacted personally if any help was needed.

Heads exercised their powers in a variety of ways but the commonly held view was that they should be independent and vigilant in the preservation of their standing within and beyond their schools. They were the main source of firm discipline, a quality foremost in the minds of many teachers and school governors, not only in the old West Riding but in schools today. The prospect of bigger and bigger schools as comprehensive reorganisation took place brought with it genuine concern about the pressures that would be put on headteachers. If the totalitarian view of the head as the sole source of decisions on all aspects of school life was taken then such apprehension appeared well founded. However authorities such as the London County Council and Leicestershire devised ways to solve the problem of excessive size. Moreover the Ministry Handbook of Headmasters published in 1959 took a less rigid view of the headteacher's influence in a school saying -

"It is the head's personality that in the vast majority of schools creates the climate of feeling; and that establishes standards of work or conduct." The H.M.I. report on Colne Valley High School is a confirmation of this view.

The file Alec Clegg kept on the reorganisation of secondary education contains material on curricula, timetables and special aptitudes which ran back into the 1930's. By 1958 he had reached the conclusion.

" ... that we fit children into the education which we provide in designated buildings rather than providing in these buildings an education geared to the needs of the children who have to attend them."

This constant emphasis on fitting education to the needs of children was the source of a sequence of initiatives in the field of secondary education. The Thorne Scheme, first discussed between Alec Clegg and his brother-in-law Gilbert Peaker H.M. Staff Inspector for Research, was tried out in the Thorne area in 1955. Pupils were not selected by taking the 11+ examination but allocated to what was thought to be the appropriate type of secondary school on the recommendation of the junior school staffs. Small panels of teachers dealt with the borderline cases. In a letter Alec Clegg wrote to Gilbert Peaker in April he wrote of this 'selection adventure' adding -

"I think we must say it is off. I am bitterly disappointed because the Thorne affair has gone off very well and it had an added advantage that I think none of us foresaw that it has brought the Grammar School and Modern School and Primary School Heads together on a constructive job in which they are all interested in a way which nothing else ever has done."

The disappointment expressed in this letter was misplaced for although the Conservatives gained control of the council they did not end the Thorne Scheme. Fuller Smith, the Conservative chairman, though not fully convinced gained reassurance over the scheme from Sir David Eccles, Minister of Education. Both had been reassured by the Chief Education Officer, another indication of his skill in preserving a large area of educational development from the oscillations of political change.

The scheme was extended to the Batley area in September 1955 and to other areas between 1956 and 1960. The erosion of the eleven plus took place alongside careful scrutiny of the Leicestershire scheme and the experiences of the early West Riding comprehensives.

The use of the Leicestershire scheme with transfer at 14, not 11, preserved a comprehensive intake for a further three years, but the implementation of this scheme in areas of the West Riding where very serious shortages of teachers existed seemed doomed to failure. Perhaps you could retain the teachers in shortage subjects such as Mathematics, Science and Modern Languages in the Senior High Schools, but recruitment for the 11 to 14 schools in these subjects in particular seemed very unlikely.

The introduction of comprehensive education in sparsely populated rural areas posed its own particular set of problems not the least of which was the recruitment of a sixth form of sufficient size. The comprehensive set up at Tadcaster had as its base a five hundred strong grammar school which recruited from a wide area extending west to east from the boundaries of Leeds to those of York, and north up to Wetherby and as far south as Sherburn. The pupils at the grammar school and the modern school in Tadcaster were badly housed so a new school was built to hold all the children from Tadcaster plus selected children from a wide area. If this school had a grammar bias in its entry the new schools built at Garforth and Wetherby had a modern one. Initially these two schools lost their able children. They went to Tadcaster until the two developed their own '0' level and 'A' level courses. The pattern of development varied from area to area and was more evolutionary than the sudden change of status which could be dictated by a political decision.

A major area of debate was the curriculum and the possible courses for a new school at Mexborough were examined in 1960 in relation to the Crowther Report. Alec Clegg felt the school should aim to attract many more young people to stay longer in full-time education. If this aim was accepted then he felt it was necessary " ... to construct a new system of education for the years between 15 or 16 and 18 which would neither suffer from those defects of the part-time route nor be academic in the old conventional sense." There would need to be a change of attitude towards adolescents. They would be treated as students rather than schoolboys and schoolgirls. Mexborough would have an open college. As the head George Sheild put it - "It is a cardinal principle that a place will be available for all who want to come whatever their ability."

CHAPTER 7

THE FOUNDATION - INFANT AND JUNIOR SCHOOLS

Social revolution was a term used by two historians to describe significant changes which took place in Britain. One wrote about changes in public education between 1870 and 1935, the other about changes in society. as a whole after 1945. The first historian added the word 'silent', the second 'shrinking'. Silent was chosen to concentrate in one word the quiet, remarkable advances made in schools since 1870. Shrinking focussed on the hopes which accompanied the massive Labour victory in 1945, and which were not realised as quickly or as fully as people expected. These two words are a reminder that within society the pace and character of change can differ. It can accelerate in public health and stagnate in education, moreover regions and districts can conform to, or diverge from, the national pattern. Furthermore a study of the origins of change may identify certain places and people as being the engines of progress. This study of Alec Clegg and West Riding Schools illustrates the continuation of the Silent Revolution until the sixties when a sequence of reports reflect how silence was changing to public debate.

A new order was built before and after the Second World War and its foundation was in the infant and junior schools. Many of the characteristics of these changes filtered through into the secondary schools. It was a slow process hence its quiet demeanour. It was not the stuff of publicity hence it ran the risk of remaining unrecognised. The details of the changes in the foundation years of public education deserve careful analysis for these were the centrepiece of the ideas and achievements of Alec Clegg and the West Riding Education Service. The changes in the West Riding were not silent nor do they deserve to be included in the evidence for a 'Shrinking Social Revolution'. They illustrate how much could be done and paradoxically how much was left to be done. Alec Clegg would have concurred with the conclusion to G.A.N. Lowndes book 'The Silent Social Revolution' P.248 - "So long as there is one child who has failed to obtain the precise educational treatment his individuality requires, so long as a single child goes hungry, has nowhere to play, fails to receive the medical attention he needs; so long as the nation fails to train and provide scope for every atom of outstanding ability it can find; so long as there are administrators or teachers who feel no sense of mission, who cannot administer or who cannot teach, the system will remain incomplete."

The forecast Alec Clegg made in the radio debate (1) that the changes taking place in the infant schools would continue into the junior schools in the remaining years of the fifties and into the sixties was realised. Some fifty junior schools out of a total of about one thousand in the West Riding were by the mid sixties achieving what " ... only two or three could manage ten years ago, and a great majority are showing clear signs of developing in the same way." These figures show what had been achieved and also, significantly, how much was still to be done. The incentive to adopt new ideas and methods was nurtured by inspectors and advisers who arranged and partook in local courses and those which made up the programme at Woolley Hall. The pressure on junior schools to concentrate attention on the achievement of as many grammar school places as possible was eased by the intro-duction of the Thorne Scheme (2) and by comprehensive reorgani-sation. Furthermore the age of transfer was being questioned on a number of grounds adding to this feeling that the opportunity to increase the scale and pace of change was now at hand.

The inspectors' and advisers' reports for the fifties and sixties give reality to the pace of change. It was slow, especially if one compares the number of innovative schools to the total number of junior schools in the West Riding. However given a new appointment, especially a headteacher, a conversion to new ideas and methods and a school could change in a relatively short time. Bentley Toll Bar school got a bad Ministry Report in 1955 yet by summer 1956 Miss Wyllie CCI was reporting improvement, noting " ... now that teaching is being conducted on individual lines teachers and pupils alike are experiencing satisfaction." At the time of the inspection the Divisional Medical Officer said "at one time at least half of the children should be in special schools". Miss

Wyllie asked him to make another visit. He was surprised at the progress which had been made and this significant comment was made on a little girl with an IQ of 63. "She should really be in a special school - yet this child is steady and stable and is happily working away and making good progress - not to mention fitting in with the environment of the school. Why should she be made exceptional, if she can pass as normal?"

When Miss Wyllie retired in 1960 she reflected on her years in the West Riding saying -

"Looking back over the years I appear to have achieved little, but I think you will get my meaning if I describe it as pioneer work at the beginning." What had been built up was a spirit of goodwill.

Mr Easto, a physical education adviser, concentrated on the Craven Area primary schools in 1955 and he felt that a majority showed a readiness to think again about " ... their aims and the purpose of their work." In the following year he found the teachers in the Spen Valley and Gaskell Division " ... much more receptive and 70 to 80 teachers took part in 11 local sessions on a movement approach to Physical Education." Yet in the same area only one out of the seven newly appointed teachers of physical education intended to teach creative dance. The tidal nature of educational change is well illustrated in Mr Easto's reports. Regularly he stressed the need for a series of visits to schools which were embarking on new ways of teaching. The other regular feature of his reports are his references to the secondary schools the " ... most disappointing and unrewarding branch of his work."

In Art the advances in the field of pottery are described in detail. Those teachers who went to Woolley on an introductory course met 30 times in 1956 and had reached the stage in December where they were involved in glaze and majolica work.

This degree of commitment would appear to be the way to ensure new ideas continued to flow into the schools, but tides have a backwash, and in 1960 this comment follows a detailed account of combined courses run by the advisers, Rocke, Thomas and Davis - "Some of our best Junior Schools have been criticised by H.M.I.'s and some criticism is justified. This occurs in those cases where work has deteriorated to the level of sensitive copying." If this was a risk H.M.I.'s identified amongst youngsters in a classroom, it was also a risk amongst heads who wished to be seen to be progressive. They copied the visible signs of progress, the carefully mounted display of children's work, topics and the integrated day - the symbols rather than the substance of child centred work. The high quality work done by youngsters which was displayed at Woolley Hall on local courses and which was used for publications such as "The Excitement of Writing" prompted disbelief amongst some teachers. Miss Jones, an adviser for Housecraft expressed concern about " ... the reaction of teachers who are shown work from other schools and their doubts about its authenticity." A mix of this sort of viewpoint with a superficial adherence to change could at its worst produce in a school what one adviser termed 'a permanent wet lunchtime.'

Some Schools Council Projects were instrumental in promoting innovation, cooperation and solid advances in schools. Aireville Secondary Modern School in Skipton had a good Rural Studies Department which built up an animal bank which was used by twenty or more primary schools involved in the Nuffield Junior Science Project. The mix of local, county and national sources of ideas and resources stood a better chance of success than initiatives which in many cases were dependent on one, or a few enthusiasts.

The work advisers saw in schools often prompted them to reflect on its significance in relation to the aims and methods of teaching. In his 1961 report Mr Barton Wood wrote of Art as "the language of the imagination". He was sure subject thinking limited imaginative expression. Art as a source of personal progress was recorded by another Art adviser who quoted the example of two boys who were transferred from Horbury Secondary Modern School to Morley Grammar School so that they could attempt a G.C.E. in Art. They were put in the bottom stream and at the end of the first term they held the first and second positions in the form. Perhaps the exceptions invite comment but it is difficult to escape the conclusion that to perceptive people teaching is a profession of surprises.

Some advisers found it difficult to report exactly on the Arts. Diana Jordan argued in a lengthy memorandum to Alec Clegg in

December 1952 that " ... real quality is elusive and a by product of distinguished teaching. " In Dance and Movement she held that "... it disappears when the teacher leaves.' Her standpoint of the delicate, transient nature of quality prompted Alec Clegg to reply that there was more continuity in quality work than she imagined.

Four years later, in December 1956, Alec Clegg wrote a very detailed twelve page reply to a request by Mrs Summers, wife of a West Riding headteacher, to visit some of the quality schools in the county. This letter was written on Christmas morning and Alec Clegg confessed he was as a result "... not popular in this house at the moment." The central issue in the letter was the transient nature of innovative teaching. He described his role in relation to the handful of junior schools as one of help, encouragement and the avoidance of publicity. The Education Committee would be given no more than a straightforward account of what was going on in these schools. In the absence of pressure these schools would have the opportunity to achieve quiet, thorough progress. He expressed his concern that the habit of formalising change led in A.N. Whitehead's words to a -

"... fall from one formalism into another; from one dunghill of inert ideas into another."

The central issue in the letter was the nature of the work in the handful of good junior schools. Reflecting on the progress made in these schools he wrote -

"We have created this ferment in schools deliberately. It is now no longer just happening - we don't just accept it as a bonus - a lucky strike we have produced and accentuated it in a few junior schools." He maintained that what had been revealed was "... a potential which we did not know existed." His letter ended -

"I don't want it to get precious. I don't want to shoot a line about it - but if my judgement is correct we shall slowly and surely change the pattern of education in this country in the next 10 years." Whatever Alec Clegg wrote about publicity the interest created in educational circles by the changes in West Riding junior schools was considerable. Training colleges sent staff and students to see the work. The former Ministry Staff Inspector for Junior Schools who moved to the London Institute sent parties up to

Yorkshire to see what he termed "unique work". The Ministry itself ran a course at Woolley Hall in early 1957 and Woolley Hall hosted a sequence of courses attended by educationalists from Germany, America, Norway and the Antipodes. There may have been only a handful of schools, but the distinctive nature of the changes aroused widespread interest.

Before the West Riding ended Alec Clegg built up a collection of films, slides and tape recordings of work in primary schools. Many of these schools were the ones which in the fifties and sixties had been the front runners in change. The numerous conversations between Alec Clegg, teachers and children give the listener rich evidence of their accomplishments which could readily deserve the title 'the excitement of listening'.

The head of Lilly Hall School, Maltby, talks about a Junk Stew with the plodding signature tune of Steptoe and Son in the background. A dustman brought a collection of junk into the school and it was put on display. It was described, discussed, handled, drawn, smelt and written about. The shapes, textures and smells were the sources of work. Another day the children were taken on an early morning walk in the mist and they collected many spiders which they took back to school to identify, to draw and to describe before they were returned to the hedges they came from. In wilder weather they went out to watch the trees in a strong wind. The teachers who made these decisions saw opportunities, took them and brought an excitement to the school day. If they used written sources they used those which were closest to the first hand. Victorian England was seen through the eyes of Henry Mayhew's characters and if the topic was studied near Christmas time a display of Victorian Christmas cards was used.

The junior school at Altofts celebrated its centenary in 1972. Teachers used the first log book to give its 105 pupils an insight into Victorian Altofts. Perhaps the children got a sense of superiority when they read of the 67 who were there in 1872 " ... most of whom were untidy and unkempt in appearance." Discussion with local people on the past brought a reality to history which probably left a permanent stamp on a child's memory. About five miles away at Airedale Middle School a four day visit to London was undertaken in the same year. Alec Clegg was a regular visitor to this school and built up a detailed collection of work done by the children in Mrs Pyrah's class. Tape recordings of the preparations and the aftermath of the visit were made and they give an insight into how individual interest can be built into a carefully programmed visit. The journey to London was broken by a visit to the American War Cemetery outside Cambridge, and followed by a visit to Cambridge itself. The individual topic books record the reflections of the children on the cemetery. One youngster wrote "Rows and rows of crosses were spread out over a large lawn." Another wrote "Thousands of bright grave stones hit me, as I peered over the hill." Once in Cambridge the tour of the colleges prompted this matter of fact observation -

"Every college had its own chapel which seemed rather stupid when they could all worship in just a couple of chapels."

The discussions that preceded the visit drew on the scattered knowledge and interests the children had in the capital. They ranged from Rugby League Finals at Wembley to a boy's interest in William Wilberforce and the Slave Trade. So when they visited Westminster Abbey it was not just to appreciate architecture but for one boy to find the memorial to Wilberforce and another to find that to Sir Isaac Newton. Others recorded their first impressions of a national monument. Before the visit one boy had told Alec Clegg that he was looking forward to four days eating sweets. Sweets came up in the discussion after the visit. Some of the children had offered sweets to soldiers on duty at Windsor Castle and were told by others they they were awful for they might get the men court martialled! Another recorded his memory of St. James' Park twelve birds' nests built in one of the gates. Like a good meal this visit had a main course and a variety of starters and sweets. It catered for individual taste yet provided a balanced diet. Visits conducted in this way are a pointer to the truth Liam Hudson sought when he wrote about creativity in his book 'Contrary Imaginations' - P.136

"Naive people believe that you create conformity by discipline and originality by being permissive. Equally naive people, it seems believe the reverse; that beauty is born of hard times, while intellectual and material advantage produces dullards. The truth, whatever it is, is not as simple as this."

Forethought by teachers produces its own discipline for the main route of their work is clear and allows them to let youngsters make diversions according to their own interests. There can be freedom within discipline. The mix will differ from child to child. Balby Street Junior School in Denaby, probably one the most depressing colliery villages in South Yorkshire, was a very good school. Not one child in the school came from a family with a professional background.

After eight years as headteacher of Balby Street Junior School in Denaby, South Yorkshire, Arthur Naylor engaged in a taped discussion with Alec Clegg. He stressed the importance of the Arts in his philosophy. He said that many of the children who entered the school were unable to communicate in any way. It was not the fault of the infant school but of the society in which they lived. His answer to this question 'What does one do with a frustrated child?' was "give them concrete materials, certain guidance and clear limits, and lastly freedom within those limits." He felt the right relationship between teacher and child would lead to a child wishing to communicate. Music, Art, Movement and Drama gave the children a chance to express themselves. Alec Clegg spoke to all of the six teachers in the school and each of them said that the expressive work had a marked carry over into reading, writing and arithmetic. Balby Street was one of the first in the country to be designated an Educational Priority School. The head's philosophy was expressed simply as 'It is the doing that matters...' If the work of schools such as Balby Street was put forward as the blueprint for advance nationwide one of the first to challenge such a suggestion would have been the Chief Education Officer of the West Riding. He appreciated the individuality of schools and of the teachers and pupils within the schools. In his view generalisation and ossification were constant dangers.

Simpsons Lane Infant School was opened in 1967 near Kellingley Colliery. Many miners and their families moved from Scotland and the North East at this time to secure jobs in the expanding Yorkshire coalfield. The teachers in the school provided a wide variety of things to look at, to handle and to provide opportunities for experiment. The head told Alec Clegg "We want to get them talking". The things that the children handled, weighed and discussed included buttons, sticks and golf balls, and they would find out how many of each weighed an ounce. The displays of objects focussed attention on colours and textures which they would describe. The school had 280 children and took in three year olds. It was a popular school with a waiting list and considerable parental involvement in its work. The welcome to parents played an important part in the slow process of creating a feeling of community in the surrrounding Coal Board and Council estates. The parents like their children provided surprises. A mother of a very naughty boy was very good with other children in school and their good behaviour rubbed off on her own son. Questioned on programming works for infants the head stressed that it was less a 'deliberate' programme but more a matter of picking the right moment when the child shows interest.

The red brick terraces of Castleford would seem an unlikely place to provide inspiration for a great artist yet this was the home of Henry Moore. In his biography of Moore, Herbert Read draws attention to three teachers, John Holland in the elementary school who encouraged Henry's natural aptitude for design; Thomas Dawes the 'unorthodox' headmaster of Castleford Grammar School; and lastly, and most important " ... Miss Alice Gostick, a woman of half French origin who was the first to recognise the exceptional nature of her pupil's talents and consistently encouraged their development throughout the decisive years of his education." The range of achievement that can result from a single source is wonderfully illustrated by Henry Moore's reaction to the gift of an elephant skull in 1968 from Sir Julian Huxley. Between 1968 and 1970 Henry Moore produced 33 etchings of this skull. The etchings were put on display at Woolley Hall not just as a tribute to Moore's imagination and skill, but as a prompt to teachers to see what could happen when they provided a promising starting point for work.

The headmistress at Wakefield Girls High School gets similar praise to that of Miss Gostick in the biography of Barbara Hepworth another Yorkshire sculptor - Page 11

"Miss McCroben must have been an extraordinary woman, capable of detecting her pupils' special gifts and guiding them, where possible, into the proper channels. For she not only encouraged Barbara's independence of mind but took active steps to secure a scholarship. These, in a sense, were decisive factors in determining the young girl's future." Perhaps the most detailed, imaginative and powerful appreciation of a teacher was written by Ted Hughes, Poet Laureate, and given by him at Mexborough Parish Church on 10th April 1980.

His appreciation of John Fisher was a remarkable tribute to an exceptional teacher as he said -

"Many English teachers can unlock this treasure house, John Fisher was one of the few who could then use this treasure to unlock people. Opening those treasures, he could open people."

"For all these he became a most important person - and for very many, perhaps, their chief spiritual guide through their most precarious and formative years.

To hold the keys to our greatest national treasure - our literature - is no small responsibility.

And our poem would have to take full account of how John Fisher used those keys - of how he, not only opened the treasure-house, but opened the treasures within the treasure. Our physical scope is recorded in our genes. But our spiritual scope, and our awareness of our nationality, is coded in the literature of our tribe - and, unless we are given possession of that, and are taught the currency of it, then we are beggars in our own community, and strangers in our own towns.

Our poem would have to render in full just how he did this.

Living for this work, as he did, even to the neglect of his own freedoms; giving his life, as he did, to teaching the best, and to teaching what was precious in the best, the high moments of his life, I've no doubt his real achievements were those extraordinary trances in the classroom - extraordinary to all who experienced them - when he raised his congregation of students into the inmost spirit of some literary masterpiece, and communicated its beauty and its power and its meanings direct, in the most startling way.

Our poem would have to recreate those moments with King Lear or Paradise Lost or the Prelude, when he imparted such stocks of understanding, such a sudden grasp of how valuable these things were - sometimes only with an exclamation or a look.

This was teaching of a sort that happens in spiritual communities more often than in schools. In those moments he was able to alter one's whole imagination, with new meaning.

And whoever alters our imagination, alters the foundation of our life; they change everything that happens to us.

We would render full justice to this in our poem. We would render, too, some account of what so many of us owe him for these gifts. And this would be a very complex and weighty part of our poem, because our debt to him in this way has gone into everything we know and are.

It was a strange power he had, to transmit so completely his own love for these creations, and his feeling for their worth. As a detail, for instance, my part of our poem would include how he bestowed on me a sudden total infatuation for the music of Beethoven without - and this is the strange part - my ever having consciously listened to one note of it.

Hearing John speak of Beethoven, I suddenly found myself possessed by this passion for a composer - whom I then had to set out to discover, but who very quickly, and permanently, took the same position in my life as he had in John's. And that is only one example.

To speak adequately of this sort of teaching, our poem would need all its inspiration, as it would to convey just what it means, and how immensely important it is that so many of John's students are carrying around the seeds of this experience. Such seeds can be dormant a long time and might even flower on in a next generation, but they are there. John sowed them and they have actual existence, and those seeds hold the survival and the future of the spirit of our culture."

It is worth quoting a scientist to end this section for Jacob Bronowski in the 'Ascent of Man' recognised that -

"...the most powerful drive in the ascent of man is his pleasure in his own skill. He loves to do what he does well and having done it well, he loves to do it better."

A yung foale

This foale is a harabe
and he has. a long
Life. heade of hum
and when he grows
up. he will be picoally
Be sadeld up and Be
ridane. Harabe horses.
Aree Good strong horses.
They Have to be Well groomd
And well fed if realey hungry.

When Brian Wiper started school at Rossington he could not read or write. Brian's interest in horses was encouraged and he began a series of drawings. These illustrate his artistic skill and sensitivity. Alongside his artistic development he began to read and write. The drawing above illustrates his skill and sensitivity.

Reference to "A yung foale". This drawing and description illustrate this parallel development.

CHAPTER 8

ALEC CLEGG AND THE WIDER
WORLD OF EDUCATION

Alec Clegg's keen interest in what was going on in West Riding Schools was matched by his interest in what was going on elsewhere. Visits to other parts of this country and abroad to America, Australasia and Europe enriched his knowledge and enabled him to assess West Riding policy against a wide and detailed educational back-cloth. The visits often prompted dialogues, return visits and initiatives such as the regular Anglo-Norwegian courses at Woolley Hall. In pessimistic mood Alec Clegg could foresee English cities suffering the disorder and misery of American cities if the problems of the maladjusted and the deprived were not addressed at school level. On the other hand he could reflect on why Australia had so few of the problems abundantly apparent in American cities and already growing in urban Britain.

When Alec Clegg visited Germany in the autumn of 1953 he went to grammar schools in Dortmund, Hamm and Unna. Also he went to primary schools in the Arnsberg area. He contrasted the financial and curricular responsibilities of schools and local authorities in Britain with those in Germany. In his account of the visit he wrote -

"The result of all this is the interesting point that, although the instruction, method and curriculum tend to be highly centralised by comparison with practice over here, buildings tend to be decentralised, and our picture of diversity in education with comparative uniformity in building is reversed over there."

Provided the money was available there was more freedom in Germany to have ambitious projects even in small villages. He described one village school as outstanding, adding -

"It had been planned with a complete understanding of the educational needs of the children and the social needs of the village. In addition to being a delightful school it housed the village fire engine in an annexe, and showers were provided in the basement for the use of the village generally as the water supply in most houses is inadequate. Finally, in order to assure that the Headmaster would be a man who would be at one with the peasant community, a cow stall and pig sties had been built under the basement under his house and sufficient ground was purchased for grazing."

The following autumn Alec Clegg went to the United States and to South America to take part in a UNESCO conference. His letters to Walter Hyman are full of insights and humorous asides on American education and life. In his first letter he ranged from a comparison of New York with Washington to what he termed, the language problem between Britain and the United States. He illustrated this fact by noting that - " ... on the toilet lid in the aeroplane was written - "No waste only from natural causes."

He gave the Hymans details on the controversies in the American High Schools, especially the issue of how to meet the needs of the brightest pupils. At Harvard University and the Teachers' college in New York they favoured the segregation of the ablest youngsters for Mathematics, Science, English and Languages. Most American authorities supported segregation in the High Schools and in this respect provided a blueprint for the way most comprehensive schools were to be organised in the West Riding after secondary reorganisation took place. Americans condemned the eleven plus examination and the stranglehold they felt British universities had on the work of grammar schools. Such information was invaluable to Alec Clegg in preparing policy statements but it lacked the 'immense enjoyment' he experienced during a visit to the Laurence College which was " ... doing marvellous work in music, art and drama." He followed this exhilarating visit with a tour of the worst schools in New York. His list of misconceptions about America would have amused the Hymans. It began with - "There are a lot of beautiful women - it is not so."

When he described the UNESCO conference in Montevideo he began by expressing his hopes of finding out how its ideals were translated into reality. His conclusion was that the conference was a farce and he ended with the words "I have never in all my life been so disillusioned."

The rich vein of humour in the letters Alec Clegg sent to the Hymans changed in 1955 when Mr Fuller Smith and the Conservatives gained control of the Council. In a memorandum to two of his staff, Mr Brown and Mr Tidswell, he summarised the instructions he had received from "our masters". The Conservatives had to be informed " ... well in advance" of any major issues which were to be brought before the committee and specific reference was made to the Further Education Section which was liable "... to spring things on us". The assertive nature of the meeting is reflected in the style of the memorandum, the only exception being the fifth out of fourteen points where Alec Clegg reported "we are to be allowed to pick potatoes." The stark nature of the programme of economy is punctured by this one sentence; a reference to the schoolboys autumnal escape from the classroom.

Similarly officers would inject humour into their confidential reports to the Chief. Mr Eyles, who dealt with Further Education, visited Paris in the spring of 1956. If this report had been 'sprung' on the Committee it is doubtful if they would have felt it appropriate to a time of economy.

His visit is described as follows

"With a view to getting ideas on the display of garments amongst other things at our evening institute exhibitions, visits were paid to the Casino de Paris and The Folies Bergere. I am not sure that all that was seen would be supported to the same extent in the West Riding. Suffice to say that much of the decor was outstanding and if transferred to this County the problem of reducing the ratio of female to male students would cease to exist!"

Humour could be the oil on troubled waters or the lubricant in the administrative machine, a machine, according to J.E.C. Tidswell who had the overall supervision of secondary schools, which led to him working an additional three hours in the office each night, plus Saturday afternoon there and between four or five hours at home each Sunday. In these circumstances a sense of humour is essential for survval.

During the fifties visitors from abroad came to the West Riding to see schools and to attend courses. In 1954 Dr Elizabeth Halsey of Iowa State University came to see classes in Physical

Education. Two years later thirty men and women teachers from the U.S.A. came on a similar mission. Movement and the Arts in Primary Schools were the centre points of interest. Invitations to advisory staff and primary teachers to organise courses in Cleveland were made by the Independent Schools Association of the U.S.A. From 1952 to 1957 teachers and inspectors from Norway came to the West Riding to see Primary school work, especially in Art and Physical Education, and to attend courses at Woolley Hall. Other overseas links, such as those with Germany and Australia, enriched the exchange of people and ideas giving the West Riding an important place in the worldwide debate on education.

In a narrower sense the wider world of education was the rest of Britain, and in particular the place of Alec Clegg and the West Riding in relation to developments in England and Wales. Studies such as the Early Leaving Report of 1954 and the Crowther Report of 1959 underlined the need to increase the numbers in sixth forms and higher education in order to meet the future demands of the professions, commerce and industry. Advances in science and technology called for widespread changes in education. As the Crowther Report concluded -

" ... it is not only at the top but almost to the bottom of the pyramid that the scientific revolution of our time needs to be reflected in a longer educational process."

Lord Robbins reflected on his acceptance of the chairmanship of the committee appointed to report on higher education in these words -

"The enterprise to which I had thus committed myself was one which was to extend me to the utmost for the better part of the next three years." (1)

The correspondence in the West Riding which was prompted by the work of the Robbins Committee illustrates that it had a similar effect on Alec Clegg. The letters which passed between him and other Chief Education Officers and friends in the universities show Alec Clegg as a focal point of deeply held views on two issues - firstly, the suggestion that there should be two Ministers of Education, and, secondly that local authorities should relinquish control of their training colleges. Lord Robbins expressed regret that on both issues his views were not accepted.

In 1958 the Yorkshire Association of Education Committees stated that - "... the scarcity of teachers for primary schools is likely for the next ten years to be a greater threat to the education service than is a shortage of school buildings." Where the teacher shortage was most acute the suggestion that the West Riding gave up the control of its training colleges could only be viewed with grave apprehension. As in so many other areas of his work Alec Clegg got detailed evidence together which he fed into the Robbins debate, especially on the future of the training colleges. The correspondence is of interest not only for what it tells us of the issues debated and the quality of that debate, but how it illustrates the difficulties which have to be faced when 'excellent proposals' (Alec Clegg's words) are to be translated into regional or local policy.

The suggestion that the control of teacher training colleges be transferred to the universities ignored the effective response the West Riding and other local education authorities had made to the mounting demand for teachers after 1945. Moreover the West Riding institutions for higher education had by the sixties an important part to play in maintaining the momentum for change. As Alec Clegg put it in a letter to the Prime Minister in October 1963. "The Local Education Authorities forced the pace as no direct grant institution could have done." The single mindedness of the West Riding to solve the teacher shortage would be replaced by university control and the likelihood that the teacher training department would be one of many competing for funds instead of being a separately funded and governed institution.

The range and detailed nature of the evidence collected for the submissions to the Robbins Committee is remarkable. Attention was concentrated on able children particularly those in the industrial parts of the West Riding. The disadvantages many faced in seeking places in higher education and those faced by the ones who got to college or university were explored in detail. The results of the 1958 investigation into the distribution of youngsters with intelligence quotients above 130 is shown in Appendices ...

As Clegg wrote -

" ... the really disturbing facts which emerged from the investigation are that when the able children from South Yorkshire do get to the grammar school they are less likely to get to the sixth form, if they get an award it is less likely to get them to Oxford and Cambridge than would be the case if they attended schools in the west or north." Further details gathered in 1959 and 1961 strongly confirmed the conclusions reached in 1958. Set the desperate teacher shortage in South Yorkshire alongside this evidence and one can appreciate the pressing need to examine the implications of the Robbins suggestions on teacher training against detailed evidence from the colleges and schools in the West Riding. The training colleges gained considerable advantages from other county council departments such as the architects. Such advantages would go if the colleges became departments in universities. Moreover, the deliberate attempt to recruit local people into West Riding colleges and to encourage service in West Riding schools would probably lose some of its strength if the change was made. Colleges had their efforts focussed fully upon the supply of quality teachers, whereas within universities the teacher training department was one department amongst many. Also a proportion of their students opted for the extra year of teacher training so at least they got a job in education. They were not enthusiasts.

Not stated, but possibly a real consideration, was the feeling many like Alec Clegg had of personal involvement and pride in the setting up of the West Riding colleges such as Bretton Hall and Wentworth Woodhouse. On the other hand courses run at Woolley Hall by university staff often prompted comment that they were remote from the real needs of young teachers likely to become probationers in a South Yorkshire modern school. Diana Jordan's confidential comments on a course run by Leeds University professors at Woolley Hall on the writing of English in spring 1958 were typical of those sent to Alec Clegg on courses of this type. She wrote -

"I cannot see that these University professors can do anything but make education more and more complex." She added " ... Yet, when we listen to writers and poets, masters of the art of language, talking at other courses everyone understands, everyone goes with them and is lifted to higher realms of comprehension." (2)

Some indication of the range of Alec Clegg's enquiries can be illustrated by the exchange of letters with grammar school headmasters outside the West Riding and with academics in universities. The head of the High School for boys in Nottingham agreed that there were legitimate complaints against universities but he expressed his unease about naming them. Sir Nevill Mott of the Cavendish Laboratory, Cambridge felt many of the local authorities were too small to be responsible for higher education. There seemed a disposition to recognise the strength of Alec Clegg's cause but limited support for the maintenance of teacher training college independence.

Opinions such as these need to be set against the exact details gathered from West Riding Schools. Sheffield University had 100 students in its geography group at the start of an academic year. It was cut down to 25 at the end of the year many students being transferred on to a General Course.

At the end of this study of wastage Alec Clegg wrote -

"Our heads can give example after example of wastage over 30% and sometimes as high as 75%."

Authorities such as Essex, Middlesex and Leeds along with members of the Association of Chief Education Officers provided information for Alec Clegg. With ample evidence to hand Alec Clegg corresponded with Sir Edward Boyle, Sir William Alexander and newspapers such as the Sunday Times, the Financial Times and the Daily Express. Other Chief Education Officers shared Alec Clegg's feeling that the universities, along with many of the Robbins Committee, were uneasy about the wealth of evidence produced and made public in opposition to university control of teacher training. One of the most succinct comments on the issue was made by F.Lincoln Ralphs, the Chief Education Officer of Norfolk who wrote - "The Report throughout seems more anxious to protect the freedom of universities to do as they like rather than to enable those in education to like what they do."

The Robbins Report echoed the conclusions of the West Riding studies of how few able working class youngsters went to universities. Alec Clegg in this his last report 'The Final Ten Years' said, "These facts stirred the Committee into embarking on a scheme, the results of which are only just known."

The Oxbridge scheme was devised so as to obtain places at co-operative Oxford and Cambridge colleges for sixth form boys from working class families. As with so many of the schemes associated with Alec Clegg it had at its heart the assessment and appreciation of character and potential rather than a bare record of exam success. The personal contacts made by Alec Clegg led to four Cambridge colleges - Churchill, Clare, Fitzwilliam and Kings' - taking part whilst at Oxford - Merton, St Catherines' and University colleges were involved in the scheme. Masters such as Alan Bullock of St Catherines' and Sir Eric Ashby of Clare were men likely to give active support to Alec Clegg's initiative. Although the scheme did no more than turn a trickle of working class boys into Oxford and Cambridge into a substantial trickle it provided proof of a wide range of untapped ability. Moreover it underlined the independence of spirit and grittiness of the young Yorkshire men who took part in this social and educational experiment. (3)

The procedure adopted within the West Riding was to divide the authority into groups of schools, each group putting forward candidates for interview by a panel consisting of two experienced heads and the Chief Education Officer. Those selected were interviewed by particular colleges, and provided they obtained the minimum advanced level qualifications, they would be admitted one year after they completed their sixth form course. The additional year was to be spent in broadening a young man's outlook and experience. The planning of this year was done by the head of the school in consultation with the Authority.

An important part of the preparations for the Oxbridge scheme was the establishment of links with industrialists and business men in the North, so that a range of useful broadened courses could be available for the year prior to a young man entering Oxford or Cambridge. The County Youth Employment

Officer wrote to a wide range of employers in June 1965. Of the fifty contacted 21 gave positive replies, 13 did not answer and the remainder said 'No' or replied in such a way that nothing of practical use was offered. Firms such as English Electric, Crompton Parkinson, Yorkshire Imperial Metals, Steel, Peach & Tozer, Rolls Royce and others agreed to take part. I.C.I. were prepared to accept nominations provided they were ... 'on the science side.'

Some firms went further and explored the possibility of European and overseas links giving the West Riding Authority confidence that suitable placements could be made. The significance of the term 'broadening' is illustrated by this key sentence in a very long reply from Rowntrees of York - "It is certainly a scheme in which we should like to participate, but I am at the moment a little doubtful whether we can provide employment which would be suitably broadening." They suggested laboratory work as a possibility.

Yet another example of Alec Clegg's careful preparation was a West Riding enquiry in November 1963 into the successes of boys rejected by Oxford or Cambridge who went to other universities. Of the 31 grammar schools who replied 17 provided details of rejected applicants who went elsewhere, seventy five per cent of whom gained either first or top second degrees. Apart from academic achievement the heads drew attention to the sporting and other achievements of this group. The case for the Oxbridge scheme was underpinned by such studies and this useful preparation was matched by the support given to students throughout the years of the scheme.

Alec Clegg was personally involved in the scheme from the initial selection of the candidate to the aftermath of the university course. He completed most of their personal files with the candidates reflections on university life and the scheme itself. The correspondence comprises sixty individual histories fattened out by the necessary forms giving details of parental income, reports from tutors and a considerable number of requests from students for prompt payment of grants. The latter are a reminder that these young men came from families whose incomes were small compared to those enjoyed by the parents of the public schoolboys who made up the bulk of most college communities.

Although the initial approach was to a Cambridge College it was Merton, the oldest college in either university and described by John Betjeman as " ... a series of higgledy, piggledy buildings set among meadows ..." which took the first two under the Oxbridge scheme. These two went up to Oxford in 1964 and the West Riding publication for the decade 1954 to 1964 said " ... their progress will be watched with interest".

Interest changed to apprehension for the difficulties forecast for South Yorkshire youngsters materialised, and one of the two left Merton College after two years. A year away and a return to complete his third year was suggested but he left, went to the University of Kent and successfully completed his degree. The detailed letters which passed between the college, the Chief Education Officer and the school show all three were deeply concerned to foster personal ease, confidence and success, but the Merton tutor concluded that he was the "....least understood student he had ever met." It was not a lack of ability but a deep insularity which perplexed the college. The other student enjoyed his first term 'immensely' but felt his broadened course, spent partly in Germany and partly in a factory, had not improved his physics. The first two entrants under the Clegg scheme had broken the ice but they illustrated the difficulties which would have to be anticipated and faced.

Dennis Potter, playwright and son of a Forest of Dean coal miner, wrote the Nigel Barton plays which were in part reflections on his experiences at Oxford University. Speaking in an Oxford Union debate the central character, Nigel Barton, probably puts into words what many working class boys felt when they went up to one of the older universities -

"No one who has been brought up in a working class culture can ever altogether escape, or wish to escape, the almost suffocating warmth and friendliness of that culture. But - and this is what I mean by the personal element - as soon as you cross the frontiers between one class and another you feel - I feel - as though you are negotiating a minefield." (4)

110

There was a social gulf which had to be bridged and most did it by hard work and personality, a large part of which was Yorkshire grit. After three years at Clare College one student gave as his last piece of advice. "Never be ashamed of a good Yorkshire accent, Take pride in it, and cultivate it!".

The extent to which the West Riding went to help Oxbridge students is well illustrated by one who took a Music Degree at Kings' College, Cambridge. The Director of Studies interviewed him before he went up to Kings' and wrote "I cannot recommend (he) be admitted to read music at Kings' ". Things did not look promising but arrangements were made for personal tuition on Saturdays by West Riding peripatetic staff and also for him to gain extra experience as a viola player. He was given unlimited use of the Authority's gramophone library and Miss Spence, Music Adviser, arranged for him to receive regular tuition in advanced composition at Guiseley Music Centre. Later in August he went to Edinburgh University to attend a Music Course directed by Professor Mellors.

The first letter Alec Clegg received from the Senior Tutor described the young man as " ... a staunch and humorous chap. I like him very much ..,". Much of his first year was spent in a wide variety of musical activities as he put in a letter " ... the opportunity like Everest, is there. Later he was accepted into what he termed "the musical aristocracy" - the University First Orchestra.. This gave him the privilege of playing under the baton of Benjamin Britten at the Aldeburgh Festival. Also he played in the college water polo team breaking the Kings' tradition for intellectual intensity and athletic apathy.

Alec Clegg received a detailed account of the strain of exams on students taking the Music Tripos - eight three hour papers plus a practical exam taken in five consecutive days. There was a strong feeling amongst students that not only was there too heavy a burden of exams but the marking was too severe. This student represented others in complaining on this issue. These matters were relayed in considerable detail to Alec Clegg ending with an apology for the length of the letter and hope that it had not savoured too much of 'The History of the fall of Caesar' or

Osborne's 'Angry Young Man'. The letter was reflective as well for Alec Clegg was treated to thoughts on music as a creative art and on the nature of inspiration. Perhaps the instinctive delight youngsters in Primary schools gained from creative work had its mature expression in many of these letters.

The fact that the Robbins Committee were persuaded to drop the proposal to put teacher training under university control could be seen as largely a successful rearguard action by Alec Clegg and the West Riding. Perhaps some would see this fact as evidence of Yorkshire intransigence, but set the initiative of the Oxbridge scheme alongside it and the conclusion must be that progress involves a subtle mix of conservation and enterprise. When he reflected on the scheme in 1973 Alec Clegg quoted a famous remark from the Crowther Report -

" ... what is extracted from the pool of ability depends much less on the content of the pool than on the effectiveness of the pump."

By the mid sixties the Oxbridge scheme was established and, as with the debate on the effectiveness of the 11+ examination in selection for grammar schools, the scheme was to cast doubt on over reliance on 'A' level results for university selection.

THE OXBRIDGE SCHEME

COLLEGES TAKING WEST RIDING OXBRIDGE STUDENTS

OXFORD		CAMBRIDGE	
Merton College	17	Clare	8
St Catherines	11	Kings'	8
University College	7	Churchill	6
		Fitzwilliam	3
TOTAL	35		25

WEST RIDING SCHOOLS SENDING CLEGG SCHOLARS TO OXFORD OR CAMBRIDGE

	No.		No.
Colne Valley H.S.	5	Ripon G.S.	1
Batley G.S. Boys	5	Harrogate G.S.	1
Skipton Ermysteds G.S.	5	Knaresboro G.S.	1
Thorne G.S.	4	Ilkley G.S.	1
Percy Jackson G.S.	3	Bingley G.S.	1
Holme Valley G.S.	3	Ossett G.S.	1
Wath G.S.	3	Whitcliffe Mount G.S.	1
Mexborough G.S.	3	Rastrick G.S.	2
Keighley G.S.	2	Castleford G.S.	1
Pontefract, Kings	2	Wakefield Q.E. G.S.	2
Maltby G.S.	2	Aireborough G.S.	1
Rothwell G.S.	2	Drax G.S.	1
Penistone G.S.	2	Elland G.S.	1
		Calder H.S.	1
		Milfield G.S.	1
		Oakbank G.S.	2

TOTAL NO. OF SCHOLARS - 60

BROAD OCCUPATIONAL BREAKDOWN OF FATHERS EMPLOYMENT

Coal Industry	12
Textile Workers	6
Farm Labourers	3
Shop Workers	3
Joiners, Electricians, Painters, Decorators, Tool Setters, Crane Drivers, etc.	5
Clerical	5
Self-employed - Newsagent, Haulage	2
Public Service	4
Steel Worker	1
Sales Representative	2
County Councillor	1
Others	<u>16</u>
	<u>60</u>

113

COURSES TAKEN AT OXFORD & CAMBRIDGE

A R T S	Oxford	Cambridge
Languages	7	-
French	1	-
English	1	1
History	6	-
Geography	1	-
Classics	1	-
Music	-	1
Law	2	2
Economics	-	1
P.P.E.	2	-
Moral Science.	-	1
	21	6

SCIENCES	Oxford	Cambridge
Chemistry	5	1
Physics	5	-
Mechanical Sciences	-	2
Maths	2	2
Natural Sciences	-	14
Mettalurgy	1	-
	13	19

TOTAL   59

60 Oxbridge candidates - 1 went to University of Kent to complete a degree.

CHAPTER 9

NEWSOM AND THE CHANGE OF HEART

Once absorbed in the detail of official reports such as Newsom and Robbins and the mass of correspondence they generated it is very easy to overlook central issues. Newsom had the title 'Half our Future' and in the foreword Sir Edward Boyle, the Minister of Education, pointed to what schools would have to do if these youngsters were to have the opportunities anticipated in the 1944 Education Act. He wrote -

"Their potentialities are no less real, and of no less importance, because they do not readily lend themselves to measurement by the conventional criteria of academic achievement."

After the report was published Alec Clegg reflected not only on its content but upon its influence on his ideas. To some readers the notes he made may appear pessimistic yet they are more a reflection of his deep and abiding concern with the lot of the majority of youngsters who went through the state education system. His view was -

"It is a pleasant and comforting thing to improve the ladder of advancement for those capable of climbing it - but it is quite another to muster concern for those who can't go beyond the first ten rungs. What an odd thing it is that the children in the special class for the retarded earn our concern and compassion - but those who are so unfortunate that they don't quite fall into it are the riff-raff, the duds, the blockheads - therefore the delinquents." He saw few signs after publication "... of vigorous effort to implement" the report, moreover he added "let us be quite clear about this - comprehensive schools won't do it." To Alec Clegg the introduction of comprehensive schools and a new set of examinations was an advance, but there was no guarantee that they would foster changes which would benefit society at large. The implications of Newsom could be examined at different levels and Alec Clegg illustrated this standpoint by looking at the context of Robert Lowe's oft repeated remark on the Second Reform Act of 1867 -

"We must educate our masters."

The detail which accompanied this statement gave a much clearer picture of class preservation.

"I don't think it is any part of the duty of the Government to prescribe what people should learn except in the case of the poor where time is so limited that we must fix upon a few elementary subjects to get anything done at all ... the lower classes ought to be educated to discharge the duties cast upon them. They should also be educated that they may appreciate and defer to a higher cultivation when they meet it, and the higher classes ought to be educated in a very different manner in order that they may exhibit to the lower classes that higher education to which if it were shown to them they would bow down and defer." (1)

Unlike the Robbins report Newsom prompted Alec Clegg to think deeply about English society and he looked back to John Ruskin, not Robert Lowe, for ideas. Ruskin's view of education was very different to that of Lowe - "The entire object of true education is to make people not merely do the right things but enjoy the right things."

With this as a starting point Alec Clegg looked at the implications of the 1944 Act " ...with its implication of complete social mobility and a theoretical rejection of the social stratification on which our society has hitherto been based." These reflections prompted by Newsom remained at the heart of Alec Clegg's work up to and beyond his retirement in 1973.

The Robbins and Newsom Reports were published in 1963, Alec Clegg being one of the Newsom Committee which since 1961 had gathered evidence on " ... the education between the ages of 13 and 16 of pupils, of average or less than average ability ... ". Six symbolic characters, two Browns, two Jones and two Robinsons were used to portray the conclusions reached in a survey of over 6,000 boys and girls. Alec Clegg referred to his work on the Newsom Committee in an article for the Times Educational Supplement in 1973 pointing out -

"The Newsom Committee took a long look at John Robinson from the bottom quartile and found out how little he weighed, how short he was and how he lived in a problem area and was not a prefect or a member of a team or a youth club."

The vast majority of Browns, Jones and Robinsons went to secondary modern schools at this time. The organisation of these schools was wryly described by David Ayerst, a member of the Newsom and Crowther Committees, in recipe form -

"Take thirty pupils, add a teacher, provide a syllabus and cook together at an even temperature for one to five periods a week according to whether the recipe is for Physics, French or Religious Instruction." (2)

With teacher shortages, inadequate buildings and growing numbers of pupils, especially in areas such as the south of the West Riding, even the maintenance of a stable diet seemed an ambitious aim. Go beyond that and you could be inviting disaster.

The number and character of the courses run at Woolley Hall between 1957 and 1965 illustrate how the West Riding sought to encourage change and quality work in its schools. (3)

Those courses which were directed at Secondary Modern Schools nearly doubled during these years. Some were joint courses attended by teachers in primary and secondary schools, others concentrated on grammar or modern schools. Joint courses invited a dialogue which, if successful, could lead to the implications of the changes at primary level being discussed and developed in secondary schools.

More important than the increase in the number of courses was the character of so many of them with their emphasis upon the first hand. Those who ran the courses and spoke on them were in most cases good practitioners rather than theorists, and courses such as number 284, which ran from April to July 1958 is a good example. It was an ambitious course which dealt with basic geology, topography and human settlements.

The practical work included map making and was linked to local field work which involved amongst other things the study of buildings, place names and field names. The course was run by Dr. W.G. Hoskins, Dr. A. Raistrick and Mr. W.R. Grist of Scarborough, an authority on bird and animal life.

Dr. Hoskins became a national figure, the first Professor of Local History and the author of outstanding studies of the English landscape. He believed in boots as much as books as a source of understanding, walking vast areas of England. Reflecting on his early life in Devon he said -

"The landscapes I looked at many years ago were even then more than just scenery. I wanted to know what they were saying. Now I know something of the code and how to decipher it." He quoted the painter John Constable, who wrote -

"It is the Soul that sees; the outward eyes Present the object, but the Mind descries." Then Hoskins adds a sentence which could be a major theme for the whole of this book -

"We see nothing till we truly understand it." (4)

Arthur Raistrick concentrated on Yorkshire and spent a lifetime studying its history and development. Like Eric Hoskins he was a walker and his intimate knowledge of the county was reflected in his prose. His imagination is illustrated by this extract from his study of the landscape of Yorkshire in the late twentieth century.

P.181 - 'The West Riding of Yorkshire". He talks of the high-tension power lines as a feature of the new landscape adding -

"Pylons stride across the countryside with their lace-like structure, each of them a smaller daintier Eiffel Tower, with the fine connecting catenaries of wire, showing as silver lines where the sun catches them."

Others who took part in this and similar courses were John Addy, a schoolmaster-student at Balliol College, Oxford in 1963 who taught in the West Riding; W.E. Tate a village school master and later Reader in Historical Sources in Leeds University and author of 'The Parish Chest'. In the Doncaster area John Lidster, from Doncaster Museum, took local archaeological finds into schools. There was a sense of theatre when this unassuming man took a skull from a small case and talked of how much it could tell us about early Victorian Rossington. There were no fillings in the teeth, a tribute to stone ground flour and an absence of the twentieth century deluge of sweet-meats. A Roman sandal worn by a soldier was so small that it underlined how over the centuries British people have increased in height and weight. The scientists who took part in Course 324 were in similar vein, Dr. T.E. Allibone F.R.S. Director of the Aldermaston Research Laboratory,

Dr. Lister, a glaciologist who took part in a Trans-Antarctic Expedition and John Gilmour, the Director of Cambridge University Botanic Gardens.

Since 1948 the School Museum Service built up a rich collection of visual and aural material for use in schools. By 1964 some 20,000 items from its collection were lent to schools each year. In addition to the loan service help and advice was offered to schools on the use of new aids such as closed circuit television and language laboratories.

Once viewed at the level of the enthusiast there are clear links between the changes which were going on in the primary schools and the aims of the Newsom Report.

The realisation of those aims would be a slow process but the Woolley Hall courses pointed the way and gave encouragement. However the process was engulfed by comprehensive reorganisation and the introduction of the Certificate of Secondary Education. The modern school with one target in view, the replacement of the subject dominated curriculum and traditional timetable by " ... a change in the curriculum and a change in educational approach" was facing amalgamation into a new, large school and the ossification of the single subject framework for a bulk of its pupils. The one route left to innovators was Mode 3 of the Certificate of Secondary Education which enabled schools to devise their own courses.

Alec Clegg and the Education Committee opposed the creation of the new exam system, but when the Minister decided to press ahead with this change in 1962 it was clear that opposition was fruitless. The likelihood that technical interests would gain control of the exam and as a consequence exercise too much influence on the work of modern schools was a major concern for Alec Clegg. He and the Chief Education Officer for Sheffield, T.H. Tunn, played a crucial part in the early work of the West Yorkshire and Lindsey Regional C.S.E. Board. The emphasis on course work embodied in the Mode 3 examination in particular was in Alec Clegg's eyes the way to avoid the traditional defects of national examinations.

The prospect of comprehensive reorganisation raised

fundamental problems in the provision of satisfactory buildings. Areas with a rapidly rising population could cherish the hope of a new school, but most areas faced turning existing buildings to a new use. Practical solutions were virtually impossible in some places and as a consequence the West Riding explored the possibility of middle schools which would take youngsters from 8 to12, or from 9 to 13. Apart from solving a practical problem of accommodation a middle school had the added advantage that primary school ideas could be developed for a further one or two years. Lastly these schools offered the prospect that the clamping effect of the national exam system might be reduced as well.

The passage of the secondary sector of the West Riding Education Service through this sea of change resembles that of a sailing ship in a strong crosswind. The only way forward was by tacking.. Fortunately the Chief Education Officer was a good tacker!

Alec Clegg was sure that the youngsters studied by the Newsom Committee required the most skilled teaching yet they got the poorest deal in almost all respects at secondary level. They suffered from the law of diminishing concern. In March 1966 he gave a talk entitled 'What comprehensive schools cannot do', in which he said of the less able child -

"He needs the best teachers, we give him the poorest; he will benefit most from a rich choice of subjects in fact he gets far less than his brighter fellows; he needs the stimulus of varied and specialist equipment, not only does he not get this but he is all too often conscious of the fact that his needs are being sacrificed to those of his abler brothers and sisters." Alec Clegg went on to warn that it would be very difficult for the advances made at primary level to feed through into the secondary sector. He said -

"But there are tremendous forces at the secondary stage which are likely to thwart any upward trend of this fascinating primary school development."

Later at a Woolley Hall course he described the implications of failing the youngsters who made up 'Half Our Future'.

"All I have to say mirrors the conviction that the task of the Secondary Modern School is at once the most important and the hardest in the whole field of education today. It is the most important because our survival as a free and disciplined people matters more than our technological expertise, and precise standard of living, and that survival depends above all on what we make of the great mass of ordinary children whose worth or worthlessness will determine whether or not we can as a nation sustain the democratic way of life."

There is always a temptation. to see the sheer bulk of correspondence on an issue as an indicator of importance. Sheer bulk is an element to consider but it can mislead. The correspondence Alec Clegg had on teacher training in relation to the Robbins Report was considerable. It was the crucial part of a Dunkirk like operation to preserve West Riding control of its training colleges, and it was successful. Other bulky files which contained routine correspondence might prompt no more than cursory examination yet some contain unexpected gems of information. Alec Clegg's work on the Newsom Committee did not result in the mass of paper associated with Robbins, perhaps because cooperation in a forward looking report bred less correspondence than mustering support for a rearguard action. The extent of this cooperation is hidden in an unlikely file of correspondence, one dealing with the preparations for the Annual Meeting and Dinner of the Association of Chief Education Officers which was due to take place on 4th and 5th February, 1965. Alec Clegg, the incoming President, built up a thick file of correspondence and amongst the letters is one from Sir John Newsom apologising for not being able to attend 'Alec's Party'. He would be on passage to Australia at the time of the dinner.

In a letter dated 9th November 1964, Sir John reflected on the impact of the Robbins and Beloe reports on education. This passage illustrates the difficulty far sighted educationalists had in turning hopes into reality.

"I should have thought the one thing we do not want at the moment is for training colleges to get more entangled with the universities. As I go around I find that, enflamed by the prospects of the B.Ed, they are spending more and more time on their academic side and far less on their vocational and this will get worse when they, both metaphorically and literally start designing their own hoods and gowns."

"But Beloe is going to be frightful and such evidence as I have seen myself shows an appalling similarity between the papers in many subjects and G.C.E. 'O' level which we all knew to be a preposterous examination. And one could weep when one thinks that this has been brought on us largely by teachers. The very people who have now climbed on to the bandwagon and denounced the 11+ are themselves seeking to impose a 16+ which, in the end, will be far more deleterious."

If the examination system was to dominate the central area of education for the 14-16 age group, and if the prescriptive nature of a majority of syllabuses was to limit the choice of work for this age group then freedom to plan one's own work was confined to the pre 14 year old age groups and the peripheral work for the 14 to 16 year olds. The only other alternative was to examine the lot and have done with it!

If the prospect shared by Sir John Newsom and Alec Clegg in autumn 1964 seemed bleak then in some measure the summer had raised spirits in the West Riding with the publication of 'The Excitement of Writing'. By 1969 the book had run to its seventh impression and was followed in 1973 by a sequel, 'Enjoying Writing'. The interesting fact, often overlooked, is that the considerable investment of time, especially by inspectors and advisers, in dance, movement, art and music had a profound influence on other parts of the curriculum. In his foreword to 'The Excitement of Writing' Denys Thompson pointed out how over concentration on grammatical skill squeezed out " ...the living reading and writing that constitute any worthy course in English." He cited '0' level scripts by Africans as examples of 95 per cent accuracy in grammar but little more than pidgin English in narrative quality. His conclusion was that - "It is likely that more research will show that anything worth testing in the use of English comes most surely as a by-product."

The written and oral work of many youngsters was a natural outlet for the creative qualities which had been awoken and encouraged. The widespread interest in these books led to discussion of how creative work could be evaluated and rewarded. Another source of ideas on new methods of teaching, new areas of study and new methods of examination was the Schools Council. Areas of the curriculum such as Science and Technology seem far removed from the Arts, hitherto the centrepieces of West Riding initiatives at junior level, but they deserve mention for they illustrate the common ground in aims and methods which began to characterise the work in some schools.

The design of rooms and the lists of anticipated capital equipment can in most instances go a long way towards deciding the nature of courses and teaching in technical and science subjects. At Rossington Comprehensive School the decision was made to leave one of the rooms designated for Technical Studies bare of furniture and capital equipment. The teacher who took over this room in the new comprehensive building had been in charge of Mathematics and Science in the Boys' Secondary Modern School. He had an insatiable curiosity in all aspects of Science. He visited many engineering works in Yorkshire and the Midlands picking up equipment which he felt would provide materials for projects in the field of technology. He bought all the Meccano he could lay his hands on and had the drawers, the bench tops and the cupboards specially made to house the wide variety of equipment and materials which were accumulated in the early years of development. He built devices to catch the sun's rays so as to boil water. He built an observatory and housed a powerful telescope in it and astronomy soon became an area of study for some youngsters. Alongside these joint projects were individual ones which were a substantial part of the course in the fourth and fifth years. It is interesting to note that many of the ablest youngsters opted for this course which was a C.S.E. one, rather than take an additional 'O' level. This spoke well for the course and for the frame of mind that judged educational provision on content and interest, not just the label at the end.

The Schools Council Integrated Science Scheme gave a broad cover of 'all' science and for successful youngsters resulted in two 'O' levels. The course gave a coherence to science and emphasised the social impact of scientific and technological change. This integration within the sciences and between the sciences and the humanities helped to keep options open for those wishing to go into a sixth form. More importantly it helped schools to create a unified curriculum for the 14 to 16 age group. Against this advantage must be set the view of some employers that a qualification in Integrated Science was inadequate when set alongside those in pure Science.

However, it is worth noting that an enquiry for the Schools Council by Geoffrey Dorling, Head of Science at Wymondham College, found that 22 of the 41 schools offering S.C.I.S.P. saw no need to modify Integrated Science to cope with 'A' level work. A majority of the Colleges of Further Education wanted single science '0' levels so at 16+ schools intent upon making changes began to face similar problems to those associated with the 11+ exam. Without close cooperation with parents and employers schools could face the charge that career prospects for youngsters had been sacrificed in the pursuit of educational innovation. Many schools preferred to remain within the comfortable circle of sustainable success celebrated annually at the speech day and prize giving.

A careful examination of the changes which took place in the junior and secondary sectors of a pyramid of West Riding schools can show their effects on the lives of their pupils. The amount of time and effort required to promote and to assess the quality of what youngsters did was much greater than anticipated. Moreover there were surprises which demanded the re-examination of many aspects of organisation and accepted practice in schools.

Rossington, dubbed the largest village in England and designed with a Garden City in mind, was by the 1950's one of a collection of unattractive mining villages which encircled Doncaster. Its two junior schools and two secondary modern schools were single sex establishments, perpetually short of teachers, and, due to the development of the coal industry always facing rising intakes of pupils. Consequently the site of the four schools contained the largest collection and greatest variety of temporary classrooms in the West Riding. Those who passed the eleven plus went to Maltby Grammar School but the majority stayed in the village modern schools, the boys leaving to seek work at the pit whilst the girls went into shops and similar jobs.

The Junior Boys' School earned a reputation for innovative work under Leslie Horner and when he left the headship to become an adviser his successor, Ted Tattersall, carried the work further and established the school's reputation well beyond the West Riding. The process of the two secondary moderns becoming one mixed school and going comprehensive began in 1965. The heart of this change was the work planned for the mixed classes which would form the school of the future. There was no eleven plus, the mixed secondary modern school moved from streaming to banding and on to mixed ability grouping and the integration of subjects for the 11 to 14 age groups. To achieve these changes one had to act as Viscount Halifax's trimmer did -

"This innocent term Trimmer signifieth no more than this, that if men are together in a boat and one part of the company would weigh down on one side, and another would make it lean as much to the contrary, it happeneth there is a third opinion of those who conceive it would do as well if the boat went even, without endangering the passengers."

The comprehensive school developed a programme of work which took the implications of what had been done in the junior schools on to the age of 16. A pattern of examinations was chosen which would evaluate the work of an eight form, and what later became an eleven form, entry comprehensive school. Integration in areas such as the Humanities, the Sciences and Crafts was planned and carried out, so too were schemes such as European Studies which embodied elements of foreign languages, European Literature, History and Geography. Set up by a linguist who taught drama it proved how youngsters who comprised 'Half Our Future' reacted to a new approach to what had been a somewhat privileged and conservative area of the curriculum.

The course was established with the Associated Examination Board and initially successful candidates received one pass. Later it was hoped that the course, like that in the Humanities, could lead to two or three line certification. The course aimed 'to encourage, exercise and develop the pupils' power of appreciation, discrimination and expression. Consequently quality is our major concern.' A depth element was provided by a project and the course was not divided into subject compartments but presented as a series of themes. The project was limited to 4,000 words underlining the aim to encourage quality rather than quantity. The team of staff engaged in a sequence of individual tutorials with youngsters so as areas of interest could be identified and project titles agreed. Many of these titles may seem unusually ambitious and beyond the ability of youngsters who in the first few years of the scheme were all from the old secondary modern scbools.

One girl who was interested in the lot of ordinary soldiers during the two world wars decided to study trench warfare in the 1914-1918 war and the jungle warfare of the second World War in the Far East. Her studies ranged over the history of the two wars and the reaction of poets and playwrights such as Wilfred Owen and Willis Hall. The discovery which excited her was the illustrations by Ronald Searle in the HMSO History of the Second World War. (5) Most youngsters associated Ronald Searle with St Trinians rather than the terrible suffering endured by those who fought in the Far East. The exams could prompt unexpected responses such as one boy's reaction to a question on the Spanish Civil War which included a black and white reproduction of Picasso's 'Guernica'. He wrote that the painting brought out

"... the confusion and pointlessness of war" and that it was "... unashamedly unpleasant, almost vulgar". These comments were seen as evidence of an alert, sensitive mind which continued to function even under exam pressures. The same boy loved drawing and was very knowledgeable on the decoration of barges on the Don Navigation. Alec Clegg saw in the work of the fifteen 11+ failures who took this course, testimony to the qualities which in many cases would have remained undisturbed but for the sustained pressure in the West Riding for teachers to explore and to encourage.

Rossington Comprehensive School is quoted in 'Half Way There' as an example of how an integrated Humanities scheme could at '0' and C.S.E. levels lead to "... great flexibility of study by individuals and groups while retaining a common objective for all students." The school was one of the six trial schools for the 'Race Pack' in the Humanities Curriculum project. This pack of information centred on the issue of racial intolerance in Britain and was considered by many as a very touchy subject to be introduced in school. The reactions of pupils and teachers were monitored by members of the centre for Mass Communications Research at Leicester University. Charles Husband came and lived with a mining family in Rossington for a few weeks talking to youngsters, their parents and many people in the colliery village. The conclusion of the study was that

"... the six schools showed a small but significant shift towards greater tolerance attributable to the teaching." Courses such as these aimed to foster interest and to educate in the broadest sense. Hence exam successes appear as the confirmation of aims rather than prizes to be put on display. Not a stunning conclusion by Leicester University, but when set against the frequent outbursts blaming delinquency and the like on progressive education it is clear evidence of worthwhile change. Inevitably the silent, social revolution comes to mind - a slow, quiet invaluable change for the better.

At the North of England conference in January 1968 Sir Alec Clegg reflected on 'The Newsom Report and its Aftermath'. He began by reminding his audience of the advances made in schools in the fifties and sixties - the improvements in buildings, the curriculum and staffing; the Mode 3 of the Certificate of Secondary Education; experiments in teaching with an outgoing approach; a recognition of the value of the arts; and the integration of extra curricular activities into the three session day. At this point there was a change of outlook as he put it -

"But here my optimism, or if you like complacency ends. The whole essence of the Newsom report lies in three words which occur in the introduction. We asked for a 'change of heart' towards the children with whom we were concerned. It has not come about ..."

He went on - "If this change of heart does not come about I personally believe that in the next 50 years we shall run into social difficulties which will make those of the last 50 years trivial."

He quoted the Provost of Kings College who said -

"Our educational system has developed into an entirely ruthless machine for the elimination of the unworthy." The consequence of this view was that the comprehensive school could become the most effective means of branding the less able.

Pyramid is a useful word in the vocabulary of education and there were a few in the West Riding which raised the hopes of the Chief Education officer, but there were many which did not. The latter part of Sir Alec's speech, like many others he made at this time, was in effect a warning that pyramids can be symbols of death, and in the case of the Newsom Report, the death of an idea.

Sir Alec with ? and Sir John Hunt

CHAPTER 10

1960

Alec Clegg once logged a day in the life of a Chief Education Officer which illustrated the mix of the regular and the unexpected. Halfway through his span of office in the West Riding takes us roughly to 1960, a time to look back and a time to look forward, rather like the uneasy half time between the Revolutionary War (1793-1801) and the Napoleonic War (1803-1815). In this case however the time is one chosen for reflection rather than to recoup for another spell of warfare. 1960 can illustrate the ideas, the work of administrators and the many people who week by week and month by month played a significant part in the sequence of events that comprised the history of the West Riding Education Service in this one year. Derek Birley in his book 'The education officer and his world' uses the word "ambivalence" to describe his position saying, Page 3 -

"... he will live in two worlds slipping uneasily from one to the other like an incompetent chameleon. It is not just that he has to deal with office matters on the one hand and the affairs of a separate profession on the other, though there is an interaction between the two which gives educational administration a special flavour and special problems. He lives in the crossfire of the demands of local government conditions and those of a costly and idealistic service. He is increasingly told that planning is the way to resolve this conflict, yet in neither of his two worlds has planning so far made any serious challenge to pragmatism as a way of life." (1)

The New Year is a time when hangover follows celebration. Hangover in the case of Grantley Hall College was the continuation of a long running story of animosity between the college staff. Allegations of inefficiency and unacceptable conduct amounting to a text of 27 sides were dealt with by Alec Clegg early in 1960 and eventually brought before the college governors in July 1960. The atmosphere amongst the staff of the college and between the Warden and some of the bodies who used Grantley for courses was described as one of "vendetta and personal animosity". The Warden maintained the charges were gross exaggeration but he did admit that his relationship with his staff was "... acutely unhappy". Alec Clegg faced a mountain of minor incidents at Grantley which in total justified that description, but if considered individually were of limited importance. Students from the Economics Department at Leeds University were charged with continuous bad behaviour such as stealing a leg of mutton from the kitchen in the middle of the night and making such a noise that the inhabitants of Aldfield, two miles away, could hear the row. The Deputy Warden was said to be either most excitable, or likely to go to sleep in lectures even when she was supposed to be chairing a session. The grumbling appendix was threatening to burst when the issues were brought before governors in the summer of 1960. By December the Warden had left and the former animosity amongst staff had proved contagious and infected the governors. They debated at length whether or not both the Chairman and Vice Chairman should be present with Alec Clegg for the preliminary interview session with candidates for the Wardenship prior to the afternoon interview by the full committee. Debate collapsed into furore over the matter of accommodation for governors at Grantley, a matter which prompted Alec Clegg to say his position there "... can be likened to a nut between two crackers".

If the troubles at Grantley illustrate the crossfire of local government then Alec Clegg's enquiries into the characteristics of youngsters of 'low mentality' show the careful collection and analysis of information which lay behind every educational initiative taken by the West Riding.

The reply Miss Wyllie, County Inspector for Special Schools, sent to the Chief Education Officer went into exact detail on the characteristics of such a child who was "... unable to manage buttons, laces, braces or to put on shoes, wash himself or go to the toilet unaided (if indeed he realises the need to do so)." Such children are either continually on the move or completely apathetic and may just sit "... like a suet pudding".

This detailed response was sent to R.Munro, H.M.I., for comment and he made the very important observation that nationally "...there is much confusion between the educationally sub-normal and maladjusted children and between the institutions which deal with such children." Collected and analysed in January 1960 this information was banked in preparation for future initiatives or responses.

At first sight the time taken and the potential value of this investigation compares very favourably with the hours of unavoidable and stressful deliberation, discussion and argument associated with the problems at Grantley Hall. Yet that expenditure of time was necessary for only thoroughness of investigation could ensure that the matter had been dealt with in the best possible manner. Moreover the preservation of goodwill between the Education Committee, the central administration and the educational institutions of the West Riding was a top priority not to be put at risk by precipitate action. The colleges enjoyed a status and independence above that of schools and as a consequence they had to descend further into a trough of difficulties before the Chief Education Officer was involved. Inevitably he was faced with a complex and difficult situation.

During January and February Alec Clegg wrote to, or spoke to, those he felt might be suitable applicants for the post of Principal of the Day Training College at Swinton. He held the view that if you had experienced a fruitful, constructive relationship with someone and you felt they would not only fit a particular post but enrich a team, then they should be made aware of the opportunity. Alec Clegg believed a good team was always much more than the sum of its parts. It had an ethos all of its own. Those who in these circumstances decided to go through the process of application and interview were not committed in any way to Alec Clegg. This point was made very clear in the confidential letters sent by Alec Clegg to those he felt might fill particular posts with distinction. The independence of both parties was stated in stark clarity yet an unsuccessful candidate might, if he or she knew of such exchanges, think them exercises in patronage - a means whereby a Chief Education Officer could surround himself with a group of carefully chosen, dutiful supporters. With the problems of Grantley in the background it is not unreasonable to assume that the Swinton post prompted Alec Clegg to maximise his efforts to get a good short list. The character of the correspondence reinforces the view that it was personal quality not deference that he sought. Ray O'Connor, the headmaster of Don Valley High School and former training college lecturer, was one of those he wrote to in January. Alec Clegg's approach prompted a process of self searching which was remarkable in its frankness. Instead of marketing himself as a prospective principal there is an honesty and sensitivity foreign to most letters of application. Reflecting on his work at Don Valley Ray O'Connor wrote -

"I am moved by a passion to develop and spread the creative and imaginative work that flourishes here, and to bring about that gentleness of school environment in which such work can develop."

Compare the nature of written exchanges such as these with the atmosphere of the final interview for a senior post at County Hall and one can appreciate that such exchanges can be very valuable precursors to the process of short listing, interview and appointment. Alec Clegg's view was frankly expressed to Dick Field, whom he had known in Birmingham, and who he thought might consider the Swinton post. In a letter which was "strictly private and personal" he wrote -

"If we merely regard this as a new venture and advertise for a Principal and let him recruit his own staff from public advertisement I have no doubt we should get a good Training College, but it may well not have the ethos that I would hope to achieve by the other method." The detailed exchanges between Alec Clegg and those he contacted as possible applicants had in each case a statement similar to this one in a letter to Dick Field "... the matter is entirely between you and me with neither of us committed in any way."

The staffing needs of Swinton Day Training college were similar to those of an Extra Mural Studies Department in a University. Staff would be dealing with mature men and women as Alec Clegg wrote -

"... they were mature and understanding and the waves of fashion which afflict most students blew over them leaving little deposit."

As with the Principalship of the college Alec Clegg ranged widely in his enquiries about likely staff who could contribute to a successful launch of the Day College. One of those he wrote to was Christian Schiller, at the Institute of Education in London University, who regularly took part in courses at Woolley Hall, a man of vision whose views were valued a great deal. This preparation paid handsome dividends as 'The Final Ten Years 1964-74' says of Swinton trained teachers -

"They had no problems of motivation and in a very short time those who had followed the course were in great demand in some of the most experienced and progressive schools in South Yorkshire."

Alec Clegg was involved in the deliberations which preceded the publication of the Crowther Report in 1959 and his private file for 1960 has a varied collection of material on reactions to the report. A concise digest of the report was published by the West Riding highlighting its main arguments and suggestions. In February an article in 'Education' by W.P. Alexander highlighted the waste of ability caused by 7 out of every 8 giving up education altogether at 15 or 16 years of age. In addition 50% of those involved in part-time education gave up during the course. The article suggested the remedy to this waste was courses which mixed study with practical experience. Copies of Hansard which covered the debates on the Crowther Report (March 1960) are included in the file and no doubt Alec Clegg enjoyed reading the maiden speech of Miss Harvie Anderson, M.P. for Renfrew East who recalled taking a group of Scotch teenagers from poor families to London before the war. They were a revelation to her - "They knew their history; they loved the ballet; they recited their Shakespeare with the company at Regent's Park rather too loudly. They were prepared to spend hours in the National Gallery and they looked down on this House with absorbed interest. They did all this while retaining a vivid interest in the dead rats which they found washed up by Tower Bridge and while keeping an infallible eye open to old gentlemen who were most likely to provide them with a free ice cream."

Miss Anderson would have found a lot of common ground between her recollections and those of Alec Clegg. (2)

It was very appropriate that Alec Clegg's reply to a request from the Vice-Chancellor of Sheffield University for recommendations for honorary degrees should be dated 29th February. The only name which "came immediately to mind" was Alderman Hyman who despite his delight in political conflict had "... devoted a lifetime to education." To leap is to throw oneself, to spring suddenly, so Alderman Hyman was the ideal leap year man!

Through February and March the reports from advisers and inspectors covered developments in various divisions of the West Riding, courses given and courses planned and matters of internal cooperation and dissent. The Art Adviser, Mr. Davis, recommended a new type of course at Woolley. Twelve head-teachers of good schools each with two members of staff should meet at Woolley once a term. They should represent all divisions of the West Riding and all three art advisers would be present at each of the meetings. The analysis Mr. Davis did of art education in West Riding Schools contained an important observation on the work of some progressive schools, which could in his view, unless care was taken " ... deteriorate to the level of sensitive copying." Like Diana Jordan he maintained a teacher could create the conditions for imaginative work but could not guarantee it would occur. The report is full of astute observations and constructive suggestions and ends with a report on two boys who were transferred from Horbury Secondary Modern to Morley Grammar School so as they could attempt a G.C.E. in Art.

The emphasis upon a sustained period of instruction and discussion rather than an occasional weekend is echoed in the reports of Henry Scott and Mrs Taylor. Henry Scott, the senior adviser for Physical Education, had concentrated on 7 schools in his first 18 months in the West Riding. His work in secondary schools had been deliberately restricted to dealing with inadequate facilities such as - only 3 out of 14 secondary schools in the Don Valley Division had gymnasia and changing facilities. Mrs Taylor described Airedale, Division 4 as "the most rewarding of all my divisions" and that she had developed movement " ... in small pockets within this Division" in the primary schools, adding " ... it has been found that if small pockets can be established, the interest in the work spreads throughout the Division."

Mr Tyler, the Drama Adviser, described his work as an uphill fight but in spring 1960 he was looking forward to the start of an International Theatre Month for he felt annual festivals were one of the main ways to encourage Youth Drama. Collections of drama equipment had been built up so that any initiatives could be given practical support. These pools of equipment, peripatetic tutors and courses such as the terminal Evening Institute Drama Courses at Grantley Hall could provide support in areas where there was an active interest in drama.

The work of the music advisers and the West Riding Orchestra came to the fore in March when a letter from Stanley Adams, the Senior Adviser, reported that the acrimony which characterised the late fifties had broken out again after a brief respite.

Alec Clegg and his deputy, Jim Hogan, spent a great deal of valuable time damping down and seeking a solution to the personal friction between the three Music advisers. The two bulky files on music are largely a tale of self justification and fault finding in others. Jim Hogan had already received complaints about an "insidious campaign from a rebellious minority" in the West Riding orchestra, from the Senior Adviser. Whilst Stanley Adams was conducting some members deliberately played wrong notes. On another occasion at the Don Valley Music Festival one musician mimicked the instructions a lady teacher gave to her youngsters. Actions such as these eventually led to one musician being sacked. The complaints against a small minority in the orchestra seem justified, but with three advisers at loggerheads joint ventures such as music festivals seem open invitations for disruption to flourish. Festivals were often accompanied by an outburst of bitter correspondence.

Alec Clegg asked Miss Milne another adviser to comment on infant music festivals, and she concluded a list of shortcomings on the way Mr Adams organised these events by stating that it was the child's individual development rather than the public performance that mattered. Sandwiched between extensive correspondence on contentious issues are some letters dealing with the development of guitar work in schools. These end with a letter from Mr Wilkinson, of Adwick, who wrote "Because of this quick progress the children really feel that musical study is a discovery and a joy." Alec Clegg's thoroughness prompted him to write to Mr Suttle H.M.I. in December on the upsurge of guitar work in schools saying -

"I want to be extremely careful not to embark upon a stunt. On the other hand I don't want Gavall's enthusiasm to be thwarted if you and folk like you think that what he is doing makes a worthwhile contribution to musical education."

It is necessary to trespass into 1961 to appreciate fully the crabwise character of any progress made by the Music advisers. Mr Adams showed no interest in guitar work yet as senior adviser could legitimately complain he had not been informed of the appointment of a guitar teacher in the south of the Riding. Alec Clegg sent an apology but reminded him of his lack of interest in guitar work. Later Mr Adams would have felt fortified by Mr Suttle's confirmation of his view that a particular music teacher was "totally incompetent". In Alec Clegg's words the man had " ... a string of references and testimonials as long as your arm from almost everyone from Beethoven onwards." Such unanimity was unusual and was in the field of condemnation not progress. When John Gavall wrote to Alec Clegg in 1972 reminiscing on his years in the West Riding he referred to his difficulties with Mr Adams adding ".. but I was always conscious that higher up the educational tree, there was an idealism to which I personally felt very responsive and which made small obstacles unimportant and all efforts really worthwhile."

Alec Clegg and his deputy Jim Hogan shared the burden of necessary intervention in the affairs of the music advisers. Often matters went to Hogan first. He could act as a buffer for the Chief Education Officer, or act in concert with Alec Clegg as a resolver of particular problems. In other areas of administration Jim Hogan, could be a trouble shooter taking the initiative in matters which demanded attention and which, once investigated, led to executive action. In this respect his Deputy reflected the chameleon characteristics of the Chief Officer. Later in the year Chief and Deputy were in Wath and they talked to an assistant teacher who had spent six and a half years in a local secondary school. He felt no interest had been shown locally in the welfare of young teachers and he illustrated this view by quoting the views of councillors who saw no need to help with housing for in their eyes teachers earned enough to buy their own. He compared this attitude with Lincoln, where he had just obtained a post, and where he was going to be provided with a house. The teacher deplored the fact that political considerations rather than educational ones determined the structure of education in the Wath area. Set against the range of work done on the supply and distribution of teachers in the West Riding during 1960 comments such as these must have made both Chief and Deputy angry for it was in precisely this and other areas in the South of the Riding that the shortage was most acute. (3)

Grape vine information on a substantial scale could prompt Alec Clegg to write frankly to heads on particular issues. In March he wrote to a grammar school head asking him to confirm either that all that had come to his ears was incorrect or that what is happening will not recur. A shot across the bows in a private letter could be an effective way of ensuring, as in this case, that regular late arrival at school ceased.

A newcomer to private files might anticipate they contained a substantial amount of correspondence giving the inside story on major decisions. Neither 1960 nor other years confirm this guess. In 1960 small matters often loomed large and their nagging presence demanded a solution. Hospitality for visitors was a minute proportion of educational expenditure yet it prompted considerable correspondence in 1959 and 1960.

A strand of Yorkshire niggardliness was highlighted in November 1959 over the payment for the Everest explorer Sir John Hunt's lunch at Woolley Hall. The initial charge was met by the member of the Education Department looking after the visitor, or group of visitors. Details of each sum of money spent on hospitality went to the Chairman of the County Council and he decided whether or not it was a legitimate charge on his hospitality fund.

The delay and doubts raised in relation to Sir John Hunt's lunch led to Alec Clegg drawing up a typically detailed study on 'Hospitality to Visitors' which pointed out such facts as the meals staff volunteered their services for the opening of schools; that if a visitor is on the train at 1.00 pm and has eaten lunch on the train the Divisional Education Officer pays for it, however if the visitor leaves the train at 12.30 pm and lunches with the Divisional Education Officer at 12.45 pm the lunch has to be paid out of the Chairman of the Council's account. Alec Clegg pointed out other examples of 'meagre' hospitality and concluded, "If the present system of complexity and doubt and meagre insufficiency continues, it is inevitable that chief officers will discourage visits from outside, and the Authority will lose much in reputation and not a little in enlightenment."

In August a letter to Alderman Hyman gave details of the provision of floral decorations at County Hall. It described how a senior member of staff collected flowers from a number of institutions and brought them to the Supplies Department who then used them to decorate County Hall. Alec Clegg suggested that a college, such as Bretton Hall, should be commissioned to provide flowers regularly and be paid for this service.

The initiative in relation to hospitality for visitors and the financial fringes of educational expenditure came from Alec Clegg, but in the matter of seating arrangements and the commemorative plaque at the formal opening of Tadcaster Grammar School, the initiative or rather the outburst came from Alderman Hyman.

The formal opening of Tadcaster Grammar School led to a very critical letter from Alderman Hyman to Alec Clegg on the design of the commemorative plaque and the composition of platform parties. Hyman thought the plaque "... huge, stupid and out of all proportion" and that the platform party was full of nonentities, In his reply Alec Clegg pointed out there was a case for different plaques for different schools and that if, as was so often the case, Committee members did not reply to invitations, they could not expect to automatically get "... a prominent seat." This incident is a reminder of Alec Clegg's description of Walter Hyman many years later. He wrote -

"He loved a struggle and would create obstacles if none existed ... He invariably took the line of most resistance." (4)

The observations Alec Clegg made to Sir Ronald Gould, NUT Secretary, on the anomalies of the organisation of the West Riding County Association of the NUT were couched in less abrasive form. Alec Clegg pointed out that Leeds, Bradford, Sheffield and other borough members were present at meetings which discussed West Riding business, but West Riding members were not present at meetings where borough business was discussed. It was agreed that they would resolve the matter at a personal meeting.

A memorandum from Alec Clegg to the County Clerk in March dealing with the effect of poor pay on recruitment of clerical and administrative staff led to a sub-committee being set up to collect information on the issue. The memorandum concentrated attention on such matters as the number of the education staff who received less than the wage of an eighteen year old unskilled labourer in the building or civil engineering industry. The sixties were a time of educational expansion yet between 1954 and 1964 the Central Office Staff fell from 244 to 206. Alec Clegg had good cause to seek increases in staff members and salaries.

Through the summer months the correspondence on Music between Alec Clegg, his deputy and the advisers continued to flow. The winter months brought a concentration on guitar work and a confirmation from Homerton College, Cambridge that small group guitar work was flourishing there - a plus for Mr Gavall, direct rather than crabwise progress. The Grantley Hall saga was moving towards its end in the winter with preparations taking place for the appointment of a new Warden. However the uncertainties on hospitality for visitors were not resolved by December so Alec Clegg declined to invite Sir James Robertson to the West Riding underlining by this action the points he had made on this issue earlier in the year.

The collection of Bill Morrell 'incredibilities' received in November may have offset a little the oft recorded disharmony amongst the Music advisers, The prize window display, in no way a temporary one, for Bill Morrell remarked on it a week after his first visit, comprised 16 jam jars (many containing brown water); 1 toilet roll; 1 box of chalks and 1 old wireless battery - not preparations for a junk stew but a genuine display!

Old pictures, old books, broken shelves and out of date notices may reflect a state of mind in a school, but a notice 'Reference Books' stuck into the back of a new book by four drawing pins in a new library in a Grammar School does deserve the word incredible. Ernest Peet, Supervisor of Caretakers, could have added to Bill Morrell's collection of 'incredibilities', yet they were probably fewer and more apparent because of the marked overall improvement in the quality of school caretaking. It is worth noting that Alec Clegg almost always gave the introductory talk for courses in Caretaking held at Woolley Hall. His involvement in the design and care of buildings ranged from courses such as these to his membership of the Council for Industrial Design and the Furniture Development Council. So at one level he was talking with men trying to maintain old buildings in some of the most depressing industrial districts of the West Riding and at another level exchanging views with Sir Herbert Read and Sir Gordon Russell.

Caretaking was a wonderful example of how what might appear to some monotonous drudgery could become a science whilst the decoration of a building could become an art. Ernest Peet devised experiments to show how dirt behaved

"... when it is dry, when it is moist, and when it is swept and dusted; what happens when it becomes bonded; what kind of surfaces attract and repel it."

Good maintenance and attractive display could even in the drabbest districts create an oasis of beauty. As one head said his aim -

"... was to create inside school an environment which would compensate visually for the ugliness outside."

CHAPTER 11

TECHNOLOGY, HANDICRAFT AND RURAL STUDIES

<u>Introduction</u>

The previous chapter concentrated on one year, 1960. This chapter follows Alec Clegg's interest and initiatives in Technology and Handicrafts during his span of office in the West Riding. It is a study of a substantial part of the curriculum which had a clear identity at secondary level, particularly in the grammar schools. Specialisation was regarded as essential in the grammar school. It was one of the sources of examination success and in similar vein many economists believed it was the source of wealth. A very different view on specialisation was expressed by Sir Richard Livingstone in his study of 'The Future in Education' - P126

"To sum up. We have lost - at any rate in the post primary school - our grip on education. It has become a mass of uncoordinated subjects, a chaos instead of a cosmos. Its dominating idea, so far as it has one, is to provide the equipment of knowledge which an intelligent man should possess. So it tends to become a collection of isolated subjects - a world of planets, stars wandering each on its irregular way, occasionally dashing into each other. For this we need to substitute a solar system whose ruling principle is the making of human beings."

Alec Clegg shared this view and his administration reflected an emphasis upon unity, not only in working practice but in relation to aims and the initiatives undertaken to achieve those aims. His early years in the West Riding illustrate how significant the scientific strand was in Alec Clegg's work and it is important to assess the West Riding initiatives against what happened elsewhere in the immediate post war years.

NUMBER OF STUDENTS ENROLLED IN EVENING, TECHNICAL AND ART SCHOOLS - 1926 - 1938

DATE	STUDENTS IN WEST RIDING INSTITUTIONS	WEST RIDING STUDENTS IN INSTITUTIONS OF NEIGH-BOURING AUTHORITIES
1926-27	40,854	6,602
1929-30	44,567	7,479
1932-33	46,948	9,207
1935-36	53,044	11,441
1937-38	57,218	12,907

The neglect of technical education and the British dependence on foreign technology was tragically illustrated in the Second World War. Swiss fuses were needed to detonate our shells, anti-aircraft defence was dependent on French height-finders and American predictors. The Royal Air Force and the Navy were heavily dependent on American instruments and even the British invention of radar relied on American valves. Perhaps some would argue these were examples of industrial inter-dependence but they were in fact illustrations of some of the shortcomings of British industry. Lease-Lend perpetuated our dependence on American supplies and victory in 1945, like the clock striking midnight for Cinderella, cast British industry back from the victory coach to the pumpkin of pre war stagnation.

The West Riding compares very favourably with the national picture of decline in technical education. Attention was concentrated on Agricultural and Mining Education between the wars. Askham Bryan College of Agriculture was largely completed by 1939 whilst mining and technical institutes were set up at Dinnington, Mexborough and Whitwood. Despite disputes with the Board of Education on the funding of Further Education, steady growth took place, After the Second World War one of the important initiatives in Science education was the opening of Malham Tarn Field Centre, and in 1948 it was opened to schools.

Many grammar schools seized this opportunity as Alec Clegg put it " ... to escape from book theory to exciting practical work ...". In Modern schools many ceased to have a mechanical science course for boys and a biological course for girls, replacing them by a general science course for mixed classes. The development of Rural Studies, especially in Modern schools underlined this move away from books and blackboards to first hand practical work. Bee-keeping, livestock-keeping and other initiatives were encouraged by courses at Woolley Hall, which had a fine demonstration apiary.

COURSES AT WOOLLEY HALL 1952-1974
DEALING WITH SECONDARY EDUCATION
(Expressed as percentages of the total of secondary courses)

ART & CRAFTS	15%
ENGLISH	10%
HISTORY, GEOGRAPHY	5%
FOREIGN LANGUAGES	3%
MUSIC	3%
MATHEMATICS	8% } 22%
SCIENCE, RURAL STUDIES	14%
PHYSICAL EDUCATION	8%
RELIGIOUS EDUCATION	9%
COURSES FOR HEAD TEACHERS	15%
COURSES FOR DEPUTIES	2%
REMEDIAL EDUCATION	2%
OTHERS	6%
	100%

Specialist Teachers - Handicrafts

For over four years, from 1952 to 1956, Alec Clegg was involved in the meetings and discussions of the Sub-Committee set up by the Ministry of Education to consider the supply and Training of Specialist Teachers.

Two of the specialist areas, Handicraft and Rural Studies, were clearly linked to Technical and Scientific education yet their place in, and contribution to, the quality of the secondary curriculum received very little attention. For Alec Clegg and other contributors to the discussions which preceded the final reports the compartmentalised approach, the neglect of Art and Design in relation to other practical subjects and the overall lack of urgency and imagination were causes of deep concern.

Alec Clegg joined the committee in April 1952 although he had written, "I am not prepared to sit on a Committee which is concerned solely with increasing the supply of the wrong thing." However the chairman, E. L. Russell, Chief Education Officer for Birmingham persuaded him to join. Within a week of the first meeting of the Sub-Committee Alec Clegg was inviting comments from advisers and inspectors on specialist teacher training and setting up a series of meetings at Woolley Hall. One issue for discussion was 'art in relation to technical training'. A comment from an Art Adviser was - "... for children concerned very much with technics a consideration of design as an all-round factor involving both the art and technical elements becomes fundamental. This means seeing design not as art applied to machines, but seeing art in machinery." The advisors commented on the two year trained or Emergency Trained teachers of Art in Secondary Modern schools describing many of them as 'exceptionally gifted'. On the other hand they were very critical of Junior Art Departments which offered - "... neither a good art nor a good general education, and need either a drastic reconstruction or preferably complete abolition." The discussions with advisers came to similar conclusions in relation to other subjects such as Handicraft and, during one session at Woolley Hall, Alec Clegg described teachers of this subject as " ... competent craftsman with very little understanding apart from their own subject." He and Diana Jordan went further concluding that -

" ... unless the child has power to create through this subject, the subject has no educational value." Damning comment but liable to legitimate challenge on the grounds that to make something, to take it home and to see it in use, even the inevitable teapot stand, was a personal achievement. However the criticism was followed by a proposal to launch an experiment at Castleford "to try to bridge the gap at the Junior School stage."

This sequence of thorough discussion on principles and practice, likely experiments and follow up work, is typical of the West Riding Education Department at this time. By the autumn of 1952 Alec Clegg had discussed specialist teacher training with all the relevant advisers, senior staff and the principals of West Riding Training Colleges. He was well prepared and in a letter to the Sub-Committee Chairman, E. L. Russell, dated 22nd October, 1952, he expressed his anxiety on the quality of training, especially in relation to the H.T.D. courses. (2) Moreover Alec Clegg had canvassed the opinion of men such as William Coldstream, Principal of the Slade School of Art who wrote, 24th September, 1952 -

"As you say it is of the greatest value to any teacher of art entering a children's school to be conversant with the broadest aspects of art teaching and to have had some teaching practice. We certainly tell this to those of our students who intend to enter teaching and, when I discuss courses of study with such students in future, I will have your letter very much in mind."

William Coldstream had had the youthful Stanley Spencer at the Slade and his view on what the Slade could do for him would have intrigued Alec Clegg. William Coldstream wrote of Spencer that -

"He was, essentially, an original personality. Original personalities are not like clever people. There is really very little they can be taught. All one can do is to put before them what may prove useful and leave it to them to teach themselves." (3)

The conclusions reached by Alec Clegg as a result of his enquiries and discussions were that the methods employed to train Handicraft teachers were inferior to those used for almost any other specialists. Moreover handicraft teachers lacked prestige in schools, especially grammar schools, and their prospects for promotion were poor. When he was interviewed by the Sub-Committee the Principal of Shoreditch College emphasised that a handicraft teacher had to be "... something very much more than the specialist craftsman and that his approach to teaching should be informed by a broad cultural outlook and academic background." His complaint was that some local authorities thought of these teachers as "... mere manual specialists", segregated from the rest of their colleagues.

What excited Alec Clegg was the view put by Clifford Ellis who gave evidence for the Society for Education in Art. Ellis maintained Britain should create "... that cultural and artistic background to the child's life which other countries such as Italy and Mexico had concentrated on for many centuries." Art to Clifford Ellis was 'an essential part of life, and not an artificial excrescence taught as a routine school subject.' He outlined to the Sub-Committee a number of experiments in coordinated training. These ideas were one source of Alec Clegg's suggestion to the Sub-Committee that -

"... I can think of nothing that we as a Committee could recommend which would be likely to have greater influence than a first class Craft Training College under really inspired direction."

Seeking ideas on possible changes in college courses Alec Clegg asked his Craft Advisers -

"What I want to know from you is - if you were Hitler and you could just decree how the teachers of Woodwork and Metalwork in this country should be trained, and you had no financial restrictions, what would you do?"

One suggestion agreed by the Chief Education Officer and his advisers was a fifty fifty division of time throughout a three year course between craft and a group of other subjects.

Three letters in mid September 1953 from Alec Clegg to E. L. Russell, A. A. Part. MBE, at the Ministry of Education and to A. C. Dean set out his concern over the training of Handicraft teachers. He acknowledged there had been "... a most marked improvement in recent years in the understanding of design" at Shoreditch and Loughborough but that the work in schools still tended to be " ... dull, unimaginative, insensitive and aesthetically unsatisfying." He was worried that the Handicraft HMI's were " ... too severely shaped on Shoreditch lathes," and he returned to his favourite solution "... a Slap up new three year college with an unusual output of, say, 60 men and women ...".

The suggestion of a mixed college is interesting for so much of the discussion before and after this date is strictly within subject compartments taking little or no account of encouraging an integration of crafts for boys and girls.

In the following year a thorough analysis of the number and quality of applicants for specialist posts in Art, Handicraft and other subjects was undertaken in the West Riding. Copies of the results and conclusions were sent to the Sub-Committee and other interested parties such as Sir Charles Morris, Vice Chancellor of Leeds University. Alec Clegg laid great emphasis on the predicament of Secondary Modern Schools saying -

"... from all appearances little is being done to increase the number of specialist teachers which will be required to deal with the situation which will arise in most Secondary Modern Schools in the last years of this decade."

Rural Studies - Agriculture

The reply Alec Clegg received from A. Thompson at the Ministry of Education to his enquiry about the supply of teachers " ... adequately trained to give instruction in agricultural and horticultural subjects in Secondary Technical Schools" was expressed in two blunt, simple sentences -

"There is no such thing for agriculture or horticulture", and that these studies were " ... often done deplorably badly in schools as a result."

The identification of this void prompted Alec Clegg to initiate a survey of all counties which provided secondary technical courses in Agricultural subjects. Eleven counties, a majority of which were rural, ran no courses in agricultural subjects. Out of the counties offering courses Kent had three centres, Oxfordshire, Surrey, the East and West Ridings had two each. The counties which did not reply included Lincolnshire, Cambridgeshire, Gloucestershire and Worcestershire. Eleven out of the fourteen counties which provided such training acknowledged they had difficulty in staffing these centres. The void was proved and Alec Clegg's input to discussions is probably summarised in a series of pencilled notes which stressed the need not only for more teachers but for training to include far more practical work. He added, probably with his garden at Saxton in mind, "As a gardener I know that the vital time when things do, or do not, happen is between Easter and the end of June, just the time when the students are spending their time on examinations, school practice and holidays ...". The same points could be applied to Rural Studies in schools.

The Sub-Committee Report on this matter referred to the urgent problem of training specialist teachers in Rural Studies and it gave optimistic and pessimistic estimates of supply. The former left a shortage of 233 in 1959, the latter at least double that figure.

There is no doubt that Alec Clegg would have given a pessimistic nod, when he read the conclusions reached by F. L. Freeman, Chief Education Officer for Southampton, on the Sub-Committee's Final Report. He wrote (25th October 1956):

"I felt that it had not got the note of urgency in it that we ought to make in regard to the immediate future ... Also I felt that there was no sort of philosophy about the document, it was far too dry as dust."

The frustration expressed in this letter was shared by Alec Clegg and it prompts the thought that the three years on the Ministry Sub-Committee played its part in the clear cut practical recommendations in the West Riding Report on Technical Education.

Technical Education Report by A B Clegg & J M Hogan 1955

The West Riding initiatives in technical education at secondary level were designed to give them separate status from grammar schools. As Alec Clegg stated in 'Ten Years of Change' -

"They (the Education Committee) believe that in the national interest the Technical schools of the future must compete on equal terms with the Grammar schools for the best brains in the community."

Details of this viewpoint were presented in a Report on Technical Education which was drawn up by Alec Clegg and Jim Hogan in 1955. They looked back 25 years to when Dr. Hallam, then Education Officer in the West Riding, sought to start an " ... alternative course in 13 grammar schools." All that was left of this initiative in 1955 were " ... a few old pieces of practical apparatus still lying about in the wood - or metal - work shops." The cause of failure was " ... The power of the classical tradition of the English Grammar School and the draw of the Older Universities ..." However another attempt was being made by setting up a Technical High School in Bentley.

In typical Clegg fashion the Report began by explaining how any expansion of technical education might be used - "Are we to have more atom bombs or more confectionery; more jet engines or more vacuum cleaners? A similar point but in different style is made by Sir Alexander Fleck, Chairman of I.C.I. in the fifth volume of the Oxford History of Technology - p.840.

'But power in itself is neither good nor evil: in the last analysis, its uses are subject to man's good sense or his stupidity.'

The report goes on to consider the sorts of institutions needed to provide for an expansion of technical education at secondary or higher educational levels. Grammar schools provided a meagre supply of scientists and technologists at universities whilst others took Ordinary or Higher National Certificate courses. The wastage rate on these ONC and HNC courses was 90%. The educational implications of the pressing need for technological expansion were summarised as follows -

"1. That the newer industries will demand more highly intelligent workers than in fact exist and they will tend to blame the educational service for not providing them.
2. That the older industries, left with employees of a poorer ability, will blame education rather than nature for this insufficiency.
3. That the great future problem of education generally, and of technical education in particular, will be to produce workers of higher quality out of less promising material."

The report focussed in particular on the problem facing the Modern Schools and the few Secondary Technical Schools if they were going to meet industrial demand for better trained workers.

To offer these youngsters a diluted form of Grammar School education would in the eyes of the authors of the report " ... be doomed to utter failure." They felt Grammar school pupils could 'endure and even survive intensive doses of academic instruction,' but entirely different methods of teaching and types of courses would have to be adopted if the right sort of expansion was to be achieved.

The conclusion reached on this issue falls very much in line with those beginning to spread in West Riding junior schools. As the report puts it - "In short, it will not do to concentrate solely on the factual side of education by which men learn to do things, and ignore the more subtle side, which makes them want to do them."

Part of the report was based on the answers to a questionnaire sent by Alec Clegg to industrial firms in the West Riding. One firm described how it recruited between 80 and 90 boys who had taken 'A' level courses at grammar or public schools. They went on a five year training course during which time six months of each year was spent in a college of technology and the rest of the year in industrial training. The advantages of such sandwich courses over a full time university course followed by full time industrial training is stressed in the report.

One can readily conclude that technical education was not only inadequate in amount but a story of extensive waste. Yet this conclusion leaves out a very significant fact which is highlighted in the report. About half of the few, some 330 students each year, who successfully completed Higher National Certificate courses in the Yorkshire region, did not come from Grammar schools. 'In other words, 330 pupils who have either been passed over at the age of 11, or who have been deemed unfit to embark upon an academic course, successfully conclude a course which is higher than the standards normally expected at the conclusion of the Grammar School Course.' This fact pointed to the need to devise courses which would attract and develop boys with such abilities. Pudsey Technical Institute was started with such an experimental course in mind.

If a careful mix of theory and practice was the route to better technical education then once in a job many would face disappointment for they might be engaged in -

"... unsatisfying fragmentary routine jobs with little knowledge of, or concern for, the finished article." This was a problem for industry to solve if it sought to press specialisation to its limits."

The wastage on City and Guilds Courses was greater than that on ONC and HNC courses for only one student out of every eighteen admitted passed the final examination. The source of many failures was difficulty with the academic side of the work. This disturbing fact led Alec Clegg to seek detailed information on vocational education. He used the 1953 publication by Leeds Incorporated Chamber of Commerce which summarised the results of a study of 168 firms in the Leeds area. Alec Clegg wrote to many of the firms in this study and reached the conclusion that -

"None of the firms approached dissented seriously from the view that general education is all important for children of school age." The remarks some firms made on Modern School recruits were of particular interest. Quite a number matured a great deal after a few years and could " ... undertake more extensive preparation of a professional character." Others, "few and far between" ... "possess qualities of originality and show evidence of real creative imagination." These observations led to the statement - "The general attitude is that, assuming a reasonable average standard of education, it is the personal qualities that count."

When the report moved from the assessment of the amount of and quality of technical education to its conclusions and recommendations for the future, it stresses the overwhelming need to provide classrooms and teachers for the additional children moving into secondary schools after 1955. There would not be the time to revise the Development Plan or to consult on any suggested changes - it was, especially in the 'black' areas of the Riding, a stark problem of finding a teacher and a place where he or she could teach.

The reports from inspectors and advisers in the coalfield areas illustrated not only the overall shortage of teachers; but the severe nature of the shortage in the sciences, mathematics and craft subjects. An ambitious scheme to improve the quality of technical education would need to face the realities in reports such as those of Mr Oakley Hughes, who joined the advisory team in 1954. In his first 12 months he made 300 visits to a variety of institutes of further education writing -

"Too often I found uninspired teaching from the staffs. This attitude showed in the lack of virility, the dreary units scattered in unsuitable premises where little or no effort seemed to have been made to produce any sense of community." The reaction of heads to suggestions of supervision and guidance and courses at Grantley and Woolley were "... received as though I was making an indecent suggestion." Reports such as this may be part of the explanation of the wastage on technical courses and indicate that significant expenditure on the development of technical education would, at a time of Conservative economy, be ill-advised and by no means as essential as trying to provide places for the rising numbers of pupils in secondary schools.

Alec Clegg would have found Oakley Hughes assessment of the further education sector a dismal confirmation of what he felt about craft teaching in a bulk of secondary schools. In October 1953 he attended a course for handicraft teachers at Woolley Hall. In a letter to Dennis Young he said -

"... I was utterly depressed by it. There seemed to be nothing of spontaneity, vitality and fun in doing the job that, it seems to me, are the essential concomitants of good craft work. I dare not say this to any of the HMI's or to my own colleagues, but certainly I feel it."

His observation on courses run by HM Inspectors in Handicraft drew similar criticism. Speaking of one course he described how each wood and metalwork teacher produced a piece of work and a set of drawings. These were collected, discussed and then reproduced and bound, one copy for each course member. Alec Clegg remarked -

"... and I suppose that from now onwards the teachers will work through this book of drawings with their classes." He felt "... that a procedure of this kind misses 90% of what I would hope would emerge from good Handicraft teaching."

In another letter he described this approach as "... pedestrian and unimaginative, leading to a cul-de-sac or dead end."

His pessimistic view of handicraft teaching was formed before the Report on Technical Education was prepared and it is very likely that it played its part in determining the character of the conclusions which sought to restrict funding to worthwhile initiatives.

With the appointment of handicraft advisers such as J. F. Hardy and G. H. Wilson in the early sixties reports on craft and technical education began to flow through to Alec Clegg. These reports dated from 1962 and in part reflect on events of the previous decade. Mr Hardy wrote of those who entered teaching with the minimum qualification with a Technological Certificate of the City and Guilds. He reported "There is a preponderance of these men in the South of the Riding: 30 of my teachers having entered this way. Often one's first concern with these men is their spoken and written English: spelling mistakes being quite common in the blackboard work of some. Their standards are those of industry." He deplored the "... disturbing lack of thought given to the less able child" by these teachers and felt that a training centre ought to be set up at Worsborough to improve their standard of teaching. The one ray of light in his report was Dinnington Secondary School where a unique course in metal sculpture using welding techniques had been established by a teacher who trained at a College of Art as a silversmith. Elsewhere boys studied engineering drawing yet, in some cases, did no craftwork at all! Reports such as this harden the view that progress in craft and technical education was, at the time of the 1955 Technical Education Report, going to be a very difficult task and reluctantly one is driven to accept the Report's conclusion of - "the compelling need to accommodate an additional 25,000 children in the schools".

The Report did promise that if those with an interest in and potential in the field of technology could be identified then "... the Committee will expand their provision for Secondary Education beyond the age of 15 wherever there is a need, and in doing so they will have in mind the nature of the employment likely to be offered to the majority of the pupils leaving any particular school and the need to effect a balance between the education offered by the more traditional Grammar School and that with a pronounced leaning towards Science and Engineering of the kind which will be offered at the new Bentley High School."

Bearing in mind the problem of wastage on technical courses this recommendation seems to co-ordinate the needs of youngsters and schools with the available resources. The eighth recommendation dealt with vocational courses such as those in agriculture. These would be supported with adequate practical facilities provided they were established on a 'sound educational basis'. Provisions such as these encouraged development but were designed to prevent waste. The final conclusion dealt with the courses at Pudsey promising to extend them to other areas if these proved successful.

The policies the West Riding adopted on technical education seem thorough and realistic yet, set against the state of technology within the British economy, they were inadequate. This conclusion is no more than using the detail from one authority to illustrate a national shortcoming. Moreover, in using an innovative education authority it serves to underline the scale of this inadequacy. In the 1970's a study of 'The Multinationals' by Christopher Tugendhat pointed out that of 29 key inventions 19 were made in the USA and 10 in Britain, France and Germany. Out of the final products 22 were developed in the USA and only 7 in the three European states. The ability to exploit scientific and technological breakthroughs depended on the number and quality of a nation's technicians, craftsmen and commercial staff. In this respect Britain deserved the title given to it in 1961 by Michael Shanks - 'The Stagnant Society'.

Running through Alec Clegg's correspondence on craft teaching is a concern about the impact of dull routine on the quality of life at school and later at work, Probably he would not have gone as far as L. T. C. Rolt did in his biography of Isambard Kingdom Brunel but by the 1970's his concern about society at large would have led him to concur with this conclusion. P.319 -

"For just as the machines, by carrying too far the precepts of division of labour, degraded the craftsman into a machine minder, so as surely and far more subtly, the process of specialisation has by perpetual reduction destroyed that catholicity of intellect without which civilisation cannot survive." (4)

COURSES AT WOOLLEY HALL - 1952 / 1974

	1952	1953	1954	1955	1956	1957	1958	1959
Infant & Junior	7	3	7	7	13	10	11	9
Secondary	6	6	13	9	11	12	11	14
Junior / Secondary	2	3	4	2	4	5	3	4
Caretaking, School Meals Supp. Services/Groundsmen	2	2	-	6	8	5	6	3
Technical Colleges, FE, Training Colleges	4	7	6	6	2	1	1	2
Youth / Outdoor Pursuits	4	1	2	1	2	4	-	1

	1960	1961	1962	1963	1964	1965	1966	1967
Infant & Junior	12	17	26	22	17	22	20	13
Secondary	13	15	16	15	16	19	19	22
Junior / Secondary	2	2	-	2	1	4	3	6
Caretaking, School Meals Supp. Services/Groundsmen	7	5	5	6	4	5	7	6
Technical Colleges, FE, Training Colleges	1	1	1	1	1	1	1	
Youth / Outdoor Pursuits	1	1	-	-	2	2	-	

	1968	1969	1970	1971	1972	1973	1974	
Infant & Junior	15	18	19	28	30	22	10	
Secondary	19	21	21	24	17	19	5	
Junior / Secondary	6	1	2	5	10	8	5	
Caretaking, School Meals Supp. Services/Groundsmen	12	7	10	8	11	9	1	
Technical Colleges, FE, Training Colleges								
Youth / Outdoor Pursuits								

CHAPTER 12

THE EXCITEMENT OF WRITING

By 1969 'The Excitement of Writing' had reached its seventh impression and had made a widespread and deep impact on educational thinking. The abundance of sincere, sensitive and imaginative writing taking place in many West Riding Schools underlined the conclusion reached by Denys Thompson in his foreword to the book. He wrote -

"This is a timely and salutary book, revolutionary in its implications for the teaching of English."

Many presume that children have to be taught and tested to achieve a command of written English. Similarly people presume that children are incapable of organising themselves and are instinctive spectators. The work of Iona and Peter Opie proved otherwise and their studies of childrens' games showed the hidden resources which were neglected by adults. Reflecting on twenty years of research in the 1950's and 1960's they could say -

"... we have not met a child who was unable to tell us something interesting, and who did not unwittingly increase the size of our files". (1) Their study of 'Children's Games in Street and Playground' led them to state -

"A true game is one that frees the spirit. It allows no cares but those fictitious ones engendered by the game itself."

A filmstrip of Bruegel's painting, 'Children's Games', can prompt considerable discussion as youngsters eagerly describe their own versions of games such as marbles. Most of these games are rooted in history and each generation has its own versions. A boy who lived near to the gravel quarries south of Doncaster described 'bombsie', a version involving the use of discarded ball bearings taken from old quarry machines. An unsuspecting owner of glass marbles challenged in the playground to a game of bombsie, and provided the ball bearing owner gets first strike he can shatter his opponents glass 'alley', a version typifying the twentieth century.

Alec Clegg wrote a fable about Fred who lived on an island with his father and mother. He did not go to school for there wasn't one on the island so his mother taught him to read and to write and to draw and to paint. His father kept pigeons and bees and tended his garden of flowers and vegetables. Fred learned a great deal from his father and his uncle who was a forester. One day a learned educationalist visited the island and was amazed at Fred's know-ledge and ability. He analysed Fred's knowledge and wrote up his conclusions in a series of textbooks. These books were sold in large numbers and were used with groups of children put in classes of 40 and housed in schools. The fable, written in 1965, ended -

"However, in due course a few, a very few indeed, intelligent teachers came to take a cool look at what was happening and they realised that for the vast majority of children the majority of our educational processes add about as much to the mental stature of our children as a diet of sawdust would add to their physical stature ...". The fable of Fred underlines the need for teachers to adopt promising ideas to their own set of circumstances.

'The Excitement of Writing' gave publicity to children's work, it showed how, as William Walsh put it, the writing " ... comes out of the child's own centre, out of his feelings and senses and his own immediate collisions with people and the world." (2)

Furthermore it underlined the inadequacies of the routine diet of sawdust. Amongst the letters Alec Clegg received was one from a teacher fighting, in her words, 'a lone battle' against 'that ghastly and soul-less business of "exercises" and "blank filling"' Added to this was all the ironmongery of machine teaching. If this letter from the Ladies College of English in Eastbourne illustrates the view of the frustrated teacher, another letter from Chief Thomas E. Olvie from the Catholic School in Omolua, Mid-Western Nigeria, illustrates not only the impact of the book in many parts of the world but perhaps an instinctive recognition, that this was the English Chief Olvie wished to develop.

Dear Sir,

With much information that you are (in) good condition sir. I kindly beging you to send me one of your book. If you send it here I will be one of your best friends in this world. I hope that failure will not be the requests answer.

Thanks sir,

I am yours sincerely.

In a letter to Miss Peggy Jones at Keighley Girls' Grammar School Alec Clegg said he was moved to get the book published so as to help get rid of "... some of the worst features of American teaching from our schools - the underlining and blank filling techniques that came in with the standardised attainment tests." (3)

His sense of humour would have received an unexpected boost when the publishers, Chatto & Windus, told him that the Association for the Training of English in the U.S.A. had decided to buy 1,000 copies for their members.

Before 'The Excitement of Writing' was published nationally by Chatto and Windus it was printed and circulated to schools in the West Riding. Alec Clegg sent copies to those he felt would be interested, and if impressed, might give the book support and publicity. He sent copies to Marghanita Laski who reviewed books in 'The Observer' (4) and to Brian Jackson at the Advisory Centre for Education. The central issue in Alec Clegg's letters was the teaching of English and in a postscript to a letter to Miss Laski on 6th November 1963 he wrote -

"My whole thesis, of course, stands or falls by whether the work produced without these examinations is in fact good." The same sort of approach to Brian Jackson drew another enthusiastic response and he called it "... one of the most remarkable books on English teaching that has ever been produced." (5)

In the letter to Miss Laski, Alec Clegg set side by side the great advances made in South Yorkshire primary schools by enlightened teaching and illustrated in 'The Excitement of Writing' with the "vast commercial racket that has been built up around

'Exercises in English' ''. There is no doubt he enjoyed collecting and repeating to these two correspondents such examples as 'What do we call a mermaids's brother?' and 'Cow is to calf as pig is to ...' or, 'Pick out the co-ordinating conjunction in the following passage'.

Another collection of correspondence which preceded national publication dealt with the head teachers of the schools whose pupils were represented in the book. Nancy Smith distinguished direct controlled experience from free writing, whilst another head said their English work aimed "... to train the children in deeper and more automatic observation and also to train them in discrimination and sincerity in their use of words." Enquiries from Australia in July 1964 prompted Alec Clegg to send the addresses of the West Riding schools so that there could be direct contact made between schools in both countries. Each piece of work selected for the book was carefully examined in case of plagiarism. Three or four verses taken from Robert Louis Stevenson were found amongst submissions and after a request from Wakefield to all schools for special scrutiny another school found that a girl had taken her descriptive piece from the 'Observers' book of Horses and Ponies. The explanation given by the girl was that she had copied notes into a rough book "... and in that way felt she was not copying straight from the original. . ''. Scrutiny at Wakefield and in the schools identified these two examples which could, if published and discovered, have been very damaging to Alec Clegg's robust case against English exercises. However one instance of plagiarism remained and was referred to in 'Where' in July 1964 (6) in a letter from Ann Arden-Clarke.

Alec Clegg went to the Junior School which the boy who had written the piece attended. He looked at the boys work and took one of his recent writing books back to his office so that Ann Arden-Clarke could be offered the opportunity to see the way the boy was writing some months later. Alec Clegg's letter to the editor of 'Where' ended by pointing out the quality of the boy's work which he said "... proves to the hilt, I think, the point that I made." He left the option to see the work to the editor and the correspondent adding "However, I don't want to go to this trouble if you think this is a relatively insignificant piece of correspondence." (7) Once more the thoroughness of Alec Clegg in promoting or defending a case is illustrated.

The concern to preserve originality led to some pieces of writing being excluded possibly because they were too unusual to be accepted as original. Correspondence about one grammar school girl is of particular interest for it raises once again the issue of the outsiders, those of unusual or rare ability who do not fit into the traditional educational framework. The headmistress acknowledged to Alec Clegg that the girl's work had bad faults but 'In fact, though, the feeling expressed through the symbolism is absolutely authentic, and the imagery "the cotton boll'd tree" and "the flouresant, gelatinous sky" - completely original The girl had a very difficult home life and was described as unusually sensitive and self contained. She appreciated 'the advantage of being a tree which is apart from the heat and pain of the animal world ...'. The girl went into the sixth form and gained a place at Margaret Macmillan Training College in Bradford - appropriately to train to teach English!

John Smith, editor of the Poetry Review, felt that 'The Excitement of Writing' brought people back from the artificial world of English exercises to " ... obvious good sense and reality." Alec Clegg's reply to him in February 1964 concentrated on the initial omission of one piece of work saying, "when I first read it I had considered that this phrase (with toothpick claws) and certain other phrases in the piece were too mature for a boy from a Coal Board estate, and I asked a member of my staff who was largely responsible for this work to go over and see the boy." When he returned to discuss the visit, not only was he convinced the piece was valid but that all the pieces from the school were genuine. Alec Clegg said that he found all the pieces from the school a "... source of interest and puzzlement", having "a sophistication which it is difficult to explain." A collection from the same school describing a visit to a power station elicited a similar suspicion until the local HMI telephoned Alec Clegg to inform him that he had been in the school the whole day when the work was produced. 'The Excitement of Writing' had revealed abilities in the field of written expression which hitherto had neither been recognised, or tapped by a majority of schools.

Alec Clegg's puzzlement is a clue to the widely accepted but superficial assumptions on the character of working class life, especially in mining areas. 'A Kestrel for a Knave', by Barry Hines, a teacher trained at Loughborough College, portrays Billy Casper as an enigma, a disinterested secondary modern boy, the sort categorised as MANUAL by Employment Officers, but in company with a sympathetic teacher able to give a succinct expression of what he felt about 'Kes'.

Billy describes the hawk when it flies - everything seems to go dead quiet - and that Kes is not a pet -

"Sir, hawks are not pets. Or when folks stop me and say, 'Is it tame?' Is it heck tame, it's trained thats all. It's fierce, and' its wild, an' its not bothered about anybody, not even about me right. And that's why its great." (8)

Another world - like that of children's games, and this was the area to be appreciated, to be tapped but like the hawk to have its independence respected.

Once 'The Excitement of Writing' was on sale nationally it prompted extensive correspondence not only amongst educationalists but an unexpectedly wide range of people. It seems that very many people could not associate learning with enjoyment and that this book opened up a completely new way for children to satisfy 'the longing to express." (9)

When he described the qualities of a good teacher of Art, Herbert Read said the main one was sympathy, "... the ability to draw out and preserve the child's own line of thought." In his letter of appreciation to Alec Clegg for a copy of 'The Excitement of Writing' Herbert Read expressed his great interest but said he felt "... the teaching of English presents even more problems than the teaching of Art, and in spite of the enlightened approach to the subject which this book describes the general condition surely is still deplorable." Herbert Read felt the publishing industry and examinations were largely responsible but he added -

"... it is rare to find teachers who teach language as an art rather than as correct grammar." (10) The Professor of Education at Leeds University, William Walsh, wrote of 'The Magic of Children's Writing' when he reviewed the book in the Yorkshire Post. (11) In different words he made the same point as Herbert Read about the innocent eye of children saying -

"Passage after passage brings home to one the remarkable capacity children have of seeing an object newly minted, unstaled by fatigued repetition and undulled by conventional expectation."

The raw sensitivity of work done by children allowed to let their thoughts flow could irritate many carefully groomed teachers of English Language, whether in a school or a college. But such work was a delight to David Holbrook who received a copy of the book after his friend, Richard Hoggart, had suggested such action to Alec Clegg - "You're right about working class language. I find vigorous and warm hearted girls in training college are marked down for their Lawrentian flow! By dried up old bitches who've never had a heart throb!"

David Holbrook drew on his experience teaching the 'C' stream in a secondary modern school for much of his book 'English for the Rejected', published in 1964. He found qualities in these youngsters that were not recognised and as a consequence rarely developed. The 'C' class was full of 'duds' with the atmosphere as Edward Blishen put it "... rather like that of a four-ale bar." David Holbrook maintained that "The unseen creative elements in education are as yet insufficiently recognised, given authority, or made more effective by adequate conditions, except perhaps in the infant school." Like Alec Clegg he deplored the extension of the exam system into the secondary modern school and saw the prospect of secondary education for all going sour with serious social consequences. He devoted the last pages of his book to a searching letter sent to him by an emergency trained teacher of wide experience, considerable ability and high ideals who had become completely frustrated in teaching and had left the profession. Alec Clegg would have been moved by this letter especially the postscript -

"P.S. one observation which I should have made is that the subjects - music, drama, etc., - my 'C' children never had are ones with special importance to them. I had many reasons for thinking that the biggest factor in backwardness was a kind of emotional starvation."

G.C. Allen, a Staff Inspector, felt Alec Clegg was too sweeping in his condemnation of examinations and made a case for internal exams which were externally assessed. He felt this was a partial, but not a complete, answer to the problem of exam pressure. In reply Alec Clegg said -

"... you have more faith than I have that somebody is going to devise an examination which is going to continue to do good rather than harm." (12)

The book was a subject for discussion on radio and television as well as in newspapers and magazines. David Attenborough, Alec Clegg's nephew, congratulated his uncle on the book and advised him to contact Rodney Bennett rather than the 'To-night' team who might sensationalise it. Margaret Brown, a former domestic science teacher, who had recently returned to Pontefract, where she used to teach, expressed her pleasure at Alec Clegg's talk on 'Woman's Hour'. She described how the district had changed and how the 'ill-disciplined, noisy, thoughtless, uncontrolled creatures', chiefly dogs and children had changed into wives and mothers. She added 'with more knowledge and experience than I'll ever have probably!'

Denys Thompson (13) felt 'The Excitement of Writing' had revolutionary implications for the teaching of English and drew upon his experience of seeing 'O' Level scripts from Africa saying - "Scores of the writers were 95 per cent accurate on grammar, without being able to understand or write much more than pidgin English." A request from Africa for a copy of the book in November 1964 underlined this point. It read -

"Please send me a copy of 'Experiment in Writing' as composed by the Education Committee. Thank you."

Denys Thompson felt that over concentration on grammatical skill could squeeze out " ... the living, reading and writing that constitute any worthy course in English."

A correspondent from Tasmania considered the impact of the ideas in the book on teaching methods in his country. He acknowledged the book was arresting and thought provoking but he cautioned against discarding present methods for the new approach which he rightly pointed out -

"... calls for gifted teachers prepared to undertake more correction of written work than is generally done at present, and a willingness to give a great deal of individual help to pupils."

Three years later in 1967 Alec Clegg received a request from the Education Officer in the British Residency in the New Hebrides. She had a budget of £200 to provide guided practice in using English for about 150 teachers and policemen living in the eighty islands which comprised the New Hebrides. She was intent upon writing a monthly correspondence course for them based on extracts from 'The Excitement of Writing'. Alec Clegg got Chatto and Windus to agree. This request was a reflection of the growing interest in the book outside Britain.

SALES OF 'THE EXCITEMENT OF WRITING'

	HOME	OVERSEAS	TOTAL
1967	3,525	583	4,108
1968	3,159	692	3,851
1969	2,895	1,296	4,191

The central issue in the teaching of English, or for that matter all subjects, was clearly the quality of the teacher, and on a letter from a secondary head in Ely (14) Alec Clegg pencilled in this marginal comment -

"If I was not such a slave to administrative chores I should spend a lot of time trying to find out more about the difference between the insincere and the real thing ... and precisely why it is that some teachers cannot produce the sincere."The shortage of teachers was so grave that quantity was able to maintain precedence over quality. However the unanticipated excellence of many emergency trained teachers underlined the fact that there was a vast reservoir of talent in the adult world as well as the world of children. This talent lay like the substantial part of an iceberg beneath the surface, undiscovered, a gold mine under the certificated surface of society.

Two unusual but striking flashes of light on this reservoir involve the East End of London, and in a way Stepney is to London what parts of South Yorkshire are to the rest of the county. Back in 1956 Alec Clegg had listened to Robert Birley, Headmaster of Eton, say that people had come to realise that -

"... all children need an education which is more than merely learning their letters." He illustrated the need for innovation and imagination in secondary education, particularly secondary modern schools, by recounting an incident which took place in Berlin in 1948 when a woman in charge of secondary schools in the city replied to a brutal speech by the Russian Deputy Commander. She countered his assertion for communist dominated schools with an account of her visit to St Georges-in-the-East Secondary Modern School, Stepney. Her case was that if that example was followed - "she could revolutionise the education in Berlin". This initiative had a profound effect at a time described by Robert Birley as

" ... the most critical moment in the recent history of education in Berlin, perhaps in all Germany." (15)

If innovation and opportunity married in Berlin in the face of oppressive government then innovation was extinguished in Stepney in 1971. The quality of the publication 'Stepney Words' prompted Alec Clegg to contribute towards the cost of this collection of poetry and writing by local secondary children. They wrote about the world as they perceived it and were particularly sensitive to injustice no matter what form it took. Alec Clegg was moved by its depth of feeling and so too was Bill Morrell who said of 'Stepney Words' it - ... leaves an unforgettable impression of a tip in the corner of a great city. It is all here - the old lady across the road, the clock-seller, the blind man, the dustman, the immigrants, the 'cold, old horse', the pigeons, the school ..."

STEPNEY WORDS No. 2

When I'm a man
I bet I can
Climb a mountain and
Fly to Japan,

Ride every racing car.
Ride into space
And finish my tea
Without Jam on my face.

Backed by Arnold Wesker, the playwright, and organised by Chris Serle, a teacher, it was printed and regularly sold in East London. It did not aim to make a profit but to give youngsters the opportunity to see their work in print. Alec Clegg wrote to the Times Educational Supplement in June 1971 praising 'Stepney Words' and commenting on the dismissal of the teacher who had initiated the publication. He said -

"Now I would not for a moment comment on the governors' decision as I am quite sure I do not know all the facts and it isn't my business any way. But it will be a very sad and my view an educationally harmful thing if what has happened deters other teachers from encouraging this kind of writing or from inducing children to show a critical concern for the circumstances of the community in which they live."

'Stepney Words' illustrates how the qualities encouraged in many junior schools carried forward into secondary schools. The tone was 'low-pitched and restrained'. The sadness and loneliness of city life was indelibly expressed. Perhaps one could accept such clarity from a child, too young to understand the significance of what he saw or wrote - but for many adults this clarity was unacceptable from adolescents who were half way to becoming discontented adults.

If one moves from innovation to invention, from the arts to the sciences from the sources of the excitement of writing to the sources of invention, then this passage from the conclusion to a book of that title is very revealing. (16)

"It may be true that in these days the search for new ideas and techniques is pursued with more system, greater energy and, although this is more doubtful, greater economy. Yet chance still remains an important factor in invention and the intuition, will and obstinacy of individuals spurred on by the desire for knowledge, renown or personal gain the great driving forces in technical progress. As with most other human activities, the monotony and sheer physical labour in research can be relieved by the use of expensive equipment and tasks can thereby be attempted which would otherwise be wholly impossible. But it does not appear that new mysteries will only be solved and new applications of natural forces made possible by ever increasing expenditure. In many fields of knowledge, discovery is still a matter of scouting about on the surface of things where imagination and acute observation, supported only by simple technical aids, are likely to bring rich rewards."

This passage prompts the realisation that the simple but important technical developments made in pre-history, the ancient world and medieval times, can be readily undertook by youngsters and can be a spur to further discoveries. The local studies scheme for eleven year olds at Rossington Comprehensive School concentrated on may aspects of everyday life of local people during these times. (17)

The considerable number of letters from unexpected sources illustrates how 'The Excitement of Writing' unlocked for many a route to self understanding and self expression. The spurt of interest and creativity the book prompted for many in education drove a Chief in Nigeria to write to Alec Clegg for advice. A similar impulse drove a young man at Pollington Borstal to send Alec Clegg what he had put into verse to express his feelings about his youth, his family and his present sad-state. (18) The deep unease of this young man may well have been reduced by sharing his verse with Alec Clegg. Starting in a private school and prestigious grammar school he ended up in Borstal at the age of twenty. The passage downhill began with expulsion for theft and three years in a secondary modern school, then leaving home and drifting to Brighton and London where he became a hard drinker, drug addict and thief. The last verse of a poem on London may well have reminded Alec Clegg of 'Stepney Words' -

> "Going back to my four walls which unfold my life,
> Thinking about this as I gaze aimlessly across the tenements,
> How many more know the fear and loneliness which this
> place holds,
> With no one to speak to,
> Not even neighbours,
> Only money motivated people known as friends,
> There must be something somewhere."

The links between the West Riding and teachers in other countries grew throughout Alec Clegg's span of office. Arthur Naylor, head of Balby Street Junior School in Denaby, recalls that there were occasions when he had as many visitors from the United States, Norway and Australia as he had parents from Denaby at one of the school concerts. When Miss Canning, Head of Simpsons' Lane Infant School, made a visit to Cleveland, Ohio, she listened to an exchange of verse between two girls, one black, one white. The poems were read to the whole school and illustrated how sensitive, honest self expression can lead to education becoming a part of, rather than apart from, society.

Who am I?

I am many things.
A thing of fragmented beauty
Coloured and formed by many hands
Each leaving a small piece of themselves
embedded into my being
A flower whose petals have ripped away
and trampled upon.
A fragile but strong flower whose roots have
penetrated deeply the soil.
Dead in appearance to others but alive to the
very core of my being.
A bird who has flown and seen many parts of
the earth
The best and the worst.
A small creature,
Whose survival depends on the strength of his wings
and instincts
A creature measures his life in seasons rather
then years
I am many things
And many things are me.

(SINA STEWART - July 11th 1973)

168

IN RESPONSE TO SINA

Yes you are many things,
If you appear dead to others -
And I am not quite willing to admit that statement
is true,
Then it is only to those who do not recognise life when
they see it.
I weep and burn with a frustrated anger at those
circumstances and people
That have caused you to feel as a flower whose
petals have been ripped away and trampled upon -
I search for some word to make whole again the flower -
But it is impossible and unnecessary -
You are many things, intangible and therefore
stronger than a short lived flower -
Warmth, perception, bright inquiring mind, good cheerful
company -
The vibrant life at the core shines through brightly for those -
Who know life when they see it.

BERNICE

Iona and Peter Opie found in childrens' games a marvellous source of imaginative play which linked the children of today with those of yesteryear. Look back to a time before public education was developed, to the early nineteenth century, to the time of the Napoleonic Wars and to the letters sent home by a private soldier who fought in the Peninsular War and another unsuspecting area of common ground comes to light. In his foreword to 'The Letters of Private Wheeler 1809 - 1828' B. H. Liddell Hart wrote P.9 -

"The scarcity of his formal education had compensating advantages. There is no seeking for style, no cramping by grammatical convention, in his writing - his way of writing is akin to lively talking. His reflection, or asides, are free from the conventional moralising then fashionable in writing. If he makes a moral comment it is genuinely felt. His pen portraits of comrades and officers bring them to life. In character sketching he is both shrewd and sympathetic."

Alec Clegg was convinced the inner sources of interest and imagination had to be encouraged and refined. A public education system which became a straight-jacket was an anathema to him. No accident the final quotation in 'The Excitement of Writing' is from a teacher of English in a West Riding Grammar School -

"... What nonsense it is to take 'English Language' as a subject at any time or stage. Better by far have children-conscious, language-conscious teachers doing no end of things with children and what's written up or talked about is 'English' ".

CHAPTER 13

THE PLOWDEN REPORT -
EDUCATION AND ITS SOCIAL BACKGROUND

A splenetic junior school teacher would be likely to accompany justified praise for the conclusions of the Plowden Committee by adding - 'It's about time they paid some attention to primary schools!' The shot would be fired at the Ministry of Education rather than the West Riding Education Committee and its Chief Education Officer. Spleen and logic could have drawn a comparison between architectural and educational planning, posing the question 'Do you know any architects who begin with the roof and then go tier by tier down to the foundations?' 'Yes' is an unlikely answer, unless it was uttered as a jaundiced comment on modern architecture. The rational 'No' prompts the additional information that the social and economic background in the post war period played its part in determining priority for detailed reports. The needs of industry outlined in such reports as this one which dealt with Scientific Manpower, the Barlow Report of 1946, pointed to an increased demand for higher education. The Crowther Report of 1959 gave a detailed account of the wastage of ability and stressed the need for education to meet the demand created by rapid scientific and technological change. Robbins went further along this track whilst Newsom dealt with those likely to be left behind using the effective label 'Half Our Future'. The priorities identified by these reports in the sectors of higher and secondary education overawed those in primary schools, moreover their importance was reinforced by the status of these institutions. One unfortunate result was that the top institutions in the educational ladder rarely felt ill at ease laying down the details of the qualities and standards they anticipated in their new entrants. Alec Clegg was continually drawing attention to the pressures that universities and colleges put upon schools; how the exam system bore heavily on secondary schools; and how the eleven plus was the great divider and brake upon innovation in junior schools. The Thorne Scheme, Middle Schools and the Oxbridge Scheme and many initiatives in social education contained a common factor - the preservation and creation of opportunities for as many youngsters as possible.

Alec Clegg submitted evidence to the Plowden Committee on behalf of the West Riding and was on a small working party which considered the aims of Primary Education. In a letter to Dr J. J. B. Dempster O.B.E., Secretary of the Association of Chief Education Officers, Alec Clegg described what he felt was the main source of the significant advances made in West Riding Junior Schools. Letter dated 13th February 1964 -

"Almost everything in primary education depends on the selection of the right people to teach there and the training for teaching which they receive. The people who are very closely in touch with primary education to whom I have access, seem to me to be coming to the conclusion that the most gifted people teaching in the primary schools have what seems to be almost inborn qualities that involve a number of aspects of personality appropriate to the care of young children. I am sure this is a very real thing and not something that is just fanciful. It is very hard to describe but very easy to recognise when you see a brilliant teacher at work in a primary school." The implications of this conclusion were followed through to the issues of selection for training for primary school teachers and the nature of the training itself.

Acknowledging that he was over-simplifying matters Alec Clegg divided primary schools into two groups - formal and informal. To add clarity to this division he took what he termed 'two extreme examples'. The formal school gave pupils "... the knowledge which they will require to see them through life". To achieve this end they were put into groups which were as homogeneous as possible. Teaching comprised patient and careful instruction on what to do; the performance of tasks by the children; and lastly meticulous correction. No incorrect work is allowed to pass and marks were given not only as a judgement on performance but as an incentive. Discipline was clear and firm but it did not exclude kindness. The school, the parents and the children were expected to see that some drudgery was a necessary ingredient in training for the adult world.

The informal school focussed on the individual not the class and, as a consequence, the allocation of time for work in school was elastic not rigid. The teacher sought to fit the work to the youngster, to plan experiences and work which would create interest and lead to self expression. The pupil was not constrained by a class framework but encouraged to express ideas in a variety of media. As Alec Clegg put it "The pace will be that of the individual or the small group." Work was corrected in the presence of the child and could often develop into an invaluable dialogue dealing not just with mistakes but with alternatives - a process of enrichment rather than conformity to a set pattern. Alec Clegg maintained that the informal schools were more successful in three ways -

1.   Their concern is for the individual, and this is important in these days when so much is done to and for the mass.

2.   They are on the whole happier and better behaved communities, and my judgement in this matter is not entirely subjective.

3.   They are superior in the quality of work which they achieve. This point, too, can be demonstrated.

In a letter to Lady Plowden in January 1965 (1) Alec Clegg sent details of a small but significant survey of a group of formal and informal schools. Each school was sent a list of their children which the heads were asked to put into three groups - A, B or C - "according to the quality of the progress they had made and their behaviour and attitude to the school at the end of their first year and again at the end of their second year." Group A contained youngsters who had exceeded expectations, Group B contained those who had made normal progress and Group C those who had deteriorated. The replies on progress were of particular interest but those on behaviour were of limited significance. The 33 children in Group A in formal schools had dropped to 23 by the second year whilst in the informal schools only one had dropped out of the 29 children in Group A. Alec Clegg concluded "... at least we can say from this investigation, small as it is, that there is no evidence whatsoever that the able child in the informal school is under any handicap, - and that is the allegation that is so often made." During the course of discussion Alec Clegg quoted the example of a class of 38 children in an informal school who had been allowed to proceed at their own pace. Most of them came from poor home backgrounds and normally about ten gained selective school places. Thirty of this class went to grammar schools moreover their art and aesthetic development had reached a high standard. Lastly there was no record of delinquency amongst them for the last three years. The gains were in the fields of the tangible and the intangible in fact their interaction was a major source of personal progress and satisfaction.

The debate in the Working Party was aimed at achieving a broader framework of reference on the aims of Education against which the evidence given to the Committee could be tested. Professor Tibble (2) warned that such a framework ran the risk of having no relation to what was going on in schools. Professor A J Ayer (3) thought there was a danger of complacency in the primary schools and that the criticism and scrutiny of secondary schools might be better directed at the primaries. Professor Peters (4) added that the innovative primary school often did not "... fully appreciate the value of the older traditions, such as knowledge, accuracy and precision."

Other members took a more practical tack concentrating on teacher training, the waste of talent in primary schools and courses and meetings for serving teachers. Edward Blishen, teacher, broadcaster and lecturer at York University posed the question " ... that teaching is more imprisoned by habits than any other occupation?" He thought most young teachers going to their first job had to repress their instinct for originality and conform to the established pattern of school life. The emphasis put upon teaching subjects led Edward Blishen to his first aim in education - "the preservation of the totality of human knowledge and experience." The second major aim was to " ... create a habit of learning; at present it largely creates a habit of being taught." He followed this observation through to sixth form work which he felt was largely a matter of ritual repetition not a matter of personal judgement and expression. His ideal situation was one where the teacher was constantly inventive and ready for the "... unconventional and surprising responses." The deeply entrenched habits in many schools were in his view a barrier to creating 'reasonable social and moral human beings.' He continued -

"Indeed, to achieve this aim we need to alter the habits of schools quite deeply, and to regard the community it forms, and its constant experiment and inquiry into behaviour, as an essential element in the total education that the schools exist to give." (5)

Alec Clegg shared many of Edward Blishen's ideas - the totality of human knowledge, the role of the teacher as a provider of inspiration to children and, lastly, the obvious implications on teacher training for students and serving teachers. The West Riding evidence which followed the sections dealing with formal and informal schools addressed in-service training saying it

"... should be one of the first charges on the energies of an Education Authority." In 1963 it was estimated that about half of the 10,000 teachers in the West Riding attended one meeting or another to consider and discuss their work. (6)

WEST RIDING PRIMARY SCHOOLS - 1964

BUILT BEFORE 1875 330
BUILT 1875 - 1902 352
BUILT 1902 - 1918 .... <u>162</u>
<u>844</u>

TOTAL NUMBER OF PRIMARY SCHOOLS 1964 .. <u>1,040</u>

Including the schools built since 1918, 574 are in the WRCC Development Plan for retention and upgrading.

A further 359 are to be replaced by new schools.

The figures in the table on p175 which were presented to the Plowden Committee on Primary School Buildings in the West Riding underlined the very pressing need for new schools. The slow pace of re-modelling or replacement led to the conclusion that one was looking to the 24th or 25th centuries for present problems to be solved. If the pace was slow then the submission made another very important point, not one of the 52 questions contained in the Plowden questionnaire dealt specifically with buildings or the design of primary schools. If the informal approach, already well established in the West Riding, was to spread then its implications for school design had to be considered. Something very different from the Board school with its box-like, 500 square feet classrooms, was required. The paper went as far as to contend-

"For the primary school child it is arguable that the right kind of building and facilities are even more important than for his brother and sister at the secondary school for he is at the most impressionable age when the influence of his environment can have a lasting effect."

Designs that were acceptable in 1965 could possibly be outdated by 1975 so a new approach was suggested involving a thorough survey of building materials and flexibility of design. The design of Finmere School, (7) Oxfordshire for 50 pupils aged 5 to 11 is one included in the Plowden chapter on buildings and equipment. It was one of the schools referred to by David Medd, Principal Architect at the Department of Education and Science, in a lecture to an N.U.T. conference on 'The School of the Future'. David Medd had discussed school design with Alec Clegg when he was in London serving on the Newsom Committee. David Medd sketched the way forward in the form of a sustained dialogue between educationalists and architects. He quoted a neat statement made at an R.I.B.A. meeting -

"A building is neither a beautiful shell, nor a functional shed, but a coherent solution to a problem of living." Appropriately David Medd ended his lecture with a quote from the Newsom Report where a boy's reply to the age-old question: "What do you think of your new school?" was "It could be built of marble, Sir, but it would still be a bloody school."

The Plowden Report devoted a great deal of attention to deprived areas and the committee acknowledged their study of these areas -

"... compelled us to consider the process of economic and social development and the contribution made to it by the schools."

The practical outcome was that Educational Priority Areas were to be set up. Schools in these areas would get extra help from government funds for additional staff and resources along with an Educational Priority Area Allowance for all teachers. By 1971 thirteen primary schools in the West Riding were designated by the Department of Education and Science to be entitled to such status and help. Apart from this group over one hundred other such schools got extra help from Wakefield, a clear indication of the feelings of the Chief Education Officer and his Committee on the needs of socially deprived areas. Alec Clegg's contribution to the Plowden Report was probably very much more than the written submission on behalf of the West Riding. Not only does his correspondence point to this conclusion but by the mid sixties he had established a position in the national educational framework which was beautifully described by Edward Boyle during a discussion with Maurice Kogan (8) -

"We used to say, when something was proposed, 'What would Alec Clegg think about this.' You get into that kind of position - this is my point - where it's like being, if you like, a liberal in the anti-racialist movement. It isn't on paper, you don't play for that kind of position; you either have it or you don't have it. There were a few people who didn't always agree with one another, or with the Ministry, like Alexander, Sir Ronald Gould, Alec Clegg, who had a position which nobody gave them; they simply had it, commanded it."

The Plowden Committee began its deliberations in August 1963 and during the same summer Alec Clegg was working on the idea of varying the age of transfer from primary to secondary schools. His summer studies resulted in a lengthy memorandum being presented to the Policy and Finance Sub-Committee in October of that year. He saw the three tier system as a useful means to reorganise in areas where existing buildings were unsuitable for the 11 to 18 pattern. There was a bonus in later transfer at 12 or 13 for primary school methods, which were of considerable advantage to the less able, could continue for at least one more year. The reduction in the pressure of numbers on primary school accommodation offered two other attractions - the reduction of class sizes and the possible provision of nursery groups. The ideas received wide publicity and the Education Act of 1964 allowed local authorities to establish schools which cut across the rigid definition of primary and secondary - in other words they could establish middle schools. Plowden confirmed these views in proposing an older age of transfer. The advantages included the avoidance of over large comprehrensive schools and at least a year's delay in the pressure of exams on work in schools.

Alec Clegg wanted a full investigation, not only into the training of primary teachers, but into the criteria used to select candidates for training colleges. The final report did draw attention to the need for - "an analysis of the effectiveness of different patterns of teacher training..." (9) Also the report floated the sensible idea that students preparing to be teachers, or social workers, should share much of their first year. The gains were clear as it said -

"Certainly all students preparing to teach need to know much more about social work and family needs, just as most social workers would benefit from a deeper insight into the work of schools." (10) The Plowden Report widened the context of discussion. It acknowledged the extra needs of schools in areas of social and economic poverty; it saw a need to integrate the services of the Welfare State; and, rightly it altered the emphasis in education which hitherto had been on the later phases of public education. So far as the West Riding was concerned the most developed area of educational progress was the primary sector, and this progress had revealed a wealth of untapped abilities along with an unexpectedly large number of children in distress.

In much of his work on the Welfare State Richard Titmuss concentrated on the effectiveness of the National Health Service. He felt that the role of the general practitioner was to provide good medical care. This depended in part upon his medical and scientific training and experiences and on what Titmuss termed 'six critically important variables'. The six are worth listing for they prompt immediate echoes in the field of education. (11)

1. The educational equipment and clinical skill of the doctor.

2. His capacity to understand sick people.

3. The range, content and power of the scientific aids available to the general practitioner.

4. The nature and extent of his contacts with professional colleagues.

5. The facilities available to him for dealing with the social aspects of ill-health.

6. The incidence of ill-health, mental and physical, and the norms of expectation or awareness of what constitutes 'good medical care' among the population as a whole.

If teachers saw their work solely in terms of subjects not youngsters they, like doctors, ran the serious risk that many abilities were neither recognised or developed. Moreover the mis-use of chemical tranquillisers, or unnecessary surgery is more readily apparent than the failure of a teacher to look for, or to develop, ability amongst those labelled the less able. If insufficient had been done in the training of doctors and teachers to alert them to the importance of their relationship with those who received their services, then it can throw up the sequence of questions Richard Titmuss poses in his essay on 'The Irresponsible society' - P. 221.

"What education for democracy is there in much of the professionalized, sectionalized diet served up today to students in most universities, technical colleges, teachers' training courses, and other places of instruction?

Are we not, indeed, witnessing a triumph of technique over purpose?

What, in fact, are we offering to a majority of the young

beside material success, the social graces, vocational techniques and, in particular, professional salvation?"

The revolution in education was no longer silent in many colleges and universities in Britain and elsewhere it was noisy. It was not shrinking, it was changing as the clear cut poverty identified by Seebohm Rowntree was replaced by the social stresses of the Affluent Society. These labels are clues to change, no more - reminders that schools work in a changing society and, that if they do not understand what is taking place they run the serious risk that they will deal with difficulties not opportunities.

A comprehensive scheme of education could have been achieved in the West Riding in the 1960's if the transfer age had been raised from 11 to 14. All children above this age would have fitted into the existing grammar schools whilst the 11 to 14 group would have filled the modern schools. However the Committee rejected this solution and decided that the 5 - 9, 9 -13 and 13 - 18 system might be the most appropriate for some areas. Hemsworth was chosen as the first area for this change and the three main secondary schools Hemsworth High School, Willowgarth High School and Minsthorpe High School were to be fed by 13 middle schools and 23 first schools. Minsthorpe High, a new school, was planned as a community school designed to play a full part in the life of the area whilst the middle schools were to extend best primary practice beyond the age of eleven. The effect of these changes assessed in 'The Final Ten Years' Page 23 -

"Before reorganisation there was no doubt that the Hemsworth area had a reputation, inside the County, for educational staleness and lethargy. For example, visitors to the County were seldom sent to its schools and the Divisional Executive had for a long time resisted the introduction of comprehensive education on the 11 - 18 basis, but once the new scheme 'got going' the tenor, attitude and enthusiasm of the teachers and committees throughout the area changed and the scheme was so successful that it was reported on by the D.E.S. in their Education Survey No.8 'Launching Middle Schools'."

At their best the middle schools could provide a phased,

constructive transition between class teaching and subject teaching, or they could become an area of sustained conflict between primary and secondary interests. From the former standpoint subject teaching could be the death knell of innovative class teaching, but on the other hand emphasis on class teaching could lead to a lack of balance between subjects and the disappearance of subjects, such as classics, from the curriculum.

The survey of 9-13 Middle Schools based on inspections of 48 schools in 1979 and 1980 was carefully phrased but the secondary camp, if there was one, would have taken heart from the conclusion that the survey "... revealed an association between higher overall standards of work in those schools with a greater use of subject teachers." This point was pushed home by the additional comment that - "In 7 schools substantial use of subject teachers was introduced into second year classes. Five of these were among the schools which achieved significantly higher standards of work." (12)

On the other hand throughout the report it draws attention to only limited evidence of the use of the local environment in school work or of encouraging youngsters to show initiative, except in school clubs and sports. It concluded - "In general, however, the children in the survey schools need more opportunities to pose questions, put forward arguments, speculate, solve problems, and discuss the work they are doing." The West Riding ended nearly a decade before this report was published and this constructive advice is in a way a wraith like memory of the qualities of a good West Riding primary school. To some extent they are afterthoughts but the issues not dealt with in detail in the report "... links between home and the school, or between the school and the social services ..." are omissions, and with Alec Clegg's forebodings on the future of society in mind, serious omissions. The context of educational debate had changed between the seventies and eighties and it is instructive to listen to the tape recordings of conversations between Alec Clegg and youngsters in West Riding schools. Being a regular visitor to some schools the exchanges have a ring of frankness about them which give the customers view of what was on offer.

In October 1971 Alec Clegg had a detailed discussion with former pupils of a middle school on their first few weeks in a comprehensive. The discussion centred on the personal links between teacher and pupils and how work was organised. In the middle school the teacher provided a very rich background of display material which often guided their choice of a topic for study. One youngster compared this freedom of choice with the work set to classes by the subject teachers in the comprehensive school. Alec Clegg asked what happened when having started their personal study they reached deadlock. The answer was that the class helped one another and that the teacher was there to advise as well. They could illuminate their discoveries, or difficulties, on the blackboard which in the comprehensive was strictly teacher territory. Cooperation between pupils not competition dominated the middle school classroom and the discussion on marks illustrated this point.

This discussion followed a description by one youngster of how the teacher and classmates helped with painting. They began with a rough sketch of their chosen object which they discussed with others. This discussion was often followed by one with the teacher on techniques and then the painter could move on to complete the work. Youngsters chose what they were going to paint in the middle school but in the comprehensive they all did the same thing and began with a pencilled outlined, which, if satisfactory was painted over. Grades not marks were thought to be the best way to evaluate work, moreover marks said one could have a bad effect and discourage some in a class. Habits such as 'asking out' were used in one middle school. When a youngster finds a word thought to be of interest to others it is put on the blackboard and its meaning is described and discussed. One 'ask out' prompted this sequence - 'evoke', 'toil', 'cumbersome', 'stimulate', 'interrogate', 'concept', 'limpid' and 'herbivorous'. Doing different things in an atmosphere of cooperation with grades was a very different situation to working in a competitive atmosphere for marks. The other aspect which was easy to overlook were the discussions between teacher and youngsters and those between the youngsters themselves. Grades awarded in this situation were part of a cooperative learning process and not part of a pass/fail mechanism.

The youngsters pointed out that if finding out by yourself was a priority you remembered much better than if it was merely an act of memory. The youngsters compared their 'strict kindly' teachers to those who in the secondary schools put something on the blackboard and let the children get on with the copying up. The 'strict kindly' one kept you at work and helped you solve your difficulties.

The Plowden Report focussed attention on the importance of primary schools and their immediate needs. It identified the pool of untapped ability, the inadequacy of IQ tests (13) and the underestimated effect of social deprivation on the progress of many youngsters. There was a clear need for its conclusions to be reflected in a purposeful national educational policy. This did not occur and the Committee issued a statement in January 1969 saying that only 'piecemeal progress' had been made and that the Department of Education ' ... has not formulated a systematic policy' in response to this report.

The Plowden Committee expressed concern at the slow pace of change, others went further and with very detailed evidence to back their views maintained the recommendations made by Plowden were no more than 'modest'. (14)

The popular title for the society which had developed in the fifties and sixties was 'affluent'. Perhaps many people were better off but there were very worrying, elusive features of society which could not be assessed solely in terms of being above or below a carefully drawn poverty line. As Barbara Megson put it in a memorandum to Alec Clegg (15)-

"Economic deprivation cannot be viewed in isolation, its side-effects can be educational, social and emotional as well."

A Liverpool mother was prompted to write to Alec Clegg on the distress children suffered in families which had moved out of the working class and who would to many social commentators represent the new entrants to the middle classes. She wrote -

"They've moved away from the working class environment, have semis, a museum of a home and a car and this is good providing you have the income to do it, but in each case husband and wife have to work, not only that they are determined their children will be brought up different to them which is also good, providing you know the right way to go about it, but everything has been got at the expense of their children, each child is a lonely child and unhappy. One 11 year old girl in particular is always on the verge of hysteria, I often feel like bringing them home with me and giving them the freedom for a while to express themselves and getting all out of their systems, but this wouldn't be allowed as they let me know I'm too soft with kids and this would be bad for them, and I'm not really, its just that I allow my kids to tell me straight what they think, or if I've been unfair or wrong I apologise and admit I'm a louse for shouting at them when I should have made some enquiries first, but I think you are right. Something should be done to protect kids and I think the only way it can be done is to educate the parents."

Postscript

A collection of letters celebrating the 90th birthday of Lady Plowden in May 2000 reflect on the long term inportance of the report by the Central Advisory Council for Education, which she chaired. The letters celebrate the personal qualities of Lady Plowden and other prominent educationalists who will not be remembered for statistical success, but the quality of the personal relationships they fostered in educational authorities and institutions.

The first sentence in Chapter 2 of the Plowden Report expresses this basic belief — 'At the heart of the educational process lies the child.' From the letters for the 90th birthday came a series of equally deep, simple statements such as —

George Baines —'children are subjects not objects.'

Rosemary Devanald — who stresses '... flexibility in the use of time'.

John Stephens —the importance of releasing and encouraging creativity.'

Jessie Clegg — 'we are obsessed with testing.'

Les Bennett — talks of the 'fearless leadership of Alec Clegg.'

Len Marsh — in the Postscript reflects on how the Plowden.

The report explored the potential within Local Authorities and teaching for innovation rather than to be trapped in a tight national framework.

CHAPTER 14

ALEC CLEGG -
EXAMINATIONS AND SOCIETY AT LARGE

For many years the straightjacket of examinations at eleven, sixteen and eighteen was a target for Alec Clegg. The replacement of the eleven plus examination by the Thorne scheme and the establishment of various forms of comprehensive reorganisation gave the junior and middle schools the opportunity to concentrate on the new ideas which had been pioneered in the West Riding. This freedom which in some areas extended to the age of thirteen increased the pressure to find ways to deal with the problems examinations created in secondary schools. This was not at all easy for higher education in all its forms, industry and commerce relied on examination results at sixteen and eighteen as major indicators of the quality of prospective students or employees. Alec Clegg must have felt the Thorne scheme and the middle schools increased the area available for educational progress yet on the other hand it produced a starker view of the barriers that still stood in the way.

The Beloe Report and the introduction of the Certificate of Secondary Education drew another large band of youngsters into the examination system. At the same time it gave clear identity to those who left school with no qualifications at all. When Professor S.J. Gould gave his inaugural lecture at Nottingham University on 'Sociology and Education' in 1965 he drew attention to the dangerous split in British society quoting Alec Clegg on the examination system -

"Let us take a cold look at what we do to the weaker Newsom child. We say: You have not been selected at 11 for this grammar school. You are not good enough for the G.C.E. stream in the modern school. You are not even good enough for one or two C.S.E subjects in the modern school. You will, therefore, be placed in one of the forms which gets the poorest teachers, the least choice of subjects, the most meagre use of facilities, the least homework, and whose members assume the least responsibility and are the first to be sacrificed when teachers are absent. When you leave you cannot train as an apprentice, you will be the last to secure day release. You will be the last to be cared for by the industrial training board." (1, 2)

Alec Clegg's regular criticism of the examination system may appear Quixotic to some for the mills of the Exam Boards continued to grind on lending weight to the view that he risked being labelled an impractical idealist. Against this assumption can be set the evidence in Her Majesty's Inspectors Report on schools in the Thorne, Hatfield, Stainforth area after the introduction of the Thorne Scheme (3) and Alec Clegg's evidence to a Public Inquiry in February 1965. (4)

English moved from exercises to the sort of original work exemplified in 'The Excitement of Writing'. Mathematics broadened to include more of the practical element such as graphs, map work, scale drawing and statistics. Libraries with a good stock of reference books gradually replaced collections of classroom text books and the spoken word gained at the expense of the written word. Drama, poetry, discussion and music began to play a much more important part in the school day. Put together these changes amounted to a revolution in the primary sector although they were carefully understated in the Inspectors' conclusion on nine out of thirteen schools in the Thorne, Hatfield, Stainforth area which were in the absence of the eleven plus "... seizing their opportunities".

Part of Alec Clegg's evidence to the Public Inquiry dealing with the proposed non-county borough of Wakefield dealt with what a large education authority like the West Riding might do, if there was the likelihood that 'externally imposed examinations' could be replaced by school gradings which were externally assessed. In most respects this was Mode 3 of the Certificate of Secondary Education. The lengths to which Alec Clegg was prepared to go to achieve this change were set out in Paragraph 24.

Para.24 - "The stock-in-trade of the inspectors is ideas, and there are times when all normal school visiting may have to be abandoned in the pursuit of an idea. Let me give an example. In many ways the curse of the English educational system is the externally imposed examination, and an immense leap forward might be made in the secondary field if it were possible to replace the external examination by a system which was statistically valid but which used the school grading externally assessed. Techniques to this end have been worked out by H. M. Staff Inspector for Research working with the teachers and inspectors in the West Riding, and it now seems that there is a possibility that these techniques will succeed. To achieve this end it would be worth while taking every inspector and adviser in the county, if necessary, off normal school work for many months." (5)

This declared readiness to back initiatives was not matched by many new ideas in secondary schools in fact many stuck to their established habits. When Alec Clegg asked Miss Imrie if Todmorden was going to accept the Thorne scheme he got the reply 'never'. She added that the headteachers were expert coachers and testers furthermore they felt creative studies a waste of time. The exam system had very deep roots at secondary level and even a comprehensive, Calder High School, made a distinction between selected and unselected pupils. Alec Clegg asked that this practice should stop. The handicraft adviser, Mr. Wilson, saw the inclusion of course work in the assessment procedure as a change which could encourage the individual development of youngsters. On the other hand adding C.S.E. to 'O' Level examinations led to exams for everyone in grammar schools and he felt they "... were even more insular and resistant to change then they were two or three years ago." (6) Harry Day, Rural Studies Adviser, saw a need to integrate his subject with other sciences especially biology so as to give a practical dimension to these studies. But he saw grammar schools as a barrier to change saying "... the root trouble is ignorance of Rural Studies in grammar schools, from whence our teachers emerge." (7) Another valid point in relation to the Mode 3 examination was that the mechanics of examining individual work was complex and time consuming, so much so that some schools were forced to go back to the straight forward Mode 1 examination.

If a school decided that a majority of, or all, the subjects taught up to 16 were to be assessed by Mode 3 examination then the additional work for teachers and pupils was considerable. The opportunity for creative individual work could be overwhelmed by the sheer weight of course work. One way to avoid overloading pupils was to reduce the number of subjects they were examined in at 16+. Another way was to enter them for integrated courses in the Sciences, the Humanities and the Arts.

Sir Alec saw the education system as a machine for "the elimination of the unworthy", and the streamed comprehensive school as potentially the means of branding the less able with greater certainty. Would language laboratories, computers and television sets make teaching easier? Could the machine do the work of a sensitive teacher? According to one of his dreams the answer was 'Yes'. Interviewed by a computer salesman he asked "What about Plowden's aspiration?' The salesman replied, 'We've thought of that and every time a pupil gets anything right a mechanical hand shoots out, pats him on the back and says "Well done, Charlie".' Then I woke up.

Charlie caused a laugh but the prospect Alec Clegg sketched out of the social consequences of an exam dominated education was a nightmare, not an amusing dream. The United States furnished ample evidence of the number who dropped out of the education system and who felt few, if any, obligations to society at large. In a lengthy memorandum to the Policy and Finance Sub-Committee in May 1968 Alec Clegg outlined his deep concern about the waste of human potential in the West Riding and the country as a whole. He saw the reduction of unskilled work especially in the contracting coalfield of South Yorkshire as a change which would turn unemployment into unemployability. His nightmare was that -

"Failure to secure work and its consequent sense of being useless in society can be a disastrous effect on youngsters. It can produce apathy, a callous determination to live on the State, or violent aggression. Perhaps the most significant fact about the rioters in the U.S.A. is not that they are coloured but that so many of them are teenagers so ill-educated as to be almost unemployable." (8)

STATISTICS ON MATTERS OF SOCIAL CONCERN
Quoted in 'Waste of Human Potential in Education'

a)   Cases of malicious wounding and assault and robbery by youngsters under 17 years of age have increased by 200% over the last 10 years.

b)   Illegitimate live births to girls of 18 have increased by 220%, to girls of 17 by 264%, to girls of 16 by 292% and to girls of 15 by 377%.

c)   The suicide rates which over the country as a whole show a decline have increased by 70% amongst young persons from 15 to 20 years of age.

d)   Children abandoned have increased by 86%.

e)   Children deserted by the mother, leaving the father unable to cope, have increased by over 100%.

f)   Children in thoroughly squalid homes have increased by 166%.

g)   Children with parents in prison show an increase of 50%.

h)   Children taken into care because of their own offences have increased by 78%.

i)   Boys sent to approved schools have increased during the 10 years 1956-66 by 74%, and the total number of boys in approved schools has increased by 28% during the same period.

The Seebohm Report on Local Authority and Allied Personal Social Services published in 1968 concluded that a more integrated service was required along with increased resources. Its emphasis upon prevention of distress was followed by this statement - p.229.

"We do not know exactly the form this will take; in no field is systematic research more needed. Meanwhile, we must act on the best available information and regard what is done as an experiment, in the broadest sense, from which to learn."

This admission underlines the difficulties which faced an education authority which looked to the future and weighed up the consequences of changes such as increased reliance on the extended examination system in secondary schools. It is difficult to disagree with the Provost of Kings' College who described the system as -

"... an entirely ruthless machine for the elimination of the unworthy". (9) 'Unworthy' could have been replaced by 'poor' if Richard Titmuss's reflections on education within the Welfare State had been used to describe those eliminated. During a lecture he gave in Washington U.S.A. in December 1964 (10) Richard Titmuss pointed out how since 1945 the proportion of male undergraduates who were sons of manual workers was 1% lower than between 1928 and 1947. The number of university students had doubled but the proportion coming from working class homes had remained fairly constant at just over a quarter. (11) His final comment was that social policy might well concentrate on 'ways of extending the Welfare State to the Poor'.

One section of the memorandum dealing with 'the Waste of Human Potential in Education' focussed on the failures amongst the ablest youngsters who continued their education beyond the age of sixteen. Nearly a quarter of a million pounds was spent annually by the West Riding on pupils who for one reason or another, 'dropped out'. The follow up in the case of one of the Oxbridge scholars (12) showed it was not lack of ability but other personal factors which prevented progress. Alec Clegg saw the need for what he termed 'some retrieval machinery to help students'. The Chief Education Officer was the retriever in the case of the Oxbridge students but he was also the point of reference to some who felt their ability, or ambition, lay outside and unrecognised by the examination route into higher education.

David Gale, who entered the Royal Ballet after leaving his secondary modern school, was interested in dance ever since the age of four or five. He had private lessons in dance and aimed to get the necessary certificates by the time he was fifteen. He failed and felt dance was out as an occupation. His parents persuaded him to go to another teacher which he did and in a short period of time he passed a series of examinations. He applied for admittance to the Royal Ballet, was interviewed and offered a place. It was at this point that an application was made to the West Riding and Alec Clegg ensured he got funding for what was to be a very successful career. It is said that the Annual Yorkshire Ballet Seminar at Ilkley owed its origins to the support David Gale got from Alec Clegg and the West Riding.

David Gale and his family illustrate how personal belief can with ability and determination bring success. The opposite set of family circumstances threatened an able girl for the first seventeen years of her life. Her parents separated before, or just after, she was born. Her mother remarried and the girl was brought up by her grandparents in Northern Ireland. When her grandfather died her grandmother neglected her so much that she was taken into care. At the age of thirteen she returned to her mother and her birthplace in the West Riding. Even though she was an 11+ success her parents sent her to the local secondary modern school. Her parents resisted her wish to go to the High School and to take 'O' Level examinations. Pressure by the girl and her school secured her a place in the High School where she got eight 'O' Levels and was thought to be a potential University student. The prospect of two more years at school and her independent point of view contributed to her step father turning her out. She was determined to continue her education and did. Another girl, daughter of William Bunting described as 'Naturalist, pamphleteer, archivist, rebel, bad-tempered old sod, and inspiration', (13) failed the eleven plus but her father convinced Alec Clegg of her ability and she went to Thorne Grammar School. At the age of sixteen she gave a lecture to the British Association when it met in Sheffield in 1956. These are three of the 'outsiders' who by their own efforts, or those of their family, illustrate the abilities which often lay undiscovered by the education system.

The most powerful causes of wasted potential amongst children are lack of security, love, support and encouragement. The caring school could do a great deal to identify the children needing help and it could contribute a great deal towards any decision on the character of the help itself. Schools which pursued aims of this type soon realised they were carrying a welfare load which stretched their human resources well beyond those provided for conventional classroom needs. Theoretically they could reach a point where investment in pastoral care replaced that in classroom teaching. The careful, systematic timetabling of many comprehensive schools gave many examples of such choices being made. Year teachers, house masters and mistresses, heads of lower, middle and upper schools were posts where the personal needs of youngsters were paramount. In good schools these posts were not merely appointments made to ensure good discipline, they were investments designed to improve the quality of community life. The by product of good pastoral care could be a contented and well motivated school community where youngsters sought to use their abilities to the full.

Perhaps thoroughgoing investment in pastoral care could be associated with more youngsters taking examinations and more youngsters getting better results. Perhaps extensive use of Mode 3 at 'O' Level and C.S.E. and the use of integrated syllabuses could lighten the sheer bulk of work for teachers and pupils. (14) Perhaps these options, if taken, could focus attention on quality and individual interests. Perhaps moreover the load of a single subject exam system could be reduced so that space for the individual to experiment, explore and relax was increased. Some of the Schools Council Schemes in integrated studies and those run by the West Yorkshire and Lindsey C.S.E. Board could provide a much more united curriculum which in turn gave space for more individual choice. Moreover teachers worked in teams and consequently ceased to be narrow specialists. The wider view of their work led to cooperation between staff and reduced the competition for able pupils when 'O' level and C.S.E. choices were made at the end of the third year in an 11 to 18 school. Schools with a faculty structure (15) could ensure every youngster had a balanced education up to 16, plus choice within each faculty. This structure avoided the so-called 'choices' which in many schools were 'exclusions' rather than choices. The choice of one subject automatically meant the exclusion of others.

The personal element in many youngsters which did not fit into the subject structure of secondary schools might not be as rare as many might assume. The exam system appears an all embracing structure which does not seek to identify exceptional, or unusual, qualities. Candidates achieve very good, average or poor results. They get, or they don't get, qualifications. In his study of a working class community Brian Jackson reflected on the work of three northern artists L.S. Lowry, D.H. Lawrence and Henry Moore. He felt they gave us knowledge "... which we might be tempted to overlook since it may not be containable within the academic disciplines on which we mainly take our stand." (16)

When he considers the communities in which these artists lived another dimension is added. As Brian Jackson puts it -

"Their evidence is much more subtle, and its roots run deeper. To no small extent our sense of what life and its values is, derives from the artist. We ought at least to pause over the community that differently stimulated all three. (17)

South Yorkshire colliery villages like Denaby are taken to be disadvantaged and can be designated educational priority areas. This designation can bring with it additional resources but if they are not used to foster the creative elements in education then the personal qualities which can enrich the style of life, even in the most depressing neighbourhoods, will not be developed. Brian Jackson's study ends with this conclusion -

"What men have slowly made - and wonderfully too - out of squalid conditions deserves cautious and imaginative use." (18)

EUROPEAN STUDIES

This course was designed as a unity and comprised elements of history, geography and literature. It aimed to encourage and develop a pupil's powers of appreciation, discrimination and expression. Each pupil did a project during this two year course. It covered the elements of the course with emphasis on depth. The upper limit was 4,000 words. One girl did a study of the Second World War in the Far East. The biography of Ronald Searle, who was captured by the Japanese and who worked on the Death Railway between Siam and Burma, provided information which was a surprise to those who saw him solely as the creator of St Trinians and Molesworth.

CHAPTER 15

CHILDREN IN DISTRESS

After he retired Alec Clegg reflected on his early experiences of administration in Cheshire and Worcestershire saying the difference was between doing a technicians's job and being part of a great human service. (1) The emphasis that he put upon the human qualities he found in Worcestershire stayed with him for the rest of his working life. Thorough administration conducted in an atmosphere of understanding and compassion, and backed on occasions by a flinty determination, ensured that causes such as distressed children were a top priority in the West Riding. The studies he initiated on this issue prompted conclusions similar to those reached by Richard Titmuss and Peter Townsend both of whom sought a redefinition of poverty. The momentum of social change in the forties was no longer there in the sixties. In fact according to some commentators it was change for the worse with the rich getting richer and the poor getting poorer. Alec Clegg saw the predicament of many children in the sixties as a major factor in determining the character of the future of Britain. (2)

As he and Barbara Megson wrote at the end of 'Children in Distress', p175: "If a child suffers in his own home and is also made to feel that he is of no account, as he moves into the adult world his chances of achieving happiness and success as a worker or a citizen, or indeed as a member of society, are likely to be very greatly reduced. It is difficult to believe that some of these factors are not already at work in the U.S.A. that they have not begun to work here, and they will not - unless steps are taken to avert it - have dire consequences for the future."

In December 1964 Alec Clegg sent a personal letter to all secondary headteachers in the West Riding. He asked for details about the youngsters who caused the greatest concern. His aim was to gather information which would enable him to convince the Education Committee that there was a pressing need for help. He wanted to know first of all "... if the problem exists and, if it does, what is its magnitude, nature and complexity." The replies confirmed that the problem did exist and that further investigation would probably underline its complexity.

From this and later studies it appeared that at one extreme were a few youngsters who were rarely, if ever, allowed to mix with other children and who found the first experience of school daunting. On the other hand there were many large families some of which lived in dirty, cramped accommodation where children had to compete ferociously for their share of affection and the limited material resources. Over protection or over exposure caused distress, yet no matter which route is taken to try to reach a generalisation on the causes of distress you find boys and girls who overcome difficulties and like good metal are tempered by their experiences.

With the appointment of Barbara Megson in 1966 as an administrative assistant a regular flow of information on distress amongst children in West Riding schools was established. The information showed the scale and complexity of the problems faced by the children themselves, their families and the schools and the communities in which they lived. Some of the children sought sanctuary within themselves others used their frustration as a fuel to disrupt the lives of those around them. The details on particular boys and girls inevitably point to the need for co-ordination within and between branches of the Education, Health and Social Services. Yet those who attempted to achieve this end quickly became aware that since 1945 the boundary between medical and social matters became more and more uncertain as the years went by.

From a strictly educational standpoint shortcomings in literacy and numeracy could cause stress to many youngsters. Seeking the causes of a low reading age one study showed a boy of 14 with a reading age just above that of an 8 year old. The boy joined the school at 13 when he and his mother moved to the area to attend his sister's wedding. His mother died at the wedding and as there was no known father his newly married sister and brother-in-law became his guardians. The head wrote later that the boy was coming round but that the problem was to accelerate progress in the remaining terms in school. At the same time as Barbara Megson's files were being filled by sad and difficult cases such as

195

this the newspapers were concentrating on what was termed the 'napkin' case.

Initially the story was of a school, a local authority (3) and a court trampling on the right of a mother and her child; of a girl committed to the care of a local authority simply because she broke a school rule by wiping school cutlery with a table napkin. The outburst by the press led to the matter being raised in Parliament and to criticism of the headmaster and the local authority by the Speaker of the House of Commons. When the facts about the girl and her mother eventually filtered through a very different picture emerged. The mother had tried on a number of occasions to be present with her daughter at dinner time and had on one occasion to be removed by the police. She brought a case against staff and had it dismissed by the Bench. The daughter had been absent for six months partly due to the antagonism of the mother towards the school. In an attempt to get the girl settled the local authority had offered to arrange a transfer and if necessary to assist with boarding school fees for the girl. On the matter of wiping school cutlery the offer was made that the girl could wipe it in the presence of a teacher. Barbara Megson ends her account of the case by saying "... it would be interesting to count the inches evoked to the reporting of it". In March it was 1,185 inches in daily and sunday newspapers!

The bizarre use of the press, the television and the courts to focus public attention on her complaints can be compared with the secretive behaviour of the 'Letter Box Family' of Bingley. The curtains of their house were drawn all day and visits from any local authority staff usually led to conversations through the letter box. The sealing off of the family from society was as bizarre as the napkin case underlining the old saying that fact is stranger than fiction.

These extreme cases stick in the memory warning of the unpredictable nature of human beings and the need to be prepared for the unexpected. On the other hand there is abundant evidence that sensitive and adequate support could help many youngsters to overcome the difficulties they faced at home and at school.

The replies to a later enquiry into distressed children in junior schools pointed in many cases to lack of parental care. Many of the children were poorly fed, poorly clothed, dirty and rarely had sufficient sleep. Their homes were overcrowded and the immorality, violence and disputes amongst the adults produced an atmosphere for stress and deterioration not personal development. Where poverty, physical and mental illness and personal disasters were the causes of distress there was a clear cut obligation on society to provide help. Personal pride and sheer stamina made many soldier on as Barbara Megson concluded -

"... fatherless families are often the worst off financially yet the children are frequently the best dressed in the school and do not appear on the free dinner lists. Apparently, these children do not suffer materially, but the strains imposed on the mother in achieving this may result in emotional stress and behaviour problems in the child."

The earlier the link between family and school could be made the better, as one divisional officer wrote -

"I am sure that Nursery Schools and classes would go some way to catching the would be criminals at an early age, soon enough in fact to turn some of them from the path of hooliganism, vandalism and delinquency." this officer drew Alec Clegg's attention to the fact that in 1953 nursery classes were closed. (4) Even in 1967 there were only five day nurseries operating in the West Riding. There would seem to be a sizable gap in time between the early signs of delinquency and their overt expression, but once again the individual cases illustrate the opposite under-lining the need for early preventive measures. A boy described as 'blue-eyed, golden haired, angelic little cherub of six' smoked twenty cigarettes a day, stole regularly and one day tried to get into banks. When he found out the time that a local firm made up its wage packets he broke in and stole some. The head described him as 'an unwanted child'. Children with unacceptable habits could improve, as one infant school headmistress wrote in her follow up letter to Miss Megson on distressed children -

"When Mandy first came to school she bit everyone with whom she came into contact. By patience and perseverance we gradually reduced the number of children who were bitten until it became evident that Mandy bit the children who were better dressed than she was ...".

Letters to heads of progressive primary schools brought many replies which dealt with the connections between child centred education and distressed children. One head felt many teachers had middle class values and were only comfortable using formal methods to classes of children. They did not relish using child centred methods, as he put it -

"There is only one way and one way only to lessen the gulf for the distressed, less able and that is for the school to use, as far as is possible, the child's own experiences as a vehicle for his education, and to find non-verbal and non-academic forms of activity in which he can discover his personal dynamic." Another head stressed the importance of holidays with teachers and how a week in the Lake District had introduced many children to a completely different environment and, equally important, a completely new teacher-pupil relationship. A humorous insight came from a Castleford Junior School head who extolled the virtues of clay work for children with personal problems. He wrote -

"Clay seems to enable this type of child to give vent to his pent up emotions by pounding it and later as his experience grows, the dexterous use of fingers produces work in quality better than any other media." The last letter in this collection summed the matter up, 'Formal methods leave little room for sympathy.'

Enquiries from County Hall to schools on matters like distressed or delinquent youngsters could prompt unease for some headteachers. Their guess might be that their response would be taken as an indicator of the quality of discipline and care in their school. Alec Clegg and Barbara Megson did devote many pages in 'Children in Distress' to schools that helped the weak and they followed that study by considering how ultra formal, rule bound schools could be encouraged to change. If apprehension amongst some heads was understandable then in terms of educational progress it was a necessary precursor of change.

A study in 1961 of Caning, Behaviour and Delinquency in Secondary Schools in the West Riding (5) came to the conclusion that -

" ... as far as the schools of this enquiry are concerned it appears that behaviour is best and delinquency least in those schools where corporal punishment is used sparingly." The enquiry was another example of the Chief Education Officer's thorough administration for the evidence came from Divisional Education Officers and County Council Inspectors. The Divisional Officers were asked to name the best and the worst schools in their areas and to obtain details of the number of children from each school who appeared before juvenile courts. The Council Inspectors were asked to report on the number of canings which took place in individual schools in the summer term of 1961. The enquiries were independent of each other and one of the other significant conclusions was -

" ... There is no support for the view that the best behaved schools in the West Riding drew their pupils from socially favoured areas." These studies point to child centred education in junior and infant schools and the minimum use of the cane at secondary level as two of the routes to an orderly and creative school community.

Special School Provision

The West Riding Development Plan of 1952 acknowledged the lack of "... adequate school provision for children suffering from mental or physical defects." The West Riding consulted with the Ministry and other northern authorities so that specialist schools covering a wide range of needs could be set up. Difficulties in finance, staffing and the absence of suitable accommodation stood in the way of the ambitious plan being carried out. The reports Alec Clegg received on Special Schools outlined how far the authority had to go before it met the aims of the plan.

Miss Wyllie, Inspector for Special Schools in the West Riding, regularly sent quarterly reports to Alec Clegg. These reports give an insight into the work of Special Schools, how far they met the needs of educationally sub-normal or handicapped children and how they did, or did not, link with other services. Miss Wyllie drew attention to the absence of places for ESN children in some divisions of the West Riding. In Wombwell and in Shipley children from day ESN Schools were reclassified at twelve as less severely handicapped and discharged to local secondary modern schools, solely because there was no ESN provision at secondary level. Elsewhere quite a number of handicapped children were sent away to other parts of the country.

By 1956 Adwick Park Special Classes had ceased to be a place for children of very low ability and became 'a dumping ground' for 'ascertained children'. In the same year there was a waiting list in the county as a whole of 600 children for places in day, or boarding, schools for ESN children. Some parts of the West Riding such as Castleford, Hemsworth and Keighley had Remedial Centres but the selection for the first two was described by Miss Wyllie as 'haphazard'. Some of the children in the first two schools should have been recommended for Special Schools. Their presence at the two Remedial Centres had in Miss Wyllie's view helped to put some parents off. Despite this difficulty all three centres aimed to build up a child's self respect by giving them successful experiences and by making them feel they were valued. The medical inspections which took place often found defects of vision and hearing that had remained undetected for many years. The case of a disruptive boy, who had defective hearing and had developed a remarkable skill in lip reading which enabled him to keep abreast of his work, illustrated the need for education and health services to work together. The boy always occupied a place at the front of the class but a new teacher moved him to the back. Lip reading was difficult from that position and behaviour and progress deteriorated. Only when a team of specialist doctors and teachers shared their knowledge of the boy were the facts fitted together and a sensible plan of action put into effect. (6)

Later reports from Miss Wyllie on the improvement of Toll Bar School, near Doncaster, illustrates how an individual approach to youngsters could affect the quality of education and meet the needs of the least able. The Divisional Medical Officer wrote of one little girl with an IQ of 63 - 'She should really be in a special school - yet this child is steady and stable and is happily working away and making good progress - not to mention fitting in with the environment of the school.'

Careful classification, whether on the basis of physical, psychological or social shortcomings, provided evidence for sensitive individual placement. If it was used rigidly to provide no more than a match of diagnosis with a special service, then it was possible that the most effective solution to an individual's needs could in some cases be missed. The need for a creative overlap between special schools and services and normal day schools was essential, not only to make sure resources were used as effectively as possible, but to create the public perception that services worked together for the benefit of individuals rather than being specialist classifiers and curers of personal ills and shortcomings.

Miss Wyllie's final report in the early sixties underlines the particular qualities which had developed in the Education Service -

"Looking back over the years I appear to have achieved little, but I think you will get my meaning if I describe it as pioneer work at the beginning. Of one thing I am certain - the organisation and administration of special schools is on a sound footing: personal relationships with Medical and Administrative Officers are cordial, and there is a spirit of goodwill generally."

Teachers had to be innovative to achieve progress with youngsters in Special Schools and G.H. Wilson, the Senior Adviser for Handicraft, confirmed this fact in his report to Alec Clegg in March 1962, saying -

"Some of the most exciting Handicraft is going on in the Special Schools; in most cases the teacher responsible in the workshop has not been trained to teach Handicraft, and for this reason he is less inhibited by the traditional approach." He pointed out that the approach of many secondary school handicraft teachers to less able pupils was to " ... offer the same things taught more slowly." His report to Alec Clegg in January 1964 contained a damning comment 'In only two schools can it be said that attempts are being made at the moment to offer something to the less able child ...' If secondary schools were going to help twilight youngsters then they had to offer something more than tedium in practical subjects to set against the stresses of home life. In these circumstances one can appreciate truancy could bring a sense of relief.

The inequalities which bore heavily on distressed children had their paralled if attention was turned from people to places. The south of the Riding was a seriously disadvantaged area. It had fewer grammar school places than other areas and a smaller proportion stayed on in the sixth forms. The trend continued for fewer sixth formers went on to universities. It was an area of slag heaps, depressing colliery villages and limited opportunities. One of the detailed studies carried out by Barbera Megson was a comparison of Consiborough and Ripon. Both could boast of buildings of historic interest and beauty - Conisborough castle and Ripon cathedral. In both places working class incomes were determined by the wages in the main occupations, coal mining in Conisborough and farming in the Ripon area. However these similarities are but a prelude to stark differences especially in relation to the lives of children.

Barbara Megson began her area survey of Ripon with a shrewd and sensitive description of the town and its social characteristics. (7)

"The Cathedral City of Ripon lives on past glories ... To exclusive medieval loyalty is added a resentful sense of inferiority. It was never 'done' to 'take' trade out of the town and, even now, a good Riponian is embarrassed by being recognised in a Harrogate shop."

Conisborough's predicament prompted the concise and worrying comment that even for a South Yorkshire colliery village it was a backward area. The West Riding Educational Priority Area Project described Denaby, the most depressing part of Conisborough, in these words -

"From the crags one can look down on Denaby, almost in plan, through a thin gauze of smoke. Here and there, a church or school stands out by its size, but the main impression is of rows of terraced houses; straight streets with small brick pavements, alternating with asphalted areas between two rows of houses. Some houses open straight on to the pavements; others have tiny front yards. At the back, each house has its own small bricked back yard, coal store and outside lavatory." (8)

Basically a vast majority of the houses were 'two up and two down'. When Barbara Megson did her survey 1,600 houses were scheduled for demolition in a slum clearance scheme. The overcrowding and run down state of the area was one of the causes of the high infant mortality rate in Conisborough as a whole - 30.1 per 1,000 compared to a national figure of 19.0 per 1,000. The starkest of her statistics on Conisborough was the figure for the proportion of distressed children at Balby Street Junior School - 31% of its pupils. Barbara Megson queried some of the figures from individual schools as over-estimates but there is no doubt, especially when compared to Ripon, that Conisborough as a whole was an area which deserved major investment in all public services. Ripon city with 2.5% of its school population being distressed children was well below Conisborough which had 13.3%.

If attention is focussed on the schools which sought to deal with the distressed children in Conisborough the problems appear much worse. The head of Ivanhoe Junior Mixed and Infant School listed remedies which could ease the problems which he faced. The first was to find ways to attract more teachers 'to areas like this' and to create conditions so that they would stay longer. Secondly there was an immediate need for more ancillary help and for smaller classes. His last point was to request more encouragement and understanding in the County as a whole for those combating social problems.

One of the few teachers who had stayed at Ivanhoe school over three years reflected on the improvement that had taken place due to the changeover to informal ways of teaching. Formally the children were untidy in appearance and the standard of work was low and " ... instead of respecting each other as individuals, they would taunt the more backward members of the class, or any child who was in any respect, different." She added " ... slowly children took more pride in themselves and their work." The school had well over 30 different teachers in six years and only four out of the eleven staff there in 1967 had been in the school over three years. The view that many parents were disinterested in the school is illustrated by the final case report of 15th July 1966 which read -

"This boy was a victim of his home background, a home void of affection and very little in the way of security. No interest shown towards the boy, who was left to fight for his very existence ..."

DISTRESSED CHILDREN IN
RIPON AND CONISBOROUGH - 1966-67

	School Population	Number of Distressed Children	% of School Population
RIPON - CITY	2,905	73	2.5
RIPON - OUTLYING VILLAGES	430	10	2.3
CONISBOROUGH	2,816	372	13.3

Conisborough clearly qualified to be an Educational Priority Area and in the final years of the West Riding it was targeted for a sequence of initiatives in social education. (9) By 1971 thirteen primary schools in the county were designated EPA schools by the Department of Education and Science, yet by the same year over a hundred West Riding schools received extra help in relation to the welfare of their pupils. This diverse welfare programme can lead one to overlook the day to day contact between teachers and youngsters in schools and that between Educational Welfare Officers and the families of truants, delinquents and those excluded from schools.

When the head of the Ivanhoe Junior School in Conisborough wrote to Alec Clegg in May 1967 he concentrated on the number and quality of the teachers available to a school -

" ... we do not require, in my opinion, extra welfare officers, or extra social workers in areas like these. What we need are extra good teachers, smaller classes, and more facilities to cope with creative and individual work. It is useless having a social worker visiting a very bad home, then the children from that home coming along to a teacher who generally rejects children; who knows only the chalk and talk method; who thinks buying sweets will buy the child; who spends all her time making the classroom look nicer by her own standards; who at 3.55 clears the children out ..."

He felt the children needed 'sheet anchors' to give them security and confidence in their own abilities.

The examples of work by problem children includes a fable which is worth quoting in full, for like some of Joe Orton's plays it teases the reader with the hard facts of life which many contrive to forget.

A FABLE

Once upon a time there was a pig and a cat. The cat kept saying, 'you old, dirty pig who would want to eat you.' And the pig replied 'when I die I'll be made use of, but when you die you'll just rot.' The cat always thought he was better than the pig. When the pig died he was used as food for the people to eat. When the cat died he was buried in old dirt.

MORAL

Live dirty die clean.

Reflecting on a teacher's criticism of a poem on junkies on the grounds it was an inappropriate topic a head wrote -

"Children won't write if they fear that honesty will be punished and too often they learn to distrust teachers. They have had too many school experiences where staff loyalty and the institutional obligations of teachers have taken precedence over honesty. They have seen too much maintaining face and too little respect for justifiable defiance."

The standpoint of those teachers who felt problem children and problem families were a burden on schools and the community at large was shared by some Educational Welfare Officers. One wrote to Barbara Megson that -

"If no greater positive action is taken to reduce the number of problem families I can foresee that we shall reach the position in our society where the dependants on the Welfare State outnumber those who are contributing to their upkeep." Other EWO's sent in details of youngsters and families which could have prompted Joe Orton to even more outrageous plots for his plays. A boy ran out of a Keighley school after crawling round the classroom on his hands and knees carrying a wastepaper basket in his mouth and pretending to be a dog. When the EWO went to the house in the late afternoon he found the boy in bed wrapped in a sheet with a lighted candle at its head and foot. The younger children and his mentally deranged mother were at the bedside attending the mock death scene. Another deranged mother turned up at a school playground telling the teacher on duty that she was the 'Danish Princess'. She became the 'Queen of Denmark' when the head-mistress arrived. The unfortunate children in these families were eventually taken into care.

In Worsborough the classic workshy father had 13 children and was permanently off work. Things suddenly changed when one of the boys won a National Competition which had a trip to America as a prize. Father made a quick recovery which enabled him to fly with his son and to spend a hectic seven days in Disneyland, Hollywood and elsewhere. Once at home he was back on the sick list. On this evidence the father certainly deserved the description workshy.

On many occasions welfare officers could build up relationships with youngsters and families which sustained them throughout their schooldays. One girl, sexually abused by her father and with two artificial legs after a serious accident, moved to a West Riding school maintaining, throughour her time at the school, constant contact with the welfare officer who had seen her through those terrible years. A sheet anchor of her traumatic life before she and her sister moved he kept in contact throughout her months of recovery. To see her work and to watch her scale the stairs in the main building of the school was to appreciate a rare determination and character. The sort of change that could take place if an adult gave a youngster " ... love, security, and the oppprtunity to succeed" (10) is illustrated in these staccato notes from one school.

"Boy 1964 - 1966 - Dragged to school, standing weeping on many occasions outside the classroom door, dirty, nits in hair, refused to do movement, reading non-existent, completely alone.

1966 - 1967 - Never been late, happy, reasonably clean, good mover, member of choir club, reading fairly good. Worships the ground on which his teacher walks - incidentally a teacher in his probationary year."

The table overleaf shows that a third of the distressed children identified in 1964 had apparently improved whilst just over a third had definitely deteriorated. The careful choice of words underlines not only the cautious nature of this study but also the toughness of the hard core of problem families. They could as Alec Clegg pointed out in the conclusion to his book 'Recipe for Failure' lead to social trouble - (11)

" ... which may take the form of guerilla tactics designed by the rejected groups to disrupt the existence of those who have rejected them, and this is already happening elsewhere."

In July 1967 Barbara Megson gave the Chief Education Officer the outline of a preventive system to deal with distressed children. The welfare service for a pyramid of schools was to be housed in a Welfare and Medical Room in the local comprehensive school. The local Educational Welfare Officer and his team along with those who did medical examinations would use this room. An integrated let of records could be housed here and the room could be a meeting place for case conferences. It was hoped that some boarding provision could be attached to the school for short term emergencies. A Youth Tutor was to be based at the school as well so that the gap between school and work could be bridged. The provision of adventure playgrounds was recommended especially for Educational Priority Areas. Furthermore they were to be kept open after school hours. Nursery provision was essential so too were Remedial Centres which could help those distressed children who were retarded or emotionally withdrawn.

The suggestion ended with estimates of future needs - 300 places for maladjusted children in Secondary Schools; if Junior Schools were to be catered for as well, another 300. Lastly, in 1967 the West Riding had no means of dealing with maladjusted children under 8, but if the authority followed the example of London and Liverpool admission to such schools at five could be initiated.

The preventive system could be seen as an important part of what was termed social education. In its broadest sense it was the give and take of everyday life at home, at school and in the community. If distressed children could be rescued by these measures from what seemed for many to be an inevitable decline into a poverty ridden, or criminal existence, then this part of social education would be invaluable. The increased range of activities available in schools such as outdoor activities was another aspect of social education which promised to enrich the quality of youngsters' lives.

FOLLOW UP ON 1964 ENQUIRY ON
DISTRESSED CHILDREN IN SECONARY SCHOOLS
(AUGUST 1966)

	COLUMN 1 WORST		COLUMN 2 REMAINDER	
	23 Replies 24 Cases	%	53 Replies 66 Cases	%
Continue Unchanged	8	32	15	23
Definite Deterioration	10	38	23	34
Apparent Improvement	5	19	25	37
In care (since 1964)	2	7	6	9
No Information	1	3	9	13

	COLUMN 3 COMBINED TOTALS	
	77 Replies 92 Cases	%
Continue Unchanged	23	24
Definite Deterioration	33	35
Apparent Improvement	30	32
In care (since 1964)	8	8
No Information	10	10

NOTE: In Column 2 cases overlap categories (eg home still bad, but child surmounting difficulties).

CHAPTER 16

SOCIAL EDUCATION
Special Services

Although social education is usually associated with secondary schools it begins as soon as a youngster goes to a nursery school and can continue through to the many branches of adult education.

The advantages of going to a good Nursery School were described in detail in a memorandum, 'The Education of the Pre-School Child reared in an Unfavourable Environment'.

Paragraph 4 - "for many such deprived children the opportunities and rich sensory experiences to be derived from a good Nursery School environment would be an incalculable benefit to their mental and emotional development. In such an environment young children are introduced to 'play' under optimum conditions and, by enlarging their range of experience, thinking, reasoning and speech develop normally and naturally."

The good infant and junior schools in the West Riding carried these ideas through until youngsters went to the secondary schools. The last decennial publication of the West Riding Education Committee, 'The Final Ten Years' starts a section on social education with the statement -

"As a matter of policy the Committee have established further education units in their large secondary schools. They recognise that there is merit in making provision for youth in a building where educational provision of all kinds also exists." These statements seem to suggest that social education was an addition to, rather than a part of, the day to day work of schools. Courses at Woolley Hall, such as those organised by the County Inspector, J.B. Willcock, later to be Headteacher of Minsthorpe School, concentrated on the discussion and formulation of a programme of social education which would be part of the normal school day. The discussion groups comprised teachers, inspectors, education welfare officers and youth tutors.

The programme of social education devised by Richard

Hauser and used in over eighty schools was the core of many of these discussions. Hauser was a sociologist who left Austria in 1938 and was with the British army in North Africa during the war. Later be carried out social work in Italy where he helped to set up the probation service. His next move was to Australia where he met and married Hepzibah Menuhin. When he settled in London he was intent on devoting his time to helping those in distress " ... by coaxing them back into communal life". His programme of social education was put together after carrying out a series of projects with prisoners, mental patients, alcoholics and lower stream children in secondary schools. As Yehudi Menuhin, Hepzibah's brother, put it -

"Richard's approach is to set the lame to lead the blind; he sees the abandoned child, the battered wife, the delinquent, the convict, the addict, the helpless aged, and all the other deprived human beings he cares for, as a network of interacting need, in which, as one problem derives from another, one victim can help another." (1)

Between 1945 and 1964 the secondary school curriculum became grossly overcrowded and timetabling became a complex and lengthy process. At the same time experiences outside school increased prompting the comment in the West Riding publication 'Education 1954-64', P.47, that -

" ... many activities now termed 'extra curricular' are likely more and more to be brought firmly within the curriculum." There was a pressing need to integrate the work of secondary schools and this was addressed in Schools Council initiatives such as Integrated Science and the Humanities Curriculum Project. Not only did these schemes reflect the need to reverse the fragmentation of the curriculum, but the need to relate school work to the world at large. The packs of information used to teach the Humanities included one on 'Race'. This was, and still is, a sensitive topic which in 1968 raised the political temperature as Enoch Powell openly called for the repatriation of black and other Commonwealth immigrants.

One of the six trial schools for the 'Race' pack was Rossington Comprehensive School and its work was monitored by the Centre for Mass Communication Research at Leicester University. The conclusion reached in the final publication was " ... the six trial schools showed a small but significant shift towards greater tolerance attributable to the teaching."

So as well as putting the work in English, History, Geography and Religious Education together into a unified scheme the course addressed vital issues in the everyday life of British people. There is little doubt this course had a significant element of social education. Lastly Alec Clegg constantly expressed concern on the bad effects of the exam system on education. This concern was met by the use of continuous assessment for all elements of the Humanities Course.

When Alec Clegg gave a talk on Physical Education in the summer of 1965 he ended it by describing two approaches to training in this field of teaching.

"If the colleges now training our teachers could really produce teachers who know how to exploit these media, what a magnificent variety of educational tools they could draw on and what a splendid source of educational power! Just think of these activities - the adventure training group, the games group, the athletics and swimming group, the gymnastic group, the dance and drama group - they are an education in themselves.

But if the colleges and the teachers they produce cannot make themselves masters of this magnificent armoury and just fall back on measurement, talent spotting, training the strong and ignoring the weak, narrowing the range of activity, fostering too much competition and cultivating failure, they will lamentably abuse an opportunity which is probably superior to that offered to any other category of teacher in the profession."

The end of the Second World War provided many opportunities for the Education Authority to buy properties ranging from historic houses and hotels to a camp school in Nidderdale. Before 1939 the National Camps Corporation had established a number of timber built camp schools for the anticipated evacuation of children from towns and cities in the event of war. The one at Bewerley Park was offered to the West Riding after the war. Initially the Corporation was paid for the provision of domestic services whilst the.authority provided the education. In 1956 the West Riding bought the premises and they were converted into a boarding school with its own staff. The school could accommodate 120 senior boys and girls for courses between 4 and 5 weeks duration. Initially the curriculum was centred on field work in geography, natural history and biology but it was changed to one of outdoor pursuits. By the mid fifties some 16,000 youngsters and 600 teachers from 257 schools had used the services of Bewerley Park. Reflecting on the activities offered which included caving, canoeing, climbing, camping, sailing and horse riding one head wrote -

"A course at Bewerley Park is a lot of living telescoped into a short space of time."

Although the West Riding supported youngsters who went on Outward Bound Courses Alec Clegg drew a distinction between them and those run at Bewerley Park. In a very frank address to the Outward Bound Conference at Harrogate in May 1965 he voiced his reservations on too much emphasis being put on competition, toughness, endurance and leadership. He drew attention to the lengths to which some physical education departments could go in testing by buying the many devices advertised in Physical Education publications. He felt it was dangerous to use the limited time for measuring success rather than using the subject for individual development. He felt no subject - "... more readily lets the perceptive teacher more easily into the mind of a child than Physical Education sensitively applied." One boy who had been on an Outward Bound Course had described it as "... something between a Boy Scout Camp and a Detention Centre." Alec Clegg followed this point by drawing attention to the other side of the leadership penny -subject people in the old British Empire, black people in the southern states of the U.S.A. and the social inferiors at home. This last point was pushed home with this shrewd observation -

"I am, however, quite sure that we often mistake for real leadership the cultivated assumption of superiority, and we still cultivate this." If his talk was designed to make his audience examine the ideas behind Outward Bound courses it succeeded, and, moreover, it focussed attention on the qualities he valued in social education. The essence of Bewerley was expressed by a head after looking through a file of reports on youngsters who had been there on courses.

"On looking again at the report file it is clear that Bewerley's success is that it gives youngsters a chance to succeed in one or more of a variety of ways." (2)

Visits to France and to Germany were regarded in many schools as an important part of their work in Modern Languages. One of the first initiatives after 1945 was taken by the Yorkshire branch of the Modern Languages Association. An exchange scheme was agreed with the Academie de Lille so that youngsters from England and France could spend time in a foreign country. The number of schools and youngsters taking part in the scheme grew each year reaching a total of 878 Yorkshire boys and girls and 71 schools in 1964.

Robert Birley, former head of Charterhouse School, was appointed as education adviser to General Robertson, Head of the Control Commission in Germany. Birley sought to make the Germans aware of their rich cultural tradition saying he was in the business of education, not re-education. Schemes such as exchange visits between British and German teachers, the provision of youth and adult education centres and libraries were bridges to the establishment of understanding between former enemies.

One of the elements in this quiet process of reconciliation was the Arnsberg scheme, set up in 1949 between the West Riding and Arnsberg in the North Rhineland. This scheme was another example of Alec Clegg's belief in the importance of first hand contact. Moreover, regular contacts between children and teachers from different countries could build personal links which, although they never commanded the attention of the media, were a constructive realisation of the fact that peace depends on people not politicians.

Much more tangible than the friendships and understanding that exchanges could foster was the daily satisfaction a good school dinner could give a youngster, especially if it was eaten in pleasant surroundings. The school meals services was expanded from 7,200 meals served daily in 1939 in the West Riding to 105,000 in 1954. Sixty-one prefabricated kitchens were built immediately after the war to be followed by 200 new kitchens by 1964. Attractive dining halls with octagonal tables and wooden chairs replaced cramped classrooms, folding tables and backless benches. The meals were much better and they could be eaten in a civilised atmosphere. The emphasis upon the quality of the environment in which children lived in schools was most noticeable in primary schools. The vision Diana Jordan had of Woolley Hall was a guide to the sort of environment Alec Clegg wanted in schools. She had written -

"Woolley Hall should be, in my view, a place above the average in aesthetic standards, but comfortable, homely and hospitable, where the visitors can be helped to appreciate the value of an environment of pleasing colour, decoration and furnishing as well as well cooked and served food." She wanted those that went to Woolley to consider it "their" college so "They should be expected, therefore, to assist in flower decorations, and responsibility to each other for the usual care which they would be expected to give to something that belonged to them."

It could seem irrelevant to a chapter on social education that a study of caretaking should be included, yet place as well as people is important in the upbringing of youngsters. Ill kept homes and schools do not bring about care and interest in one's surroundings. Well kept ones, tastefully decorated and clean, can encourage those personal qualities which in day by day life contribute to ease not irritation. Miss Jones, a housecraft adviser, always seemed alert to the way in which the staffs of schools had made the best of, or ignored, the potential of their school buildings. In two architecturally similar buildings in Goole the interiors were very different in character, one welcoming and well decorated the other barrack like and dismal. Don Valley High School's potential was realised and made attractive by its head, J.R. O'Connor. Miss Jones wrote in April 1960 -

"There is always an exhibition frequently changed, centrally placed and of current interest, immaculately set out under the guidance of the specialist teachers together with the headmaster." This plaudit has to be set against her observation in the same report that "... few of the new schools use their entrance halls for display."

One of the main contributors to the improved conditions in schools was Ernest Peet, Supervisor of Caretakers, appointed to this post in 1948. Over the years after 1948 Ernest Peet organised and conducted training courses for caretakers and designed a number of devices for cleaning schools, such as mechanical scrubbing and polishing machines. His inventions were based on careful studies of the various operations which made up the work of school caretakers. A good example of such a study is floor cleaning which, until his arrival in the West Riding, involved the daily brushing and regular washing and oiling of the wooden floors. This practice softened the wood opening up the grain to dirt. Moreover in an effort to reduce dust when brushing wet sawdust was used which opened the grain even more. Ernest Peet bad over 100 floor panels made and tested for wear and the performance of cleaning and maintenance techniques and materials. These studies resulted in the adoption of two simple procedures throughout the county. The significance of this and other studies and innovations on the cost and quality of cleaning and maintenance is illustrated in the notes of an interview between Mr Perrudin (3) and a Ministry of Education representative in 1959. It was apparent that caretakers trained by Mr Peet and who used his techniques not only reduced the expenditure on cleaning but contributed to cleaner and more attractive schools. The work of Ernest Peet was that of an innovative housekeeper and it contributed a great deal to the environments in which youngsters spent a great deal of their time. Mr Freeling, adviser for boys' Physical Education, was very aware of the need for attractive, clean and safe facilities for his subject and wrote of Ernest Peet's "... persistent crusading for improved schemes of cleaning and decoration."

The very detailed report Alec Clegg presented to the Policy and Finance Sub-Committee on 7th May 1968 was entitled 'Waste of Human Potential in Education.' He sought to identify the nature and scale of the waste, its causes and consequences and to suggest ways in which it might be reduced. More and more of Alec Clegg's memoranda and speeches contained a social and economic background drawn from his travels and contacts with educationalists all over the world. He noted that by 1958 technical, professional and management workers exceeded. the number of manual workers for the first time in the history of the United States. A report in France showed that in 1960 manual workers comprised 60% of the work force but by 1975 the anticipated figure would be only 20%. These rapid, clear cut trends were reflected in the coalfields of South Yorkshire where by 1988 a drop of 70,000 in the workforce was anticipated. Alec Clegg saw a grim future ahead where - " ... failure to secure work and its consequent sense of being useless in society can be a disastrous effect on youngsters." He cited nine pointers to serious social decline in Britain such as a 70% increase in suicides amongst the 15 to 20 age group; an 86% increase in abandoned children; and a 200% increase in cases of malicious wounding, assault and robbery by young people under 17. Alec Clegg used statistics such as these to illustrate the increasing seriousness of social problems. Similar figures appear in Mitchell Gordon's book 'Sick Cities' which dealt with urban life in America. He described the problem of the schools in the central areas of cities as follows - P.220. (4)

"Here a catalogue of welfare functions is thrust upon school systems to meet the needs of underprivileged youngsters who must be fed before they can be taught and assured before they can be interested, of teenagers who lack the diligence or wherewithal to acquire the learning so vital to secure employment in an increasingly automated economy, and of adults who do not themselves understand the use of education, much less desire its assiduous acquisition by their youngsters." Alec Clegg could have matched the next comment with West Riding experiences.

"Bigger burdens and smaller budgets also handicap central city school systems by placing them at a disadvantage in the competition for quality teachers." (5) Interestingly American schools sought success in the 5 not the 3 R's - reading, 'riting, 'rithmetic, reason and responsibility.

The study of waste within the West Riding's educational provision began with those who failed at university, on average 154 per annum. When those who dropped out of further education courses are added nearly a quarter of a million pounds out of the annual education budget has gone to waste. Alec Clegg felt some retrieval machinery was needed and deplored the standpoint taken by the Department of Education and Science. The West Riding did in certain circumstances make loans to students who had failed the initial stage of a course. The Department no longer approved this practice in 1968 so the dice were loaded against the student and the local authority. The objection to loans hit the working class student harder than others and as the Robbins Report (6) pointed out a manager's son had twenty times as great a chance of going to a university than the son of an unskilled manual worker of equal ability.

For the vast remainder of the school population of the West Riding the areas where wastage was likely to be greatest were those identified as ones of educational priority. The memoranda suggested these should be identified by two County Council Inspectors using the criteria laid down in the Plowden Report. Once identified Alec Clegg outlined a variety of ways in which these areas could be helped.

One of the most significant causes of youngsters failing to achieve their potential was lack of parental support which in some cases extended to parental hostility. Schools which kept parents at arms length and saw themselves as apart from rather than a part of the local community missed an opportunity to engender local interest and support. Certainly in educational priority areas it is fair to say schools had a duty to foster such support so that parents understood the opportunities that could be created and the difficulties which could be overcome. The thorough studies prompted by the Chief Education Officer into the lives of children in distress enabled him to be exact in his descriptions of parents who did not provide security, love, support or encouragement for their children. Investment in the infant schools was essential so that the problems were identified and addressed as early as possible.

It was as Alec Clegg put it " ... preposterous that the committee should have to wait for disaster to overtake those children then pay the cost." In case any committee members felt he had overstated the case they were invited to spend a day with an Educational Welfare Officer or a day in one of the EPA schools.

The changes in English society put much greater demands on schools than in the past and in the last two pages of the report deal with proposals to reduce the waste of human potential. The lack of accommodation for maladjusted children was more pressing in Yorkshire than almost any other English county, and it was much greater than the figures suggested for doctors hesitated to certify children as maladjusted because they knew there were no places for them. One additional school was proposed in this report. The short term needs of some children and families could be met by the provision of small boarding schools attached to comprehensive schools. Alec Clegg felt it was difficult to justify giving boarding school places to selected pupils whilst providing none for the non-selective whose need, though different, might be much greater. A social education centre for teachers was suggested " ... in a converted, unpretentious building in a selected area." Scawsby College was to be associated with this project if it was launched. The appointment of a teacher counsellor was anticipated and his or her brief would be to help youngsters over their personal difficulties. The process, too slow for Alec Clegg but too fast for others, of integrating the work of the Education and Medical Services took another step with both officers 'agreeing to support the ready communication of information between their departments. Educational Welfare Officers were to be relieved of as many of their clerical duties as possible especially those who worked in Educational Priority Areas so that they could do "... the essential work in the field." Another sensible initiative was to encourage older girls in secondary schools to spend holiday time with primary children with learning difficulties. Lastly Alec Clegg wanted the committee to agree to the appointment of a member of staff who would address the problems identified in the report.

Two quotations from books by Barbara Wootton focus attention on the changes in and the problems faced by public services in Britain in the fifties and sixties. Like those of Alec Clegg her books were challenging and like Alec Clegg she learned a great deal from the first hand as well as from research. Alec

Clegg insisted on going into schools each week talking with teachers and children. Barbara Wootton served as a magistrate as well as being a professor. She talked of " ... the unanswerable questions which forced themselves upon my attention as a magistrate." In her book 'Social Science and Social Pathology' she drew attention to the confusion between specialised and segregated treatment for handicapped and maladjusted children. On Pages 332-3 she raises an important issue -

"But, in the case of a child who is classified as 'maladjusted', it may well be questionable whether the diagnosis is firmly enough grounded to be maintained at all costs - especially since this may merely result in his being deprived of any special attention whatever, for want of vacancies in the particular type of institution which is deemed appropriate for him. One cannot help wondering whether without the label, and with sympathetic handling in some other environment, his problems might not still have been solved. Certainly it seems unfortunate that, as often in fact happens, children should wait months for admission to schools for the maladjusted at times when approved schools have plenty of vacancies." Personal problems had to be chronic for some children before they were dealt with and in many cases parents were ill at ease with them being categorised and then segregated. The child was seen as abnormal and to be given special treatment in a special institution. Such segregation could have adverse social effects and had to be seen against Barbara Wootton's final comment, "The only consolation is that many - perhaps even most - children prove in the end to be capable of resolving their own difficulties in their own way without special treatment of any kind." Alec Clegg's inquiries showed such resilience did exist but not on the scale implied by this remark. However her detailed study of 'The Social Foundations of Wage Policy' would have certainly earned his support. She showed that those who worked the longest hours got the lowest wages and that those who earned over £10,000 or more, a high salary in the sixties, maintained that their income was a personal matter and put a taboo on publicity. The warnings Alec Clegg gave on the quality of social life were echoed in her conclusion - "The pattern of incomes moulds the shape of social life and sets the limits of social intercourse; and everywhere that pattern bears the mark of greed and envy and of ruthless bargaining. Now is the time to show that in a civilised society those marks need not be indelible."

CHAPTER 17

INITIATIVES IN SOCIAL EDUCATION

During the years between 1968 and 1974 there was a sequence of initiatives which illustrate how the West Riding sought to find practical answers to the problems raised in the memorandum on the Waste of Human Potential in Education. The view that Britain experienced a shrinking social revolution after 1945 was by the late sixties being replaced by one that identified a destructive element in society. Conflict was replacing cooperation and in home affairs one could have said the Welfare state was being replaced by the Warfare State. Militancy was not confined to the trade unions it grew in the universities and colleges. New universities such as Warwick, East Anglia and Essex and colleges such as Hornsey and Bingley in the West Riding experienced eruptions of student protest. The students at Hornsey College of Art in North London maintained that "... the best way of finding out about the world is to turn it upside down." At Bingley the students demanded the right to choose where they lived and the repudiation of 'the parental authority of the college'. The discontent at Bingley led Alec Clegg and his staff to consider very carefully the nature and rate of social change. In a letter written in October 1969 the demands of the Bingley students were likened to a cataclysmic storm rather than a forward flowing river - Wagner's Ride of the Valkyrie rather than Smetana's Vltava. (1)

The outbreaks of disorder amongst students need to be set against the loss of confidence in the ability of central government to promote constructive change, to reduce social inequality and to replace disillusion by hope. However in the sphere of education change was taking place, especially in the secondary sector. The move towards comprehensive schools prompted by circular 10 / 65 was a positive step which held out promise for education and society at large. The conclusion in 'Half Way There' summarised this point of view.

"The one thing we can be sure about is that this old order is slowly disappearing - in schools, in universities, in Britain and all over the world. Educational institutions everywhere are not only seeking wider intakes, new patterns of self-government and curriculum reform, but seeking them in the context of the local and wider community need." (2)

Simpson's Lane Infant's School is a good illustration of the new order which was evolving in the West Riding. The school was opened in 1967 to accommodate children from a large estate of Coal Board and Council houses. The families who moved into this estate came from Scotland and North Eastern England and the menfolk worked at Kellingley Colliery. There were 280 children in the Infant School and there was the prospect of a rapid rise in the intake of children due to a local birth rate which was four times the national average. Many of the Scottish families came from a predominantly Catholic community in Lanarkshire, most of whom had four or more children. As the families on this estate came from long established colliery communities with distinct, individual qualities many of them felt insecure and unsettled in their new surroundings. The social implications of these rapidly developing communities were partially appreciated in the initiatives taken at Simpson's Lane School. The school provided a far sighted foundation yet when set against the conclusions of studies such as 'Coal is Our Life' one realises how far economic considerations dominated national policy. The study of Ashton (3) drew attention in 1956 to the cultural poverty and isolation of the community. The second edition published in 1969 pointed out that the boom conditions of the fifties had gone and that 1969 was a more 'sobering' vantage point. The authors maintained their viewpoint of the very limited horizons open to the working class, illustrating their standpoint by a fact which would have drawn an immediate nod of appreciation from Alec Clegg. Page 9 -

"Perhaps one statistic will serve to illustrate the effect of the kind of factors which we described in 1956: in 1969 the chance of a working class girl entering University is one in 600."

The West Riding was increasing its range of social provision in schools but needs were accelerating at a faster rate. Alec Clegg realised this fact and regularly drew attention to the pressing nature of social problems.

Simpson's Lane Infant School was an open plan building broken up into smaller spaces. These little corners were very important for they provided private spaces where children could, if they wished, be alone. Miss Canning, the Headteacher, put great emphasis on parental involvement in the work of the school. They were involved in planning some of the work and providing a lot of the material that went into displays. The children were encouraged to use all their senses in their work not just looking at, drawing or describing the objects in a display but discussing, weighing, feeling and comparing them. Buttons, sticks, golf balls - how many made an ounce. What were the textures of shells, stones or bark like? Were they rough, smooth, spiky or sharp? These displays prompted discussion and led to creative work which gave youngsters pleasure and confidence, and it helped to allay the feeling of insecurity some had in a community far away in distance and social habits from their original homes.

The social worker appointed to work in the communities which sent their children to Miss Canning's school became involved in a wide range of activities and saw the head as "... the king-pin in any scheme involving a social worker". The sub-headings in a detailed report entitled 'Spy for Social Security' by the school social worker began with matrimonial conciliation, maintenance and relationships. Trying to patch up family differences, and in quite a number of cases being successful, and helping mothers to obtain regular maintenance conveyed to parents that the school was "... concerned for them as individuals". Winning the confidence of parents in these matters was only part of the web of relationships a school social worker could build up in a community. There could be many tensions in this web which could be the source of considerable strain. The areas of responsibility of the head, the teachers, the Education Welfare Officer and others services can overlap beneficially or be a nagging source of disputes. The social worker at Simpson's Lane found it useful to work jointly on some cases and independently on others, an indication that individual needs could be catered for in a sensitive way. A social worker's achievements are difficult to assess. As the one at Simpson's Lane put it "... Preventative work

223

cannot be measured" and any progress was "... slow and subtle ... and in some cases there will not be any progress, merely a halting of deterioration, a holding operation."

The recommendations made by this social worker at the end of his report centred on the setting up of a country wide framework of social workers in schools with their own director and advisory service. The advantages of having a social worker in schools in Educational Priority Areas was clear, but the understandable wish to define a new area of social endeavour added another category to the multiplicity of services dealing with problem families and their children. The integration of effort could become more difficult and the recommendations "... to set up a system of consultation and supervision 'and' to act as a public relations officer and a link with outside agencies" were vital.

Alec Clegg visited schools such as Simpson's Lane often. In each case films and tapes of their work were made and the headteachers were engaged in carefully prepared dialogues on the work of the schools. A central point in these discussions was the emphasis upon individual development and creative work which in turn led to thorough progress in reading, writing and arithmetic.

The effect a far sighted and resolute head could have on the work of a school was described by one of the teachers who had spent six years at Conisbrough Ivanhoe Junior Mixed and Infants School. The head's policy was described as "... rather revolutionary, and highly idealistic". Initially, the implementation of the policy was very difficult as the children were described as untidy with a low standard of work and intelligence with little, or no, family interest in their progress. Slowly the children took more pride in themselves and their work, the school suffered a setback with the influx of a large number of children from a slum clearance area and the task of raising personal standards and horizons had to be repeated. The cultivation of personal pride, family interest and support in the early years was the route of social education. In a talk 'Recipe for Failure' Alec Clegg described the needs of a child in school as -

"... caring concern, recognition of work and an expectation of achievement which is high but within the child's competence." (4)

The head of Cutsyke Infant School went further saying - "We should beware, too, of putting a label on these children. their crying need is to be accepted as persons in their own right, loved for what they are and respected for the potential, however small, that is in them."

When youngsters moved into the secondary schools they found themselves in a very different atmosphere. No longer one teacher, one classroom and one community of between 20 and 30 boys and girls, but a traveller who was registered twice a day with a form teacher. Then the pupil set off on a curricular tour of a very large and specialised building. In the same talk 'Recipe for Failure' Alec Clegg drew attention to the difficulties faced by secondary schools where so much emphasis was put on academic attainment. This emphasis often marginalised other considerations with the result in his view that these schools "... have not yet found the right educational diet for the children of average and below average ability, and indeed what is offered to the abler children may not be the best for them either, but merely something that their superior abilities enable them to cope with."

Alec Clegg had a discussion in 1971 with youngsters from Airedale Middle School who had recently moved to the local comprehensive school. They found that competition rather than cooperation characterised the new school with much more emphasis being put on grades and marks. In their view these features could cause jealousy, envy, spitefulness and despair amongst those who did not do so well. One boy stressed how important it was to him to be able to have the freedom to choose what he wanted to do. 'Asking out', one of the features of Mrs Pyrah's class in the Middle School, was compared to the formal lessons of the comprehensive with their collections of facts followed by questions.

These comments are more than a criticism of teaching methods at secondary level. They underline the need to thoroughly integrate the work of feeder schools with the secondary school. The establishment of middle schools gave an opportunity for fire kindling to be maintained for at least another year before the anticipated pot filling process began with the 'O' Level or CSE examinations looming ahead. The need to integrate various levels of education was achieved in the Cambridgeshire village colleges where secondary, adult education, youth and community services were all housed in the same group of buildings. Minsthorpe Comprehensive School in South Elmsall had many similarities with the Cambridge colleges, although it was larger in size and different in its administration. Village college or community school, both sought to provide a wide variety of educational and social services to the community. A grant from the Carnegie Foundation helped the West Riding to provide   facilities in the Carnegie centre such as extended education for shift workers, education and hospitality for unemployed youngsters and a pre-school playgroup. A support group with members from a wide range of public services was set up to help youngsters with difficulties. Lastly a community festival group was set up to arouse local interest and provide entertainment.

Alec Clegg was wary of being dogmatic about Minsthorpe in 'The Final Ten Years'. He felt it was dangerous to give an exact definition of the term 'community school' for it could encourage a stereo-typed framework which in many cases would not meet the needs of individual communities. Once again, as in the case of the work in infant and junior schools, he believed the framework should fit the community rather than the opposite. Minsthorpe was to evolve but it did not have the span of time enjoyed by schools and teachers in the West Riding primary sector. Moreover by reflecting the Chief Education Officer's criticism of the examination straightjacket and concentrating on Mode 3. of the Certificate of Secondary Education the school invited the criticism of ambitious parents. A school which aimed to cut out 'O' Level entries and concentrate on Mode 3. C.S.E. was to many parents a denial of the route via 'O' and 'A' Levels to higher education and reasonable job prospects. Another important consideration was that the staffing implications of innovative Mode 3. examinations were considerable in the preparation and execution of syllabuses and the continuous assessment of work. The conclusion Alec Clegg reached was that "... many schools are groping towards the idea of a community school ..." (5) and he looked forward to a transformation in the next decade. Unfortunately it did not take place.

Unlike the schools which concentrated their resources on examination and sporting success those which gave priority to individual development and the quality of social life faced a daunting prospect in convincing the public of their aims. Can you match a rich harvest of 'O' and 'A' Level passes and cups won with an increased number partaking in outdoor and indoor activities? Declining truancy rates? And fewer young offenders? It will appear to many parents that the ablest were being penalised for the sake of the less able and worst behaved in the school.

Specific schemes such as the Red House Project at Denaby Main did not face the difficulties which were almost inevitable when the general policy of a secondary school was directed away from traditional goals such as the maximisation of exam successes. The Plowden Report had defined the characteristics of an Educational Priority Area and five research projects were to be funded by the Social Science Research Council. Four were in large cities, the fifth was at Denaby Main which more than met the criteria for an Educational Priority Area, with a high proportion of semi and unskilled manual workers, many large families in receipt of state benefits, poor housing and a large number of distressed children. The project began in January 1969 and aimed to improve educational standards, teacher morale and community involvement. The project had a three year span and was centred on the Red House.

Once the home of the Denaby Main pit manager, the Red House was bought, it was converted into a community centre and opened on 9th January 1970. The earliest work there was the establishment of a pre school group designed to serve three infant schools. Later developments covered infant, junior and secondary age groups along with parents, teachers and other people in the community. The house could not handle large groups so it had to act as a stimulus for developments elsewhere in Conisbrough and Denaby. However during an average week over 150 children used the Red House whilst over 1,000 different children used it for varying spans of time in a year. (6) As with many other West

Riding initiatives things evolved, but as the team at the Red House discovered evolution went with integration as educational, social, economic and political development went hand in hand. The general conclusion on the Red House project was that "it did not lead to a dramatic change in the levels of performance in the schools" but it " ... did create a new atmosphere in which schools were willing to experiment with new techniques and developments." Furthermore the initiatives taken at the Red House had practical results such as the appointment of pre-school home visitors in other areas of the West Riding.

The Terrace in Conisbrough was the site of the Alternative School Experiment, involving Dartington Hall in Devon and Conisbrough Northcliffe School. Dartington Hall described as -

"... a progressive co-educational, independent boarding school, beautifully equipped and generously staffed, well endowed and expensive," (7) was involved in an exchange scheme with Arthur Young's school in Conisbrough. The Dartington Hall Trust owned the Terrace which was used as a residential hostel. The West Riding provided financial support for the venture which was to involve youngsters from Dartington and groups from Mexborough Grammar School and Conisbrough Northcliffe.

One aim of this scheme was to explore approaches and methods of providing an interesting and constructive education for those youngsters in the bottom 30%, those unlikely to gain any 'O' level passes or even to register any success in C.S.E. The boys attached to the Terrace were to stay there for almost the whole of their final year only attending school for specific activities, or classes of their own choice. As no female staff were available from Northcliffe School girls were excluded from the scheme. A programme of work was drawn up which included the conversion of the Coach House to a workshop and rest room, the cultivation of two allotments and the decoration and maintenance of the Terrace. A teacher from Northcliffe was in charge along with the Terrace staff and between 12 and 15 boys were involved in these activities. In addition to the work at the Terrace there was an expedition each week which was a mixture of education and recreation. The expeditions included visits to Grimsby Docks, an Army Training

Centre and an Art Exhibition. Courses were arranged to meet particular interests such as one in metalwork which involved three boys going to Dartington Hall. Five others walked the Pennine Way, others produced and performed a Mummers' Play in local schools and a small group made weekly visits to St. Catherine's Hospital for subnormal patients.

Presented in this way like the icing on a cake the scheme appears as a travel agency attached to a do-it-yourself enterprise. This conclusion is a gross misrepresentation of the realities of the grassroots of social education. The scheme was well staffed and they had a building and grounds which could provide opportunities for the boys to create an identity, to build their confidence and to share in what was to them a wide range of experiences. The daily discussions and briefings along with the details of their work and visits may initially seem repetitive, long winded and trivial yet they are the facts on the lives of a group of boys who would have been perfect examples of the bottom 30% as Barry Hines describes them - "the limbo generation of school leavers too old for lessons and too young to know anything about the outside world." They hate and are hated. (8) They are a third of the future with no future.

As soon as these daily exchanges and their diaries record a willingness to complete tasks; to show compassion to the mentally ill; to decide to take an interest in international affairs; to set up a framework of rules for the Terrace and to try to make them effective, one appreciates the changes taking place in these boys. From another standpoint their initial attitudes and interests show a yawning gulf between everyday social life amongst Conisbrough teenagers and the school. The everyday life of the community can only be fully understood if the mundane everyday bits and pieces are studied, and like panning for gold, once the promising pieces are identified and considered they can be starting points for a few more steps forward in social education. The view of a local Youth Employment Officer was that those who had been to the Terrace were better than their peer group, a pointer to the modest success of a scheme which was described as "... an attempt to generate in them a greater sense of their own worth and potential." The boys on the scheme were members of the faceless minority "... who slip through most normal schooling without being touched by it." In the early autumn weeks of 1973 they found close contact with adults traumatic. The staff-pupil ratio was usually 3 to 15 and it led initially to the boys wanting the teachers as they put it "... off their backs". Used to working out their problems by 'violence and bullying of the verbal and physical variety' it took intensive counselling in the early weeks to gain their confidence. Simple tasks such as sweeping the floor and washing up were either ignored or beyond them, but gradually a change took place. They recognised a reduction in verbal or physical bullying but did not applaud the change. They explained it as a result of the excess of staff and the fact that in the Terrace you could be spotted easily. By November 1973 this account by one of the staff of a visit to Derbyshire illustrates the changes in attitude which were taking place.

19th November 1973. "Though Wednesday was a very cold winter's day the weekly outing was still undertaken and despite the uncomfortable conditions the group enjoyed a day climbing and sketching in Derbyshire. Three boys climbed in the vicinity with Neal. The sketching party were then taken to 'the plague village' of Eyam and spent a very interesting two hours sketching the village and finding out the various places of historic interest. They then continued with sketchings of the countryside around them before joining up with the climbers and returning home." The report goes on -

"Return journeys are as much a part of the experience as the actual pursuits - amongst the babel of ribald comments, humorous stories and playfully conceited recollections there is serious constructive criticism of sketches, quiet concern at the difficulties encountered in the day's climbing and sensible criticism of some aspects of the day." One boy talked about the Watergate affair and declared "I'm gonna have to start reading the newspapers and watching the news." Stories about St. Catherine's Hospital were exchanged but overall the conversation was dominated by a great feeling of compassion.

This passage echoes the qualities Alec Clegg admired in good junior schools and raises yet again the choice between pot filling and fire kindling. The Terrace showed that the fires could still be kindled even in the last term with the least able and the least motivated. Is it out of place to consider if these personal improvements are more important than a meagre collection of C.S.E. passes? A change of outlook, an increase of confidence instead of an also rans certificate confirming you completed the course.

Despite being an innovative Education Authority the West Riding had its pockets of reaction. The years during which Mrs Gunn was Principal of Bingley College (1964 - 1967) were ones of tension and difficulty. Legal wrangling continued for many months after her dismissal and contributed to the problems which faced her successor, Ernest Butcher. When Mrs Gunn was appointed Alec Clegg had reflected that she would "either be brilliant or a trouble to me." The latter was the case and it was not until January 1969 that settlement between Mrs Gunn and the West Riding was finalised. As at Hornsey College of Art in 1968 the Bingley students' protest had its origins in complaints which were expressed as demands for freedom. The two main demands were -

"That every student at Bingley College should have the right to choose where she or he wishes to live."

"That the alleged parental authority of the college be formally repudiated."

The students added that if the demands were not fully met a general meeting would be held "... to discuss action designed to force the college authorities to submit." James Jupp summarised the basic features of protest and discontent in the late sixties in these words -

"... that it rejects the adult world; that it is confined effectively to those between puberty and thirty; that it creates its own leaders and symbols; that it demands 'liberation'; that it requires less and less adult cooperation for its sub-society to function; that it frightens the adult world to death, and that it is basically harmless despite a dangerous and even self-destructive aspect." (9)

Alec Clegg's concluding remarks to the staff at Bingley College on 10th October 1969 had the same clear, cutting edge as those in a meeting with his inspectors and advisers many years before. (10) At that meeting he said that if honesty and integrity did not rule the relationships between the officers of the West Riding then those who neglected these qualities should leave. Two of the Bingley lecturers had provoked student protest and spread calumny against the teaching profession. Alec Clegg had brought their action to the notice of the National Teachers' Council to be set up to safeguard professional standards. He felt that the youth and inexperience of the students had been manipulated and abused, as he said at the end of the meeting ... I do not think I have spoken in this vein in 25 years."

One of the main spurs to seek support for a Teachers' Council was the article in the publication 'Bingley Now' by one of the College staff. One passage on 'coercive social control' gives not only the flavour of the article as a whole but the disposition of some in the student body.

"All systems of class domination rely ultimately on forcible, organised coercive sanctions, which require revolutionary action to smash. In British higher education the suffocating porridge-like ideological environment - 'repressive tolerance' or 'privileged liberalism' - masks the coercive aspect of social relations in education. But any school or college which attempted to dispense absolutely with the apparatus of terror and blackmail, which is what confidential reports, examinations and grading and disciplinary arrangements amount to, would find itself crushed out of existence. In this sense, the British State education system has not got room for one really good school or college, and 100% of our schools are bad. One revolutionary school would challenge the idea of authority in its present context."

The Black Paper view of student disorder was that it was the inevitable consequence of progressive education and the absence of discipline. Students were engaged in "... no more than the self-defeating operation of sawing off the branch on which they were sitting." To Alec Clegg the Bingley protest was a very vexing problem which demanded thorough investigation. He shared the view of Bernard Levin which appeared in a newspaper article headed, 'Why do they reject us?' Levin advised his readers "... for our sake as well as theirs, we have got to start finding out what ails them. For in doing so, we may begin to understand what ails us."

In January 1969 the third year confidential record cards at Bingley were stolen. In July the strike took place and the discussions which the Yorkshire Post (11) described as proceeding "sensibly and amiably" broke down in September because of the presentation of a new set of student demands. The issues were limited in themselves but they had been raised to the status of fundamentals by two lecturers and militants in the student body. A lemming like strand runs through much that was said and written at this time. The disposition of the Principal to seek a solution on the issue of student participation was to some an open door, and what satisfaction is there in kicking an open door? Like Harriet Crawley, another militant (12) who declared her strongest feeling was "... also the least original" and added "we are going to have a riot", the Bingley militants welcomed confrontation.

Was Bingley College, opened in 1911, and one of the oldest in the West Riding, suffering from what the Franks Report termed 'infirmity of purpose', or was it a place of 'repressive tolerance' a term used by E.P.Thompson? (13) It was neither. There was a hangover of conflict from Mrs Gunn's Principalship; there was a group of militant lecturers and students; and lastly there was a backcloth nationally of student unrest. Alec Clegg expressed his feelings in some detail to A.A. Evans, General Secretary of the A.T.C.D.E. (14) -

"I am writing to you about a matter which is at the moment causing me the utmost concern. It has become the accepted view that young people training to be teachers should be given a very large measure of freedom to express their views on current social and educational problems. I have much sympathy with this practice, even though it worries me whenever I fear that this freedom is being used as a licence to disrupt the learning of others. I am sure it is right nevertheless that students should be accorded this freedom in order that they may learn to assume responsibility. Members of staff by the very fact of their position are presumed already to be responsible. This being so, I am bound to ask myself what the right course of action ought to be when a member of a College staff writes the paragraphs set out below in a Broadsheet which is intended to circulate amongst all the students in the college in which he is employed."

This concern for the students was reflected in Alec Clegg's talk to the Bingley staff a month later when he pointed out that the leading protesters had recanted and that the foundation of a more constructive future had been established. 'The Final Ten Years' summarises the position at Bingley in this short, peaceful paragraph 1 -

"Students are more and more encouraged to run their own affairs and they are represented on the governing body of the college, and on its Academic Board, and they share in equal numbers with the staff the membership of the college Standing Joint Committee."

PONTEFRACT HANDICRAFT CLUB AND BATLEY COMMUNITY PROJECT.

The Bingley students could look forward to a professional career, relatively well paid and secure. Those who attended Pontefract Handicraft Club for boys were in most cases 'twilight' children who were now 'twilight' youth. The club was inspected in February 1967 and the HMI's described it as "an important pioneer venture". The premises were in a dark, narrow lane near the centre of the town and the club was run by its founder, a local probation officer. It had three part-time leaders and a number of voluntary helpers. Opened in 1961 it had about one hundred members, some thirty of which attended each night. The club did not keep detailed records of members and lacked the sort of framework the HMI's anticipated. They wrote "... that this work for young children at risk (among whom girls deserve equal consideration) is of great significance, but needs to be done with responsible skill as well as devotion." Perhaps it was the informality that contributed to its success. The venture was very different in organisation from the Batley Community Project which aimed to integrate immigrants into a Yorkshire township.

The sixties saw a large scale influx of immigrants and by January 1967 there were 130,000 immigrant children in Britain.

The Department of Education showed only 841 of these were in the West Riding, a mere 0.3 per cent of the county's school population. This overall figure masked the fact that most of the immigrant children were in Batley and Keighley. In 1968 7.2 per cent of school children in Batley were immigrants and the schools faced great difficulties in meeting the needs of youngsters who had completely different social, religious and cultural backgrounds. Alec Clegg wrote to the Permanent Under Secretary at the Ministry pointing out the pressing needs of these two areas and he secured their support for what came to be known as the Batley Community Project. The scheme was not launched in full until 1972 when the demise of the West Riding was already in sight, and as a consequence the main emphasis was put on establishing as wide a range of contacts in the area as possible. Alec Clegg was disturbed over the differences which cropped up between the Project Director, Miss Would, and Batley Council and he reflected that "I see the whole purpose of an experiment of this kind is not necessarily to fortify the establishment but to find alternative ways of bringing in the community." (15)

Donald Wade produced a detailed report on Community in Yorkshire in 1971 and its findings (16) set out many of the difficulties which the Batley Community Project might face. He pointed out that immigrant community leaders "... could be more co-operative with people who are trying to help them" and that Indian and Pakistani immigrants, although nearly 100% Muslim tended to be suspicious of each other. Although only in its infancy when the West Riding ended the Batley project underlined the difficulties which had to be overcome when trying to build constructive links within a multi-ethnic community. Alec Clegg compared Batley to Denaby reflecting that the Red House project succeeded because of the support it got from the local community. He was sceptical on the chance of success at Batley. When Miss Would left in 1974 and was followed by the resignation of the Assistant Director it seemed all the West Riding had to hand on to Kirklees was a stalemated initiative. The impending end of the West Riding must have been the mental equivalent of death by a thousand cuts for Alec Clegg. The correspondence of the winter months of 1972-1973 illustrated the tension between Miss Would and the Batley council and small scale incidents such as the local attitude to gypsy children at Havercroft Primary School must have made it very difficult for Alec Clegg to maintain his belief in educational progress.

THE CARAVAN FAMILY

What the treatment of the caravan family illustrated was the narrow minded attitude of the local parish council and the absence of cooperation between public services as Alec Clegg put the matter " ... a splendid example of the confused failure of these services to find a solution to a social problem." The local view of the caravan family was that they were filthy layabouts living off the state and that the three children should be sent to a boarding school and the adults ordered to leave. The headmistress of the school washed and cared for the children and ensured that they built up worthwhile relationships within the school. This was social education of the highest quality yet this care prompted this observation from the Director of Social Services -

"One cannot help wondering whether Mrs Deighton, through her kindness and efforts to improve the physical care of the children, is not in fact drawing attention to them and singling them out as being different from other children. It may be that they are so dirty as to be objectionable to the other children and their clothing so poor that it would single them out in any case."

The Education Committee refused boarding school provision for the children and it emerged at this time that Social Services had details on this family going back to 1970. This caravan family illustrated the difficulty the various parts of the Welfare State had in dealing with people who did not fit readily into one of its divisions. A generous school aiming to offer education in its widest sense was to face possible accusations of trespass into other divisions, or extending its work far beyond the boundaries of normal, everyday schooling. In this way the shrinking social revolution was catching up with Alec Clegg. Richard Titmuss in an essay on 'The Irresponsible Society' asked these questions -

"What education for democracy is there in much of the professionalized, sectionalized diet served up today to students in most universities, technical colleges, teachers' training courses, and other places of instruction? Are we not, indeed, witnessing a triumph of technique over purpose? What, in fact, are we offering to a majority of the young beside material success, the social graces, vocational techniques and, in particular, professional salvation? (17)

It is this sort of comment which prompts one to suggest the source of Alec Clegg's unease about initiatives such as the Batley Community Project and SNAP, a well resourced community initiative in Liverpool. The Shelter Neighbourhood Action Project had as one of its aims the provision of help in an Educational Priority Area, but a West Riding report on its impact on schools was blunt and to the point. It said-

"It might make better sense, for these children, if the schools were to try more open, libertarian and experimental methods which provided emotional freedom and flexibility, rather than to remain stuck in their present unprofitable groove of pressuring the children to perform by rote."

Alec Clegg and his inspectors and advisers located grassroots developments in schools that promised genuine progress. They discussed them, resourced them and sought to interest others with a view to their extension. In this way change evolved with each school having the opportunity to translate an idea so that it fitted their own set of circumstances. This mode of advance was very different from the imposed framework into which people were fitted often to their discomfort. Social change unlike economic change is not a matter for legislation. It is slow and like England's weather difficult to predict and full of surprises, good or bad.

CHAPTER 18

SOCIAL OPPORTUNITY

By the time the final years of the West Riding were slipping by, English society was developing into what Michael Young termed a meritocracy, a different kind of unequal society. Alec Clegg used this term in his lecture, 'Recipe for Failure' in which he said -

"We pay lip service to the idea of equality of educational opportunity but we do very little to initiate the kind of positive discrimination which might help to iron out the differences of home, social background, speech, wealth, authority and geographical area, which make anything like equality impossible."

The old order which ranged from the aristocracy to the working classes was being replaced by a new one where the richest twenty per cent owned three quarters of all personal wealth. J.K. Galbraith offered this consolation to those who resented this gross inequality -

" ... that if one feeds the horse enough oats, some will pass through to the road for the sparrows." Alec Clegg sought initiatives to offset the inequalities which he saw developing within the education system. (1)

The West Riding authority had initiated the Oxbridge scheme to give working class boys the opportunity to enter the exclusive top strata of English universities and had started a number of schemes to help the less able and the distressed. Whether schemes created opportunities or prevented personel decline, they increased or preserved the cohesion of society. They were the means to create equality. In the footnote to his last full report on the work of the West Riding Education Service Alec Clegg drew attention, in eleven concise paragraphs, to its quality and range of provision, and how in an area "... deeply involved in the older basic industries" it was essential to provide youngsters with "educational compensations." The quality of the relationships between the Committee, its staff and schools in general could well earn the term fraternal. A.H. Halsey uses this word with care in 'Change in British Society', Page 160 -

"I mean it to denote social groups whose members share the same essential ideals of conduct - recognition of, and care for, the needs of others - which are associated with our noblest conception of the family." A.H. Halsey could appreciate the social strengths of Denaby, the feeling of community and self help. However he saw these social assets being destroyed by the run down of the coal industry. As the study of the West Riding Educational Priority Area project concludes -

"Areas like Denniston (Denaby) cannot survive as the result of educational change alone, however effective this may be. A co-ordinated programme of educational, community and economic development is needed if we wish to reverse the trends and preserve the social, human and educational investment that has gone into such areas." (2)

A common factor of all the 'experiments' in the West Riding was the wish to enrich the quality of life of those who took part. The Oxbridge Scheme, like the Red House initiative, was one of these experiments and some of the most interesting and important information is to be found in the letters sent to Alec Clegg by the participants during or after their stay at an Oxford or Cambridge college. Statistics on the subjects taken, the results achieved and the jobs they acquired only tell part of the effect of this scheme. Quite a few years before the Oxbridge scheme began Alec Clegg reflected on the boys and girls who put in for 'County University Awards.' His experience of the annual sequence of interviews led him to write about their personal qualities and interests. To many of them exams were a goal not a gateway and to those who came from the industrial areas an interest in music, the theatre or other cultural activities was very rare. The narrowness of interests and a 'complete lack of curiosity' was a feature of over half of all the candidates, a fact which Alec Clegg found 'incredible.' These depressing facts prompted him to set down what he thought secondary education, in particular the grammar schools, should aim to provide.

Firstly, youngsters should have " ... the ability to earn their living along lines in which they will make the best contribution and which afford them the best hope of self-fulfilment." Secondly, they should " ... be able to take advantage of all that will enrich them as human beings", and lastly they should "have retained the enquiring mind." (3)

Success at university and in the career that followed ensured prosperity in the meritocracy but Alec Clegg foresaw that at fifty they would "... be patient and resigned and be trying to ensure that their children are better informed." (4) Running through so much of what he said and wrote is the concern for the quality of life and a much broader appreciation of what education could do to achieve an improvement.

Much of the correspondence between Alec Clegg and those who went on the Oxbridge scheme is a collection of searching dialogues on education and society. The scheme was termed an experiment but it proved much more for these dialogues were descriptions of social reality and testimony to the potential of working class boys. The personal opinions and feelings of these young men give an insight, not only into the impact of the two universities on working class boys, but on their impact on the universities themselves.

Two who went to Clare College, Cambridge, felt it was another world, very different from their homes in Stainforth in South Yorkshire and Golcar in the Colne Valley. Both found the freedom in the college difficult to come to terms with, for unlike the sixth forms they had to orgainise their own programmes of work. One of their friends in the college was the head boy from Eton who had an aristocratic background and whom they described as at ease with everyone. He was helpful, affable and intelligent and gained a first. He was compared to the sons of the nouveau riche who were acutely conscious of the fact that their parents had sent them to public schools and on to Cambridge so that they could acquire status. They were young men over anxious to assert their place. The part Eric Ashby, Master of Clare College, played in the scheme was in the view of these two Oxbridge students very important. Lady Clegg confirmed that her husband and Eric Ashby were in regular touch about the progress of the scheme. Alan Bullock, Master of St Catherines College at Oxford was another in regular contact with Alec Clegg about the scheme. Alan Bullock's biographies of Adolf Hitler and Ernest Bevin could be looked upon as guides to the potential of working class boys, one destructive the other constructive. Both had qualities which took them to the peak of power and it is arguable that the absence of conventional education gave these qualities plenty of scope to develop. Ernest Bevin as one biographer put it was "... the embodiment of all natural and unlettered men drawing upon wells of experience unknown to the more literate." (5)

If Alan Bullock could appreciate such potential then Eric Ashby in his study 'Technology and the Academics' expressed a viewpoint of what universities stood for which has an unusual and unexpected correlation with best primary and secondary practice in West Riding schools.

P.95 "Over and above their obvious functions to conserve and advance and transmit knowledge, they have, by adapting themselves to the scientific revolution, reunited education and discovery - two fundamental activities of the human mind. They have disseminated, through the teaching of science, a new formula for tolerating error. Through their responsibility for research they have taken their place among the pace-makers for technological change. At the same time they resist some of the disintegrating effects of modern technology. In an age which is being pressed into uniformity by mass-communication, mass-production and concepts such as manpower, universities stand for the encouragement of variety, individuality and dissent."

Merton College, Oxford, took the largest number of Oxbridge students, seventeen during the life of the scheme, whilst Clare at Cambridge, Alec Clegg's old college, took ten. No other college took double figures and neither of these colleges could say the Oxbridge students represented anything more than a regular minority over a short span of years. The rural and southern parts of the West Riding provided the students for Merton. Those who went to Clare came from a group of schools in the west of the authority such as Colne Valley, Holme Valley and Penistone. In

September 1971 the Times Educational Supplement contained an article on the scheme in which the term 'guinea pigs' was used. Only one of those who took part in the scheme used this term in the letters sent to Alec Clegg. If the scheme was a social experiment rather then a social opportunity then the rich interaction it produced would be reduced to the simple conclusion that it was a success - working class boys could fit in socially and academically with the life of Oxford and Cambridge colleges. Some of Alec Clegg's critics took a similar stance in relation to educational initiatives in areas of deprivation in the West Riding. The initiatives were started in these working class areas rather than in places such as Harrogate or Ripon where there could be an outburst against progressive ideas. The superficial nature of such reactions, seeing either people or places as educational laboratories, deserves the reaction of one youngster quoted by Stan Barstow in the introduction to 'Enjoying Writing'-

"Let reservations stay where they belong
In first class carriages."

The impact of Merton College on a student from Castleford can be appreciated in his account of his early days in Oxford. He described his room on the top floor of one of the college houses on Merton Street. He felt it was worth the effort required to scale three flights of stairs to reach his room so as to look out of the window to see Magdalene Tower and the Botanical Gardens. He felt at ease and remarked that Merton was one of the few colleges where ex-grammar school pupils outnumbered those from public schools. When he left Oxford his last letter to Alec Clegg contained the reflection that his three years at Merton had had a profound effect on his intellect and his social consciousness.

Another from Wath, in the southern coalfield area of the Riding, was an outgoing character who according to the panel who interviewed him could have sold vacuum cleaners to people who lived in houses without electricity. This Oxbridge entrant was a very energetic character who wrote sincere and buoyant letters in one of which he expressed his view that the launch of the scheme was "... superbly timed as it coincided with colleges liberalising their modes of entry. The scheme acquainted colleges with the potential which lay outside their normal catchment areas and he felt the scheme had 'broadened the horizons of Merton tutors'. Oxford to this young man was an "actors' paradise". He toured France with the Oxford University Dramatic Society in a production of Hamlet. The highspot of the tour was a performance in Monte Carlo before Princess Grace. He became President of the Merton Drama Society and in the eyes of other Oxbridge students at the college was one of its outstanding members. His own view was the scheme sent people like himself to Oxford or Cambridge with a sense of mission which was an "...added factor for stability and assurance and gave psychological reinforcement - an intangible and essential part of the scheme". Despite three operations at the Radcliffe Infirmary which described him as a unique case and threatened to keep him there as a permanent 'visual aid' he worked very hard and just missed a first class honours degree. His three years at Merton were in his view Elysium and an indication of how an outgoing, intelligent young South Yorkshireman could flourish in a cultured and friendly Oxford college.

A very different Oxbridge student to go to Merton was the son of a Nidderdale shepherd who lived near Pateley Bridge. He was a boarder at Ripon Grammar School who after being accepted for Merton spent nearly a year teaching in a German school. After his first year at Oxford he wrote to Alec Clegg describing himself as ... ill informed and unable to discuss or argue very cogently, and rather uncertain as an individual." He felt that his first year, although a struggle, had enabled him to get rid of some of these shortcomings. Oxford he maintained "... made me a thinking citizen". He went futher saying "... it has most definitely given me a completely new perspective of things - indeed, if I can say so, of life as a whole." He had two very good tutors who were demanding and made him work hard. He sampled many activities ranging from acting and punting to the debating society and the anti-Powellite march in London. The exchange of letters between this young man and Alec Clegg became a dialogue on education which in the early seventies with the end of the West Riding in sight must have been a welcome shaft of sunlight. Observations on the Oxbridge students at Merton that - "Their case only proves how futlie streaming (which is what going to Oxbridge or indeed going to university adds up to) can be at 17-18, no less futile than its earlier brothers the 11+, G.C.E. 'O' and 'A' levels etc., ... it seems a very great shame that the scheme should have been stopped, for it was at least an inroad into the bastions of privilege ...". His last letter described his intention to teach in Bulgaria and then to move to a school in Essex.

Another student with a rural background was the son of a Lithuanian father and an Austrian mother. They lived at Sowerby Bridge and the father was on regular night shifts cleaning toffee making machinery so that it was ready for the next days production. The young man was described as one of unusual intellectual maturity but frustrated by the absence of a corresponding maturity in expression. His broadened course was in Africa on the V.S.O. scheme which he said made him appreciate wider horizons and " ... possibly most important of all, to increase one's tolerance towards others." He found his first year at Oxford very stimulating and like the others in this Merton quartet described in detail the enrichment of his life. For these, and the majority on the Oxbridge scheme, it was not a matter of offsetting the effects of social poverty but a chance to realise personal potential in a rich set of circumstances.

Many years before Alec Clegg's scheme began a railwayman, Ernest March, won a scholarship to Oxford and described his feelings as an undergraduate in these words which would be echoed by those on the Oxbridge scheme -

"No undergraduate is made to feel that he is merely a cog in a vast machine. He retains his own individuality, and is treated as an individual. His work is judged by the amount and quality of himself that he expresses in it." (6)

One of the last to go to Merton found a great difference between life around Skipton and what he experienced in Oxford. At school he knew the answers to questions but was prevented from giving an articulate reply by his stutter. He got the nickname of the 'Addingham Heifer' on account of the long 'er' which preceded every answer he attempted to give. He overcame this impediment and when at Merton a letter from Alec Clegg recalled his interview for the scheme saying "I wondered who it was that was doing the interviewing, you or me!" At Merton the 'Addingham Heifer' found he could fit in well 'absorbing and reproducing aspects' of the college environment without losing his own individual character.

Those who went to Clare College, Cambridge, shared many of the views of those who went to Merton. They enjoyed the wide range of activities, and the beauty of their surroundings. Their letters convey an excitement initially rooted in apprehension which changed to a deep enjoyment of the contrast and opportunities of college life. Amongst those who went to Clare there were two students who saw the university as an important source of inequality in English society. The Clegg scheme was to them the first small chink in the armour of upper class dominance of the two older universities. The appreciation of the quality of the education they received was in some cases accompanied by criticism of outdated rules and traditions. One wrote in his last year of an enjoyable three years but he looked forward to no more proctors breathing down his neck and the prospect of owning his own car and staying out after midnight when he wanted to.

One student at Clare could look back on his school career like a non league club which ended up in the Cup Final. He had been a secondary modern pupil who gained a place at Penistone Grammar School and took Mathematics, Further Mathematics and Physics in the sixth form. He decided to take Economics at Cambridge writing in one of his letters that his aim at university was " ... to educate myself so that I am a more worthwhile human being. At one time, and certainly at the time of our meeting, I would have thought that the pecuniary reward and a possible position of power were the prime motivating forces."

It was this sort of letter which typified much of the correspondence between Alec Clegg and the participants in the Oxbridge scheme. He described letters such as this one as moving and instructive and in his reply to this student in January 1974 he forecast that in two months time, when he retired, he would be going through the letters to extract the wisdom. To Alec Clegg the sincerity of so many of these letters prompted him to write to another student that " .. a letter of the kind you wrote is to me much more encouraging and convincing than any examination results which you may get."

The Oxbridge scheme showed how working class boys could scale the peaks of the educational system. Reports such as the one on 'outstandingly successful students at the Airedale and Wharfedale college of Further Education illustrate how the least likely youngsters could match, or surpass, the achievements of those who went to Oxford of Cambridge. They may have seemed condemned to the social lowlands but they advanced well beyond the foothills and were yet another illustration of Alec Clegg's concern on the amount of untapped ability in the West Riding and England as a whole. The vast majority of the group of twenty five in this Further Education Report were failures at school academically. Their personal qualities seemed limited as well. One girl was 'all but expelled' from a grammar school and a fat boy teased so much that he was sent to a special school. The boy had an illiterate father and an epileptic mother. Who would think the girl would gain seven 'O' levels at the College and be the outstanding nurse in her year at a Leeds Hospital, or that the boy would not only gain 'O' and 'A' level qualifications but would gain a Bachelor of Education degree at York? It is important to consider what motivated these young men and women to draw upon undis-covered personal qualities and skills, and to set aside the sense of failure which must have faced them every time they looked at a school report or testimonial.

Two very successful nurses were described as 'academically unsuitable' and 'below average ability' before they were accepted for training. A boy expelled from a grammar school ended up at Hatfield Polytechnic and got a good Honours degree. It is very difficult to regard this group as late developers. They are examples of undiscovered talent in just one part of the West Riding. Two girls from secondary modern schools gained 'O'levels at the

College, went on to take O.N.D. courses and then to Colleges of Education. At the time of the report one of them was a Head of Department in a grammar school.

Many of the boys who went on the Oxbridge scheme became teachers and, understandably, the pre-nursing scheme at Airedale and Wharfedale College of Further Education was overwhelmingly populated by girls. The reason why these girls chose this career and why so many amongst the Oxbridge boys teaching are questions well worth addressing. None of the letters to Alec Clegg give direct answers, but it is very clear that many had an attitude to society and a view of the quality of personal life that fits well with a public service.

The achievements and ideas of these two groups contrast sharply with the social characteristics of Britain described in the recent addition to the Oxford Histories covering 1945 to 1990.

The author concludes that Britain had a divisive educational system and suffered " ... endemic social inequality, almost without parallel in the industrial world." Set against Kenneth O. Morgan's (7) view of a harsh and divided society the efforts of Alec Clegg and the West Riding were imaginative and successful yet they were no more than dents in the estblished patterns within British society.

OCCUPATIONS OF THOSE WHO WENT ON THE 'OXBRIDGE SCHEME'
Analysis of the replies received from participants in the scheme in 1973

RESEARCH FOR A HIGHER DEGREE	17
TEACHING	16
COMMERCE AND INDUSTRY	13
TOTAL	46

CHAPTER 19

THE WEST RIDING - a source of educational progress

The West Riding was one of the five local authorities (1) which questioned the tripartite system of grammar, technical and modern schools, and the County's Development Plan quoted from the report of the Advisory Council on Education in Scotland which stated -

"The whole scheme rests on an assumption which teacher and psychologist alike must challenge - that childern of twelve sort themselves out mostly into those categories to which these three types of school correspond."

The independent viewpoint of the West Riding was based on a detailed and wide ranging enquiry into the pattern of education in Britain and other Countries. Between 1945 and 1974 detailed research was a continuous strand of the county's education service. Such information gave Alec Clegg and his staff promising routes for development, potential difficulties and some ideas of how the ideal and the actual could be made one.

Information on New Zealand, gleaned in 1947, showed there were no grammar schools there and that admission to secondary schools was on a territorial basis. The establishment of an entrance examination by the headmistress of a popular Girls' High School resulted in the rejection of 80 pupils. Newspaper reports on the matter prompted the Prime Minister to order the Director of Education to take a plane to Auckland and to put a stop to such practices. Another instance of direct central action was based on the belief that universities played too big a part in the School Certificate. The government decided this should stop, and that a system of accredited schools should be started so that students were admitted to universities on the recommendation of head-teachers. Alec Clegg may well have endorsed the idea of one secondary school serving a given area and the restrictive nature of university requirements on the curriculum, but he would have been very apprehensive about the excessive exercise of control by a central authority.

Two years later, in 1949, the Control Commission in Germany sought West Riding participation in a youth exchange scheme with Arnsberg in the Northern Rhineland. Before, and during the war, the Hitler Youth Movement dominated the education of young Germans. It aimed to educate them physically, intellectualy and morally in the spirit of National Socialism. The Arnsberg scheme was one part of the Control Commission's policy to introduce young Germans to the life style of the youth of a democratic country. The interchange between pupils, teachers and administrators in the two countries was an important part of the slow process of converting occupation into partnership, and the readmittance of Germany into the European community. Hitler's Germany had a tripartite system based on ability and although the outdoor camps appeared innovative and dynamic the whole system was tightly controlled to serve the sinister inculcation of Nazi dogma.

It is worth reflecting on why the West Riding participated in the Arnsberg scheme when only a few years earlier the enormities of Nazi policies were exposed at the Nuremberg Trial. The definition of genocide, and this was deliberate German policy, was as follows -

"A co-ordinated plan of different actions aiming at the destruction of the social foundations of the life of national groups, with the aim of annihilating the groups themselves. The objective of such a plan would be disintergration of the national feelings, religion and the economic existence of national groups, and the destruction of the personal liberty, health, dignity and even the lives of the individuals belonging to such groups." (2)

In Germany inhumanity had been raised to the level of a principle. How was this to be changed? By applying the principle to Germany? By permanent military occupation? Or by building links at grassroots level and relying on the new generations in European countries to discuss the future and learn from the enormities of the past. This passage from 'Education 1954-64', p.90., points to the underlying aims of the Arnsberg exchange scheme.

"It was, however, obvious that no sigificant help could be given by England unless German teachers could experience at first hand the concern of our schools for the individual and the importance which we place on individual responsibility." It went on to describe how the dialogue between teachers in the two countries made "... a real exchange of ideas and critical and objective discussion of the problems affecting the education of children on both sides."

The West Riding did not ignore Britain's allies in the 1939-45 war. Permanent links were established with Lille in Northern France, with educational institutions in the United States and in Commonwealth countries such as Australia and Canada. In 1951 the very successful exchange scheme, between the Yorkshire Branch of the Modern Language Association and an area around Lille, was extended after discussions between the Association and the West Riding. The West Riding undertook to run the exchange scheme which embraced all the counties and boroughs between the Trent and Tees. An exchange committee was formed and between 1955 and 1964 the number of Yorkshire children and schools taking part rose from 256 to 878, and from 46 to 71. Moreover the scheme was extended to include student exchanges between a Yorkshire and a French training college.

The letters Alec Clegg sent back to Alderman Hyman and some of his staff during his visit to the United States and a UNESCO conference in Montevideo, contain plaudits, typical humorous asides and criticism of education and society in the New World. He was entranced by the work in music, art and dance at the Sarah Lawrence College, but felt physical education in schools was 'execrable' due to being corrupted entirely by the big football game.

He was shown some of the worst schools in New York and often in later talks on the concerns he had about British society, he drew attention to the social dangers British urban areas would face if we did not heed the lessons offered by cities like New York. Clearly he hoped to find UNESCO operating as the means to worldwide social and cultural advance, but he wrote -

"I have never in all my life been so disillusioned. It is the first time in my life I have had to trim my conscience to a party line and I don't like it."

These remarks underline Alec Clegg's independence of mind, a quality which played a significant part in establishing the West Riding as an imaginative and far sighted authority in many parts of the world.

The visit of Dr Elizabeth Halsey, of Iowa State University who was Principal of the Department of Physical Education, to West Riding schools in 1954 triggered exchanges of teachers. Thirty American teachers attended a course at Woolley Hall in 1956, and, as with the Arnsberg exchange it was not just the visits to schools and the lectures, but much more the quality of the dialogue between the Americans and their English counterparts which was the most valued feature. In her personal report to Alec Clegg, Diana Jordan, Warden at Woolley Hall, noted that what seemed common ground in theory between the two groups was quite different in practice. There was enough time for the Americans and the West Riding teachers to test and to exchange their views for the course lasted from 28th June to 14th July. The Warden described the later stages in these words -

"... we were all caught up in the common and deeply felt interest in the emerging capabilities of all children so little suspected under past methods, and so convincingly demonstrated under present teaching. We got 'home' completely the last week through the schools though I feel sure that the teachers who came on the weekends did a great deal to stress the importance of the child and not the subject."

The exchange of ideas and experiences was a feature of many courses at Woolley Hall and it contributed a great deal to the image of the county as a whole.

The number of visitors and the number of youngsters involved in exchanges with foreign and commonwealth countries increased a great deal during the fifties and sixties. Statistically the figures are impressive enough yet lying behind them is a wealth of understanding and goodwill, which if Alec Clegg's reports are any guide to their value, were of fundamental importance. His visit to Australia, which lasted from August to October in 1957, illustrates this point. At the invitation of an international group of educationalists led by Professor Tibble of Leicester, Sri Mathur, a school director from India and Alec Clegg went on tour in Australia. Apart from travelling 30,000 miles, 6,000 of which were in Australia, Alec Clegg gave fifty lectures and took part in many seminars and discussion groups. It was incredibly tiring so much so that he said "I fell asleep in the middle of a sentence that I was uttering and awoke not knowing why I was saying what I was saying." Despite the pressure his report to the Education Committee (3) gave a concise picture of the education system of Australia. Each state controlled its own service and the Director of Education, unlike a British counterpart, was not faced by bodies of elected representatives. Assessment of teachers was directly linked to the framework of promotion. An inspector would test a teacher's classes and if satisfied, or impressed, would support an advance in the promotion queue. If a teacher moved to another state, he or she had to revert to the end of a new queue. This system was condemned by Alec Clegg "... lock, stock and barrel". The necessity to concentrate on repetitive drilling in arithmetic and spelling was a brake on individual initiative and teachers had to win time to give children the opportunity for individual expression. It gave Alec Clegg considerable satisfaction that his collections of class work from West Riding schools illustrated qualities not matched in Australian schools. On the other hand he was deeply concerned at the oppressive effects of the Australian inspection system. The state which impressed him most was Tasmania, especially its rural education which he felt was better than that in the West Riding. If the rigidity of the system of inspection drew justified criticism he appreciated the integration of the system for school counselling, which covered such matters as child guidance, youth employment and special school provision.

Alec Clegg registered embarrassment on being questioned on the state of Yorkshire cricket by Bill Woodfull, a Melbourne headmaster and former Australian cricket captain but he was fascinated by the prospect of visiting Sri Mathur's school on his return journey to England. He described Sri Mathur as a man of

"... remarkable spiritual and intellectual gifts" and gave a detailed account of the unique qualities of his 600 strong girls' boarding school which recruited from all over India.

252

It was the work in crafts that made the deepest impression and once again it underlined Alec Clegg's conviction in their importance to education as a whole. He wrote -

"It was when I came to see the craft work of the school that I found something which I believed to be superior to what we do. The reason for its superiority was not so much its quality as the fact that it was so purposeful and apposite. The connection between the life of the youngsters and the crafts that they were producing was so clear and obvious, and their variety was remarkable. They span, they wove, they cooked and laundered, they plated their own cooking vessels, and they made their own cosmetics with great skill and variety from natural products. Their needlework, embroidery and pottery, painting and music, were all delightful, and I shall never in my life forget the impressiveness of my host's 18 year old daughter as she sang and accompanied herself on a sitar. The whole aim of this school was to effect a synthesis between the spiritual values of the East and the material progress of the West, and to the visitor from the West it was, of course, the former aim which impressed itself most vividly on the mind." In the same way as the noise of the wild peacocks on the corrugated iron roof remained in his memory, so too did the way the school, in every activity aim beyond ... the mere intellectual content or mastery of a skill." Alec Clegg's friends , the Elmhirsts, who set up Dartington Hall and later were involved in the exchange scheme between Dartington and Conisbrough had a similar, deep reaction to ideas from the East. The Indian poet, Rabindranath Tagore advised them when Dartington (4) was set up to "... Try to attract some budding poets, some scapegraces whom no one else dares to acknowledge. Never mind how small the flame may be, provided they have enough of a gift to light the lamp." Alec Clegg's distrust of rigid administrative frameworks which restricted rather than supported those who worked within them was illustrated in Canada in 1966 as well as in his visit to Australia.

His two month visit to Canada as a visiting Commonwealth fellow in the late summer of that year confirmed his opposition to externally prescribed syllabuses, which in his view reduced teachers to the status of low grade technicians. Moreover, as was the case in Canada and the USA there was a temptation to teach "... what can be packed in mechanically or measured objectively or programmed." As such work increased the opportunity for young-sters to develop their creative abilities would be seriously reduced. Teachers had to get through the syllabus before any enrichment of education could be contemplated. There were loopholes but these depended on personal links such as a close friendship between a school principal and an inspector. The situation common to many schools was expressed by one teacher in these sad words - "Of course, I wouldn't teach like this if I didn't have to ...".

Alec Clegg saw advantages in the Canadian system of putting children in classes on the basis of the standards they reached in their work. At first sight it seemed better than streaming yet those of limited ability were likely to end up in trade schools. These schools aimed to use the incentive of vocational training to engender an interest to stay on at school. However, they faced the problem of low status as one principal said to Alec Clegg -

"This is a school for slow ones and this is something we have to live with. I know some children carry piles of books that they don't use in this school and that others get off the bus two stages before it as they don't like people to know they come here, but we are doing a good job all the same." (5) If the English tripartitie system segregated the top 30% into the grammar schools it appeared that the reverse was the case in Canada. Alec Clegg had some reservations about the craft teaching in some of the trade schools which set '... a premium on rote learning and machine management', light years away from what he had seen in India in 1958.

When he turned his attention to the Canadian universities and educational research his apprehension on the restrictions on the class teachers was reinforced. Excessive, detailed research on quantitative factors in education to the exclusion of the elusive qualitative elements prompted him to quote James Koerner's comment that -

"It is the non quantitative and unscientific parts of education that are in all probability the most important for the training of teachers." (6)

The link forged between English and Danish handicraft teachers was an exchange where the West Riding was more of a learner than a teacher. Danish furniture design, craft equipment and craft teaching offered a rich collection of new ideas which had a significant effect on the interiors of colleges and schools and the nature of craft teaching. Another Scandinavian link was with Norway and this was started by Synøve Ryz, a gifted teacher of young children who went round West Riding schools with Diana Jordan, and impressed the Warden of Woolley with her interest in how children learn and not what they should learn. The next visitor was Else Marcussen, an Oslo Physical Education Adviser, who was "... as interested in children's powers of expression through painting, drawing and modelling as in Physical Education." (7) The third visitor, Halfrid, confirmed Diana Jordan's belief that this trio could be a source of changes which could strengthen the all round development of young children. They shared Diana Jordan's belief in the importance of movement which she maintained "... is the only activity in which body, mind and spirit can work in unison. I believe it is one of the most significant ways in which we can help children to preserve and keep their unity, their wholeness as people, before the pressures of the world today begin their disintegrating influences."

The reports sent to Alec Clegg by Diana Jordan on Woolley Courses and by G. H. Wilson on craft in schools described changes which had a common feature. Diana Jordan reflected on an Anglo-Norwegian Course, which was the thousand and seventh at Woolley, that -

"... Physical Education had begun to flow out of its accustomed channels and provide another way of helping the general growth and development of young children." G. H. Wilson wrote that progress during his first three years in the West Riding had been slow and painful, but that in March 1966 things changed and could only "... be described as a landslide." Permanent links not only brought new ideas, but where there was common ground, progress was reinforced by the confidence gained from friends abroad.

The first edition of 'The Excitement of Writing' was

255

published in 1964. This and later editions prompted regular comment in newspapers and magazines, along with a considerable amount of private correspondence between Alec Clegg and educationalists from many parts of Britain and other countries. The majority expressed great enthusiasm for the book and whilst some warned teachers against the uncritical acceptance of new approaches, others forecast that change could surprise some teachers at the hitherto unexpected abilities which would be set free. Robert Nye, a novelist, wrote about the book in 'The New Statesman' on 10th November 1972 and talked of the firstness of one five year olds boy's writing -

"I like to be a barber cose you Get a Rayt Lot of Moniy and in yor shop you Get a Rayt Lot of Pepel in yor ShoP Thay av bayds I will Put bill krim on thar her I like to cut mashtashase Sum men will brinG their little boys to av ther little boys her kut I like to Put sheyvinsowP on ther fayses and sheyv it off I want to be a barber naw I will Giv them shotbackandsayd krucot squerneck I sel rasabLads shavin Loshan shavinsowP and biLcriym i shal chath the Men 3 shiLig and hold men 2 shiLig and boys 6 Pans" (8)

Robert Nye said the boy had "... an ear for the pitch and pattern of speech which any dramatist might envy, a boy persuaded to write as if he talked on a piece of paper, neither bridled by the convention that a child's world be cut down to the size of words he can spell nor wrongly fed by teachers eager for results with lists of expressions considered appropriate to the writing of an essay on a given subject." Later work by the same boy was equally fluent but much more accurate, so firstness could survive and be refined.

Robert Nye was careful not only in his description of this little boy's writing and its implication for teachers but also on the difficulty of retaining the quality of firstness. As he says -

"Delight in the shape and sound of words, excitement in the act of piling them up and knocking them down, seems something invariably lost with the onset of puberty in all save the cases that count."

Poets he felt became poets at the age of twelve but they were very few in number. The few who had the ability "... to preserve the capacity to make things new, while knowing the old."

In the same autumn of 1972 Sister Barbara from St John's School for the Deaf at Boston Spa wrote to Alec Clegg describing the achievements of a boy and a girl. The boy had a deaf mother and two deaf brothers so Sister Barbara felt sensitivity in language would be one of the last things she could expect from him, yet as she said he "... produced a lovely piece of writing the other day." The girl, Julie, wrote a very acute description of autumn leaves which contained this passage -

"Some leaves were all screwed up, which looks as if they **were trying** to keep away from the cold. I feel the leaves some of them felt soft and others felt like soft potato crisps. When I smelt the leaves they had an aromatic smell."

In 1973 'Enjoying Writing' was published. It contained poetry and prose by youngsters between eleven and eighteen years of age. Firstness had matured, excitement had turned to enjoyment and the thoughtful boy or girl could, like the poet Douglas Dunn, meet -

"... That hard frontier
Where pencil, paint, wood, stone
And numbered rhyme
Converse with music on the edge of time." (9)

The flow of letters prompted by 'The Excitement of Writing' is clear evidence of the West Riding gaining widespread acknowledgement as an authority which through Alec Clegg, his staff and schools had made people realise the potential which lay, so often undiscovered, in the nations children.

The impact of the West Riding on other authorities covered material as well as the educational aspects of the service. The design, furnishing and care of schools and colleges were major areas of innovation. The teacher training colleges, the new schools, such as middle and comprehensives, provided many examples of what Professor Bronowski said ought to be the main guide for an architect -

"... that a building should be a coherent solution to a problem of living." (10) An architect who played an important part in middle school design in the West Riding was David Medd, who was the Principal Architect at the Department of Education and Science. (11) Alec Clegg's participation in any discussions or decisions on the design of furniture was no doubt influenced by his membership of the Council for Industrial Design which brought him into contact with people such as Sir Gordon Russell and Herbert Read. His visits abroad enriched his fund of information as well. The emphasis put on good internal design, decoration and display in schools led to the establishment of the School Museum Service which by 1964 lent over 20,000 items to schools. These items ranged from original works of art to stuffed animals. Films, slides and archive material were provided as well enabling teachers to range widely in their mode of teaching. Folders of childrens' work were built up so that inspectors and advisers could use them on courses and schools to promote new ideas.

Ernest Peet was appointed Supervisor of Caretakers in the West Riding in 1947 and between that year and his retirement earned a nation wide reputation for his ideas and inventions. Such ideas as sanding and sealing wood floors which were maintained by films of water based wax became standard practice in Britain and abroad. He designed and patented tools for applying floor dressing, window cleaning and wall washing equipment, squeegees and low cost mechanical scrubbing and polishing machines. Woolley Hall was his base for innumerable courses for his own staff and for visitors. In 1971 Ernest Peet organised thirty courses on a variety of aspects of caretaking and cleaning. As a lecturer and consultant his engagements ranged from universities and hospitals to the Ministry of Education itself and to Windsor Castle. Again by 1971 19 counties and major boroughs had used his expertise to run courses on caretaking and cleaning.

In 1969 Alec Clegg was invited to become a member of the Anglo-Soviet Consultative Committee on Bilateral relations. The Arnsberg scheme of 1949 sought to build links with a defeated enemy. The Anglo-Soviet initiative sought to build social links with a potential enemy. The invasion of Czechoslovakia in 1968 led to the cancellation of the first meeting and threw doubt on the committee building up any social contacts with the Soviet Union.

The bringing together of the two social systems and the two power blocs in Europe would clearly be a slow and touchy process. A weighty amount of correspondence passed between the Committee secretary and its members much of which was dictated by secretarial habit rather than the build up of connections between Soviet and British groups. The Committee put its emphasis on fostering relationships between non-governmental bodies, but this aim was haunted at every stage by Soviet anxiety that social initiatives were dangerous. They could cause shifts in the delicate balance within satellite states and between the two main world power blocs. It seems absurd to see dangerous political repercussions in proposals for cultural, educational and sporting exchanges but the tenor of the correspondence underlines the appropriateness of the term, the Cold War. In a frigid peace initatives to cooperate had to be carefully assessed and, if acted on, carried out with extreme diplomacy.

The joint meetings in 1969 and 1970 built confidence and a frank and friendly atmosphere was there in the spring of 1970. Alec Clegg worked on possible initiatives in the spheres of teacher, student and pupil exchanges, drama, music and other cultural activities. He obtained details on the minority of schools in the West Riding which taught Russian to 'O' and to 'A' Level and was well prepared for the Joint Meeting to be held in October 1971. These promising preliminaries were frozen by the indefinite postponement of the October 1971 meeting and for Alec Clegg this Soviet connection was at an end.

The presence of Alec Clegg on the Committee was valued not only by the Chairman, Lord Trevelyan, G.C.M.G., C.I.E., O.B.E. former H.M. Ambassador to the Soviet Union (1962-1965) but by others such as Lord Hunt, C.B.E., D.S.O. leader of the British Everest Expedition and Chairman of the Parole Board. Lord Hunt had spoken on courses at Woolley Hall and when Alec Clegg joined the Committee wrote "... I see myself playing a very inadequate second fiddle to yourself." A friendly overstatement but an indication of the place occupied by the Chief Education Officer and the West Riding in the eyes of many prominent public figures.

CHAPTER 20

CHANGE WITHIN AND WITHOUT -
THE WEST RIDING IN THE NATIONAL CONTEXT

Alec Clegg distrusted rigid administrative frameworks which could trap the occupants and offer little encouragement to personal initiative. The education services he saw abroad were in most cases constituted to provide a common national service. In Britain there was not only a public and private sector, but considerable scope for initiatives to be taken by education authorities and individual schools. Alec Clegg saw this pattern of education as an opportunity for the particular needs of each locality to be met. Furthermore local innovation was a potential source of general progress. Sybil Marshall's account of eighteen years at Kingston County Primary School, near Cambridge illustrates how the skill and achievements of a village schoolmistress can influence not only the locality but the nation. (1) There were similar examples in the West Riding such as Brodsworth Church of England School which had a firm foothold in the old rural order centred on Brodsworth Hall. The school is described in 'The Changing Primary School' and the resourceful headmistress turned it into one of the most innovative schools in South Yorkshire. She took note of Alec Clegg's advice to avoid letting the eleven plus dominate the work of the school, as he put it 'Open it out or shut it!'. The other teacher at this school was unqualified but very good. She became another example of what Alec Clegg did for those who had the quality but not the qualification. He supported her for a placement on a teaching course and she qualified very well. To the pessimist examples of innovative schools were no more than a scatter of spice on an overall pattern of mediocrity. The evidence of the Plowden Committee showed this was false.

PLOWDEN SURVEY OF PRIMARY SCHOOLS

(All 20,664 Primary Schools in England apart from 676 which were too new or 'for some other reason could not be classified' are included).

Categories	No. of Schools	No. of Children	% of total Primary Population
1. 'In most respects a school of outstanding quality.' The pace-makers.	109	29,000	1.0%
2. Good school with some out-standing features. Far above average but lacking the special touches of rare distinction.	1,538		9.0%
3. A good school in most respects without any special distinction.	4,155		23.0%
4. A school without many good features but showing signs of life with seeds of growth in it.	3,385		16.0%
5. A school with too many weak-nesses to go in Category 2 or 3 but distinguished by specially good personal relationships. Some had large numbers of immigrant children and cannot hope to attain the achievements of 2 or 3 BUT 'do splendid social work'.	1,384		0.6%
6. A decent school without enough merit to go in to 5 but too solid for 8	6,058		28.0%
7. 'Curates egg school' with good and bad features. Likely to drop into 8 but can move up. Disparity often between upper and lower part of the school. Infant / Junior Schools.	2,022		9.0%

Categories	No. of Schools	No. of Children	% of total Primary Population
8. A school markedly out of touch with current practice and with few compensating factors.	1,309		5.0%
9. A bad school where children suffer from laziness, indifference, gross incompentence and unkindness on the part of the teachers.	28	4,333	0.1%

The table represents a solid core of thorough work headed by the hope that schools in the middle groups will seek to join the pacemakers. At the bottom is a group of 28 schools which like their counterparts in the hospital emergency wards are likely to need the educational equivalent of surgery. The appreciation that schools can move up and down this group of categories, and that there can be acceleration in the process of ascent or decline is clear. Also it is clear that the quality of relationships in a school community plays a very important part in this process. The importance of social work in townships like Batley to the development of its schools cannot be underestimated. Hence Category 5 is more one of promise than dismay.

The Plowden Report dealt with primary education in the mid-sixties and it recommended changes which could lead to improvements. The Committee members saw their duty was "... to see the primary school not only in its strictly educational context but also as a part of society and of the economy." Hence they dealt with issues such as educational priority areas, and the relationship between education and other departments such as health and social services. Understandably little was done on long term social trends such as those dealt with in 'The Symmetrical Family' by Michael Young and Peter Willmott. The first chapter of the book entitled 'The Slow March' expresses the principle which they felt lay behind many social changes. P.33 -

"... many social changes start at the top and work downwards." Society is likened to a column with those in the van identified with the future whilst the rear represent the past. Think of the column crossing a bridge which is the present, with the pacemakers at the front. If the column is orderly, sociable and well motivated it can progress. Like schools in the West Riding those in the column would not be in step, but on a bridge this is an advantage for its framework and the individuality of the travellers is preserved.

Social change, whether it is good or bad, can be accelerated by emergencies. The 1939 - 45 war certainly prompted a speed up in social change. Peace brought a slow down and a chance for stability and goodwill to become the foundation of steady progress. A mix of ill researched initiatives coupled with gross acceleration could bring acute disorder. The term accelerated evolution could describe the changes which took place in the West Riding between 1945 and 1974. Alec Clegg endeavoured to ensure that the bridge to the future did not suffer the synchronised tread of innumerable feet.

One of the sources of the transformation of the primary schools in the West Riding was a vacation course held at Bingley College in 1948. Arthur Stone and a group of H.M.I.'s ran the course. They could be looked upon as the pacemakers. The effects of the course were described by Alec Clegg as "... neither immediate nor dramatic," (2) but there is no doubt that it played its part in prompting the changes which took place in a few schools in the south of the county. Alec Clegg visited these schools and said of one -

"I will never forget going into the school in South Kirby where paintings, the like of which I had never seen before were on display at child height." He had a similar experience watching a movement class in Castleford.

The opposite to the pacemakers in the West Riding were described by Brian Plummer in his 'Tales of a Rat Hunting Man'. (3) [2]He was a Biology teacher who spent a short time in 'Mexborough, Glorious Mexborough'.

Brian Plummer was interviewed by a headteacher whom he described as "... a quaint old man straight out of Martin Chuzzlewit who had been born at the age of sixty five and had oddly archaic views about everything" Brian Plummer retained his sanity by hunting rats which flourished around the nearby maggot factories. His bizarre social life enabled him to survive the head and his staff who in his view were "... ready for premature burial."

The inertia in some schools was a constant source of irritation to some advisers and to Alec Clegg.

The identifiaction and encouragement of the pacemakers was one of the functions of the advisers. Local in-service training and courses at Woolley Hall and elsewhere enabled new ideas to be discussed, refined and in many cases followed in other schools. In his study of 'Innovation and Research in Education'(4) Michael Young suggests that -

"... educators should learn about themselves by trial and error, by doing new things and watching what happens." The impact of this approach would he felt "... be greatest in the classroom." The concluding sentences of the book echo the beliefs of Alec Clegg and his administrative team - (5)

"If the signal coming from society has been read aright there will be a new combination of forces, one which should (I believe) enable educational reformers to come nearer to the achievement of long-standing objectives - to teach children, and allow them to teach themselves, without institutionalizing them; to encourage intellectual growth without withering the spontaneity which young children bring to school; to treat children as individuals rather than as junior members of a mass society; to replace authority by something more like a partnership between adults and children, learning together. The hope is that a more scientific approach to education will do something to make it more human."

Those heads and teachers content to remain as immutable onlookers to the column crossing the bridge could, with reorganisation in some of the divisions of the West Riding, find themselves deprived of the power to stand in the way of progress. The promise of new appointments and an injection of new ideas depended on the process of selection, and, unfortunately the custom of favouring local candidates was well entrenched in some parts of the West Riding. Castleford in the mid sixties illustrates the sort of difficulties which had to be faced by the central administration. The area had its pacemakers such as Mrs Pyrah, but it posed Alec Clegg and his staff serious problems in the field of appointments. The favouring of local candidates led in one case to the County Committee considering the refusal of support for the choice made by the Staffing Committee. The anticipated confrontation between them did not take place as the chosen candidate withdrew. Caretaking and teaching appointments were the subject of a series of detailed reports. These reports led to Alec Clegg seeking to change the constitution of the Staffing Sub-Committee so as to reduce the possiblity of poor quality local candidates being appointed. The correspondence between Alec Clegg and the Clerk to the West Riding led to him advising Alec Clegg that, not only would this resolution of 15th February 1949 which established the present representation have to be rescinded, but that there would be strenuous objections from the Association of Divisional Executives. As the Clerk put it "... They would say that most of them are honest and why should we beat all of them with the same stick." The solution seemed a stick in the right place. Local opposition to Central Office surfaced in January 1965 when local councillors were put under intense pressure to reject the 5-9, 9-13, 13-18 reorganisation scheme. Ernest Peet sent many details of what he regarded as locally biassed appointments for caretaking posts and delays in making appointments which had very adverse effects on schools. The presence of such irritation between local and central committees could reassure the immutables and prove a barrier to change. Moreover the build up of a national reputation for quality education could be put in jeopardy if one or more of the West Riding divisions earned a reputation for favouring local candidates.

Alec Clegg's letters contain many surprises but few can match a twelve page one to a friend who was due to visit some West Riding schools early in the new year of 1957. He wrote the letter on Christmas morning, December 1956, and in it mapped out future developments in the county education service. He foresaw the changes already taking place in the primary sector spreading through the junior schools and gaining a foothold in the secondary sector. He wrote -

"It will take us another five years to establish this theory for good and all in the junior schools and 15 years to get it going at the secondary stage dependent of course on the enlightenment of our secondary heads." He wanted to avoid publicity for he was afraid that sensible change could be portrayed as a stunt. As he put it -

"I don't want it to get precious. I don't want to shoot a line about it - but if my judgment is correct we shall slowly and surely change the pattern of education in this country in the next 10 years."

The letter to Mrs Summers ended -

"This is the longest letter I've written in 10 years and I hope I never write another and I've spent Xmas morning doing it so neither you nor I are popular in this house at the moment." His anticipation that many junior schools would adopt new methods did take place. Moreover the middle schools and a number of comprehensives built new approaches to syllabuses and teaching methods on the changing primary foundation. Hindsight showed the pace of change at secondary level was probably faster than Alec Clegg foresaw on the Christmas morning.

Woolley Hall was to a large extent the parliament of pacemakers where administrators, inspectors, advisers and those in progressive, or would be progressive, schools could meet to discuss new ideas. By the sixties the advisory service was firmly established and the Wardens at Woolley began to detect an element of repetition in some courses, which threatened to turn the new ideas into dogma with an official West Riding policy stamp on it. This was the last thing Alec Clegg wanted, but it began to happen in some of the courses aimed at Junior School staffs. It was good sense to use the local environment as a source of interest, but if it was reduced to an annual routine with rules for presentation and display, the element of individuality for each youngster was reduced. Similarly innovation in the secondary school could, if reduced to a succession of photocopied notes and questionnaires, be not very different from textbook based exercises. In some schools the photocopies were often more difficult to read than well printed textbooks, and time was often wasted inking in the indistinct passages.

Teachers had to realise that personal translation held out the promise of lessons retaining a quality which could generate and hold interest. Robert Nye's firstness could be applied to teachers as well as pupils at almost any level in education.

One of the areas of the secondary curriculum which was closely related to the local environment as a source of primary innovation was Rural Studies. Harry Day, adviser for this subject, sent detailed reports to Alec Clegg and those covering the years 1955 to 1966 illustrate the practical problems of an imaginative adviser. He went to 55 secondary schools in three months in 1955 and followed this with a tour of primary schools. The Woolley Hall courses he and other advisers set up aimed to encourage a wider approach to living things. In 1962 he wrote that "... the thing that most depresses me about Rural Studies is that the bigger our secondary schools become the more the subject tends to be reserved for the older, less able boys." The Schools Council scheme in Integrated Science promised to pull all aspects of science into one, but it faced considerable opposition in schools and industry. The two ordinary level certificates which rewarded the successful pupils were regarded as inferior to passes in single sciences. The consequence was that serious doubt was cast on Integrated Science as a route to vocational success.

The urbanisation of Britain and its social consequences lay behind much of what Alec Clegg advocated in the field of social education. Harry Day drew attention to the failure of many county boroughs in West Yorkshire to encourage Rural Studies. He argued, "... This country will be pretty well urbanised by the year 2000 and the non believers must realise that Rural Studies provide a solid contrast to the artificial, mechanised world they are so busily creating." Courses which moved the subject away from school gardening to the environment in a wider sense, included one held at Ruskin's old home at Brantwood, Coniston during the summer of 1965. This course led to a request to the Forestry Commission to make Selby Forest available to nearby West Riding schools. The isolation of Rural Studies as a subject for less able boys was broken down by initiatives such as the use of naturally grown materials in Needlework. Other points of integration were identified so that a genuine integrated curriculum could be steadily built up. Ferry Fryston, a new secondary school, explored such areas of development in the sixties. Aireville Secondary School, at Skipton, had a similarly progressive Rural Studies department which built up an animal bank. This bank was used by some 20 junior schools in the area in conjunction with the development of the Nuffield Junior Science Project.

Courses at Woolley ranged from those which prompted secondary teachers to examine their attitudes, methods and standards to those which concentrated on new ideas and how they might be put into practice. The team which took one of the early courses aimed at grammar school staffs was described by the Warden in these terms -

"Each speaker will deal with a separate aspect of the general problem of enabling children in Grammar Schools to learn for themselves and of encouraging them independently and successfully to undertake further study." (6)

This course had a star cast which aimed to dig at least some of the immutables out of their ruts. During the next year, 1960, courses involving Dr Raistrick, an outstanding local historian; Eric Simms, a man with a national reputation for his studies of wildlife and the Warden of Swillington Ings brought to Woolley that rare mix of enthusiasm and deep, practical knowledge. Their knowledge had the characteristic of firstness and could give to teachers that spark which could fire change.

Courses such as these, which could involve junior, middle and secondary school teachers, could suggest ways in which the changes initiated in infant and junior schools in the fifties, could be continued in the secondary schools. The ways forward could in many cases be in association with Schools Council Projects which gave them the prospect of local and national acceptability.

Perhaps the changes in the aims and contents of courses reflected changes in the personnel of the advisory service. Whatever the cause the regular courses, which the Warden of Woolley saw as mere repeats, were overtaken by courses based on new ideas. The new pacemakers replaced the old but their style was perhaps, to those reading this description two or more decades later, unexpected for pacemakers are generally associated with ambition and the urge to push ahead. A course entitled 'Pattern and Structure in Nature' run by Harry Day typifies this style. He began with a tribute to Basil Rocke, Art Adviser, who Harry Day felt had profoundly influenced his views on education. The Warden of Woolley described this team of speakers as first class "... sensitive, gentle people, completely identified with Harry Day's philosophy."

In 1957 Alec Clegg drew up a detailed reply to a Fabian Society questionnaire on comprehensive education. He had contacts with Fabians such as Michael Young and John Vaizey in the sixties and a lengthy correspondence with Roy Hattersley and Shirley Williams in the seventies. The Fabian Society's view on social and economic change was characterised by the tortoise which could have equally well served as a symbol of educational change in the West Riding. However the assumptions which lay behind some of the questions put by the Fabian team drew strong criticism from Alec Clegg. He could agree that the comprehensive school was a thoroughly sound idea, but he added "If it is mishandled it might achieve both educationally and socially the exact reverse of what its supporters intend." The newly set up comprehensives would in many cases fuel a powerful pressure to match, or to surpass, the academic achievements of the grammar schools which they replaced hence, "... the effort which needs to be available for the whole schools will be sucked into provision for the ablest." The lower 60% of the intelligence range could suffer and, if as the Fabian questionnaire assumed a national standard curriculum was established, any chance of inspiring this large group would be almost completely snuffed out.

As in so many of the articles he wrote, or speeches he gave, Alec Clegg dwelt on fundamentals -

"It is one thing to teach a child to read; it is another thing to teach a child to want to read ...". "In other words, it is the form and the letter of education which is the least important, and only this can be tested. The substance and the spirit is not examinable, or only examinable by the most skillful methods which cannot be suppled to the mass."

By the time Michael Young and Michael Armstrong wrote 'New Look at Comprehensive schools' (7), in 1964 the West Riding middle school scheme centred on 5 to 9, 9 to 13 and 13 to 18 upper schools was one of the alternatives for comprehensive reorganisation. Not only would this scheme make sense from the standpoint of available buildings in the West Riding, but as the authors put it - Page 17 - "It is not only the top of the high school, to some extent it is the whole of the school which is influenced by exam pressure, that ever present threat to sound education. If only children could be insulated from that pressure until they actually had to start an 'O' level they would be much better served; and the way to do that, of course is to extend the primary school - in any case the star of British education - up to 13."

By 1971 the Young Fabian pamphlet on 'Aspects of Education' (8) had as one of its studies 'Selective principles operating within schools'. Streaming was seen as "... an equivalent to the now disreputable 11 plus examination", "... and the Labour party was advised to consider legislation against streaming within schools". The rigidity of streaming in many comprehensive schools, and the detrimental effects it had on middle and lower ability youngsters, had been a subject of considerable research. The National Foundation for Educational Research Report on streaming concluded that streaming did not make any difference to the achievements of bright youngsters, but it had an adverse effect on the social and emotional development of the average and below average children.

In 1972 preparations were underway for a Fabian publication which aimed to cover a wide range of issues in social and economic policy. Alec Clegg was asked to prepare an article on Education. In a humorous letter to Shirley Williams in May 1972 he began by asking -

"There is just one thing that I should like to know - how do you intend to introduce us all - not necessarily I take it as committed adherents to your party - because in my case this would not be true. I have in fact voted for all three parties in my time in the West Riding and successfully kept out of office each party I have voted for."

Alec Clegg gathered detailed information from members of his staff, such as Reg Eyles and Barry Willcock, and from councillors blending their views and his into a very concise summary of the West Riding's achievements, or problems, up to 1972. This summary was set against a shrewd assessment of the national position. The realism which characterised much of what Alec Clegg wrote was echoed in one sentence in Roy Hattersley's draft of the introduction.

It read - "That final victory is not possible for a socialist party which crawls into power under the smokescreen of Conservative unpopularity." The exchange of views with the Fabians between 1957 and the end of the West Riding shows how Alec Clegg fitted snugly into Shirley Williams description of him as a "... professional political neutral, who advocates a radical educational policy to all the parties." Such a policy had been accepted by political parties in the West Riding in his early years. By the seventies it was a national feature linked with Alec Clegg, and underlined by his participation in a series of national reports on education.

Perceptive politicians valued the independence, foresight and experience of Alec Clegg and Sir Edward Boyle was not making an over the top remark when he described Alec Clegg as the conscience of the Education Service. In a conversation with Maurice Kogan in 1971 (9) he explained this claim saying that - "Sir Alec Clegg, C.E.O. of the West Riding ... carried weight simply by sheer force of being who he was, the person he was, and who made himself the spokesman of the Newsom child and the spokesman of the less fortunate in our society. He didn't just go on about the less fortunate, he became the accepted conscience of Curzon Street this way". He ended -

"There were a few people, who didn't always agree with one another, or with the Ministry, like Alexander, Sir Ronald Gould, Alec Clegg, who had a position which nobody gave them; they simply had it, commanded it."

Maurice Kogan saw a lot of common ground and continuity in the work of Sir Edward Boyle and Anthony Crosland at the Ministry of Education in the sixties. In his words -

"Boyle and Crosland's personal and political beliefs fitted and contributed to the complex movement of ideas affecting the education service in the 1960's. Their particular style and contribution were, however, individual."

The position at Curzon Street must in some ways have seemed a reflection of that at County Hall, Wakefield. In his preface to the Newsom Report, Edward Boyle wrote that -

"... there is above all a need for new modes of thought, and a change of heart, on the part of the community as a whole." Only with such changes would all children -

"... have an equal opportunity of acquiring intelligence, and of developing their talents and abilities to the full." Sir Edward Boyle remoulded many of the educational views of his party, but his stand on race relations and the abolition of the death penalty contributed to a Conservative reaction against his educational views. This reaction was epitomised in the first two Black Papers. Crosland had a clearer programme than Boyle, but he opposed quick surgery to end the tripartite system.

Maurice Kogan described the position of these two Ministers in the British educational system in this passage which again had echoes of the political situation in the West Riding. (10)

"Because Ministers have chosen, and local authorities have naturally reinforced their choice, not to wield all of the authority they possess, two consequences have resulted. First, there is remarkable, and beneficial, variety in British education, as compared with, say, France. Secondly, Ministers cannot carry through policies simply by virtue of clear thinking. They have to carry the system with them. Both Boyle and Crosland saw this and were good at it."

All this was likely to change if the recommendations of the Royal Commission on Local Government (11) were accepted by the Heath Government which took office in 1970. One of the recommendations was that the West Riding should end as a local authority and be parcelled out to thirteen new authorities. Alec Clegg maintained that this change would mean that - "... every school in the West Riding would eventually be placed in an authority drawing on more meagre resources that those which the present County Council command." (12) The West Riding was the only authority which faced total dismemberment and the prospect that many of the special services, vital to impoverished areas, would disappear was particularly grim. No writer of tragedy could have conceived a worse scenario than to spend the final years taking apart a lifetime's work.

Executioners are not popular people and it was during her span of office at the Ministry of Education that Margaret Thatcher took the decision to implement the recommendations on local government reorganisation. She supported the Chancellor, Anthony Barber's measures to cut taxes and subsidies and she robustly defended the decision to cut expenditure on school milk. On the other hand she ensured that any doubt about the future of the Open University was ended, and that investment in school building, particularly nursery schools which had been recom-mended in the Plowden Report was carried out. An executive rather than an executioner in these matters, and judging by many of Alec Clegg's apocryphal or actual remarks one who prompted humour as much as criticism. He was reported to have remarked during one of their early meetings that she appeared "immaculate without conception" and that her short skirted lady assistant wore a pelmet. Perhaps the nearest to an assessment of the new minister was expressed in a letter to Roy Hattersley in December 1972.

"Although I am all for much of what she proposes I fear that she is going to split the teaching profession still more widely into university sheep and college goats. She is going to erect a teaching hierarchy based on theoretical qualifications only and I suspect her in-service training programmes may well be carried out by pundits who have been far too long out of the classroom, and all these points worry me."

The death of County Alderman Mrs Fitzpatrick in spring 1972 and the departure of his deputy to London underlined for Alec Clegg how the personal elements which comprised so much of the West Riding's rich framework were ending. The last two years were to be the sternest test of Alec Clegg's qualities as a skilled administrator and creative educationalist. 1974 would see the end of one of the most successful post war education authorities in Britain. This was a disaster but deliverance could be at hand if its style was carried into the new authorities.

CHAPTER 21

RIDING FOR A FALL
The end of the West Riding

The decade before the West Riding ceased to exist saw a sequence of public enquiries, two of which dealt with changes in the Wakefield and Barnsley areas. Alec Clegg gave evidence at both of these enquiries and in both cases he stressed the advantages of the large innovative authority and pointed to the many positive features of the West Riding which lay beyond the bare statistics. By the time he summarised the case against the reorganisation of local government in the Times Educational Supplement in April 1971 it seemed that, no matter how convincing his arguments were, the die was cast against the survival of the West Riding.

The public enquiries involving Wakefield and Barnsley illustrate some of the local pressures for independence, an independence that could in some respects be dogmatic and short sighted. Another factor rarely if ever declared but always there for consideration was the impending retirement of key players such as Alec Clegg. It seems that circumstances not ideals and the chance of educational advance dictated the end of the West Riding. The Chief Education Officer's final service would be to parcel out to the inheritors the material and intangible assets of the West Riding. For ambitious local politicians with new local authorities in their sights the opportunity of being a bigger fish in a smaller pond was attractive. The promise of advancement on top of survival was a factor which could deprive the West Riding of the support its achievements deserved.

The proof of evidence given by Alec Clegg to the Public Enquiry on 9th February 1965 was prefaced by an important correction of the figures used by Mr Barnes when he gave evidence on behalf of Wakefield. (1) The inference drawn from the figures was that Wakefield, unlike the West Riding, was able to attract its quota of teachers whilst the West Riding remained a hundred short of its target. Mr Barnes used the quota figure for the wrong year and Alec Clegg was able to point out not only that the West Riding met its quota, but that it exercised its right to exceed that figure by a limited amount.If this is an example of the inevitable factual exchanges of public enquiries then the remainder of Alec Clegg's proof was exact and convincing in favour of a large authority. It provided special services such as teams of professional musicians, peripatetic staff, the School Museum Service, institutions such as Woolley Hall, the inspectors and advisers and the Library Service. Initiatives in any sector of the Education Service could be assessed, and if promising, put to others as a possible line of development. Comparisons could be attempted but at the start of the proof Alec Clegg pointed out.

"It would be an extremely difficult task to attempt to make any comparison between the achievements of any two Local Education authorities. A team of sociologists and educationalists would have to spend months if not years analysing the social composition of the population, testing the native endowment of the children, and following this up with tests of achievement at different ages and levels, studying the delinquency rates, staffing ratios, rates of pay, and administrative arrangements, and much else. And when all was done the comparison would not be valid because in the education service there are so many imponderables such as the effect of strong personality on the child mind and the variable factors are legion." (2)

The modes of reorganisation in Wakefield and Barnsley at secondary level were criticised by Alec Clegg. Wakefield decided to admit all children aged eleven to what were their modern schools, and to guide at least a third of them at the age of thirteen into the grammar school or the Wakefield direct grant schools. Alec Clegg felt the scheme was 'a monstrosity' and quoted the Crowther Report which maintained -

"What is extracted from the pool of ability depends much less on the content of the pool than on the effectiveness of the pump". Guidance not selection was the Wakefield recipe for the reorganisation at secondary level, whilst Barnsley opted for a double selection procedure centred round their conviction of the importance of the Central School. They maintained the Central School did "... so much for the boys and girls who have failed to obtain admission to Grammar Schools ...". The evidence given by the West Riding to these two public enquiries is detailed, well-presented and convincing yet one cannot escape the feeling that the dogmatic independence of some areas of the West Riding would not go away. It would reappear as soon as proposals for local government change were put forward.

The bleak future for the small, new authorities which would replace the West Riding was described by Alec Clegg in the Times Educational Supplement in April 1971. (3,4) He began with a question which was to be answered by an emphatic 'Yes' five columns later.

"Are we going to turn Newsom's 'problem areas' into the smallest and poorest local education authorities in the country, and if so does this mean that the areas of greatest need will be areas of least resource?"

The problem areas were not slums but districts of poor housing, poor amenities, low rateable value and where most of the available work was for semi skilled or unskilled workers. The reading attainment of children in these areas was eight months behind other areas and the areas had more difficulty than others in retaining teaching staff. Fewer children from these areas went to grammar schools and those that did often left at 15. The Crowther Report showed that sons of manual workers who went into the army, and who were in the top two ability groups had in a majority of cases left school at 15. The Plowden Report called for investment in these problem areas which went "... well beyond an attempt to equalise resources." The typical families which lived in problem areas comprised about 27% of those who lived in Sheffield and Leeds, but 43% of those who lived in Featherstone and 46% of who lived in Castleford or Hemsworth.

The reorganisation proposals would see only two of the minor local authorities in the Wakefield district with below 30% of these families. With fewer amenities and low ratable values these new authorities like Wakefield seem to be poverty stricken areas deliberately designed by the state. The smallest of the proposed new authorities were concentrated in the North (15) and in the Midlands (4) with none in the South. Alec Clegg followed this detailed study with alternative proposals for larger metropolitan authorities. In spite of the cogency of his case Alec Clegg envisaged the inevitable black clouds of the future ending his article with these words -

"With these alternatives open it seems incredible that a scheme could be adopted which from the point of view of education is for some districts not only the worst that has been conceived but one which is patently in complete conflict with so much expert advice and which is likely still further to handicap some of the most deprived areas of the country".

When Alec Clegg considered the administrative implications of the end of the West Riding yet another collection of difficulties was highlighted. Senior staff, such as Area Education Officers, would have to seek even more senior posts if they were to maintain their salaries. Furthermore the specialist posts, which met the needs of large authorities such as the West Riding, would face either erratic, or insufficient, demand for their services in a small authority. A good example in 1972 was building where the government released money for projects undertaken in relation to the raising of the school leaving age. The building industry faced the prospect of being stretched beyond its capacity and as Alec Clegg pointed out (5) -

"When this happens an authority which is going out of existence, which cannot enforce a penalty clause, which has lost the bait of future contracts and which has to invite fixed price tenders for jobs which won't be finished before the demise of the employer, is almost bound to suffer grievous delays."

The style of administration which might be adopted in the new authorities drew this comment:

"... there is more than a danger that the new districts will seek to pile management with a capital 'M' on to administration with a capital 'A', to recruit 'managers' rather than education officers, and to take other deleterious steps for which they will quote the Bains' view that it is 'undesirable' to require a local authority to appoint particular committees. Lastly he felt that any mistakes and problems experienced in the early period of reorganisation could, and would, be blamed on the West Riding stewardship before 1974." (6)

When one sets the very detailed evidence gathered by Alec Clegg on reorganisation against its justification by the Department of Education and Science it is difficult to escape the conclusion that the die was cast, there was no need to counter, just wait until 1974. The Department of Education and Science put its case for ending the West Riding in a letter dated 30th November 1971. (7) It stressed that the pattern of local government "... bears little relationship to present day conditions and the Government decided, therefore, that a change in the administrative pattern of the West Riding was called for." It went on to stress that the new authorities should be big enough to provide an efficient services. Its final belief was that "... much will be gained from having education authorities large enough to provide an efficient service and yet sufficiently locally based to be in close touch with local conditions and individual educational establishments." The factual details of the West Riding Education Service and the intangibles that contributed to its reputation are neglected in this reply and one turns immediately to the final remarks of Gosden and Sharp's account of 'The Development of an Education Service. The West Riding 1889-1974'.

P. 232 - "Originally the reformers believed that there should be no statutory requirement to have education committees. Pressure from education interests, however, led to second thoughts and the statutory requirement for education committees survived the reforms. Even so, the practice of corporate management has led in some authorities to the determination of educational policy by persons who have neither experience nor understanding of, nor contact with the school system. Opponents of the new approach argue that the emphasis has come to be placed upon local government for its own sake and no longer on the quality of the individual services it provides, that education is no longer seen as a national service administered locally. It is certainly a fact that although statutory education committees have survived, many of them were made to withdraw from their national organisation, the Association of Education Committees, so that that organisation has come to an end. It will be the task of future historians to assess the impact of these events."

The last years of the West Riding provide a flood of evidence of what people from all walks of life felt the authority and its Chief Education Officer stood for and provided. It is evidence of how a public service had met a remarkable range and number of individual needs. Its achievements prompt one to reflect that changes in frameworks provide no guarantee that existing qualities will be preserved, or that new qualities will be encouraged. If what is already in existence is ignored then the Department of Education's view of reorganisation and its implementation was little more than allocating what called for delicate surgery from a blind man to a butcher.

A VIEW OF THE FUTURE

One of the main themes of the final years of the West Riding was the deep concern Alec Clegg had on the condition of English society. He saw a pressing need to take effective action to reverse the damaging trends such as the rise in the number of divorces; in the number of abandoned children; in the number of children living in thoroughly bad homes and the number of illegitimate births. Consideration of these worrying changes prompted him to reflect on the condition of the Welfare State, which twenty five years earlier had aimed to remove some, even many, of the worst symptoms of injustice. In his view it had "... merely succeeded in propping up a generally poor status quo." (8) Richard Titmuss went further in expressing his concern on the Welfare State writing in the late sixties that it was viewed by many as "... unnecessary doctrinaire burden on private enterprise." (9)

The information Alec Clegg received on social matters in the West Riding came from a variety of sources. Mr R Woolfe, Research Officer, provided him with details on such issues as maladjusted children, juvenile crime and delinquency and he could indicate which areas and schools faced the biggest problems. What Mr Woolfe could not distinguish was the effects of school experience on these problems. Headteachers, such as Miss Canning of Simpson's Lane Infants School, gave details of individual youngsters and their particular needs. She followed these details with a series of proposals of how these needs could be met. Her programme of educational and welfare provision began with the suggestion that by 1973 every class in her school should have a non-teaching assistant. The remainder of the programme comprised the addition of a Family Planning Clinic, an Ante-Natal Clinic, a Toddlers' Clinic, a Coffee Bar, a telephone, and Marriage Guidance and Medical Rooms. These suggestions echoed Alec Clegg's wish to integrate the work of educational, medical and social services in the interests of youngsters and their families.

The exchanges between Alec Clegg and Leonard Elmhirst on the Dartington Conisbrough exchange scheme and on the work of the Carnegie Centre at Minsthorpe show how at secondary level the 'sphere of education was being enlarged to deal with the needs of problem areas. Apart from discussing the progress of these initiatives they considered the establishment of Liberal Arts Colleges which could be attached to Universities. Alec Clegg discussed this issue with Catherine Avant, (10) who dealt with Youth Employment in the Inner London Education Authority, and he was intent upon carrying the matter further at Leeds University.

Miss Canning gave a clear idea of the extra services and resources needed in a problem area on top of the provision of innovative teaching. High quality nursery, junior or middle schools with additional services could go a long way towards nurturing a genuine interest in education. But would this interest continue, or would it lapse in the comprehensive schools? One answer was given by a fourteen year old boy from Skellow in an essay he wrote entitled 'Schools 1000, 2000, 3000 - where will they end? His mother died when he was five and two years later his father died, then he was brought up by his grandmother. His step-grandfather resented his presence and rarely if ever talked to him so his life up to fourteen contained many elements which constituted a child in distress. Yet he was described as 'very well adjusted despite a hard background.' The character of the schools, their organisation and his classroom experience drew the following comments -

"The only distinguishing mark, from school to school being the colour of their blazers, or the quality or consistency of their football teams."

"In England the lessons tend to get extremely boring, kids are herded into classrooms, sat at the same desks, scribbling the same obscenities on the same lids, while the same teachers dictate the same lessons in the same monogramic tone."

"It is hard enough for teachers to learn the names of kids they teach twice a week. In some cases they teach up to 250 kids ... How can teachers recognise and help individually the kid who is not backward, just a little bit slow? These kids (and there are a great many of them) have the ability to do well, and can gain awards, but only if they are brought out of their shell by that bit of extra attention, by that bit of individual coaching." He continued -

"These kids, are the unhappy ones and the ones who waste themselves by leaving at the earliest opportunity through the simple reason of being unhappy." He felt the whole set up was boring and that education had lost its flair and enjoyment. The letter ended - "To educational bigwigs - Smaller schools please." The implication of the plea for smaller schools was that they would be happier and more personal places. However there were impersonal small schools and for Alec Clegg and his staff it was what went on within the school framework that mattered rather than the framework itself.

Perhaps the grammar school base of the comprehensive where this boy went played a significant part in the ethos of the school, whilst comprehensives which grew from modern schools developed with ample experience of the needs of the majority. Alec Clegg was interviewed by Jonathan Stedall in March 1970 in preparation for a searching television programme on private and state education. The programme contained fascinating detail on the high quality private Sevenoaks school and on the education in Rossington from nursery schools to the comprehensive sixth form. These schools had a rich record of progress and the Skellow essayist may well have found they met his needs and provided him with enjoyment. If the range and number of lectures and the sales of books such as 'Children in Distress' (11) are added to his appearances on television and radio then the importance of the West Riding and its Chief Education Officer to English educational ideas is abundantly clear.

The apprehension Alec Clegg had on the future of educational administration was confirmed in a letter from a former West Riding adviser who took up a new post in Sheffield in 1971. The adviser reflected on his experience in the West Riding and compared it to his new job saying -

"We have gone 'management mad,' however, and relationships with Heads and teachers are nowhere near the type we achieved in the Riding." Alec Clegg was regularly reminded of the part personal relationships had played in the West Riding by a steady flow of letters, many of which reflected on decisions which had altered the writers' lives. Typical was one from a young man who had gained a 2:1 in Horticulture from Wye College, London University. Originally he had been at Bowland Secondary School but was backed by the West Riding for a transfer to Clitheroe Royal Grammar school where he took 'O' and 'A' level examinations. He wrote - "It would, however, have been impossible to have got anywhere without the assistance of the W R C C - materially and 'spiritually' (for I felt the W R C C actually took a personal interest in my case and my progress.)

A letter from a mother of four young children in Kings Lynn who had spent her childhood in Brampton Bierlow had as its centrepiece the personal support she received from Alec Clegg to get a place at Barnsley Technical College. Her father was a miner suffering from silicosis and her mother had had to undertake a variety of part-time jobs to keep the family solvent. Her memory of the secondary modern school she attended was expressed in one telling sentence -

"Dirt, poverty, boring misery, and the daily call of 'hands up free dinners' to a child in second hand clothes, left us with a gaunt nervousness which I still struggle to suppress." She passed two 'A' levels and seven 'O' levels and felt the minor award, travel expenses and lunch vouchers that Alec Clegg had got the committee to agree had been a turning point in her life. She worked with the National Union of Railwaymen and combined it with an extra-mural course at London University. Her next move was to Westminster where as she put it - "I moved to the lower rungs of the Cabinet Office, working for the statisticians on questions for the Cabinet Ministers, and staying about four years." One cannot escape the conclusion that letters such as these pin-point the importance of personal connections and also how much talent may have lain undetected in administrative frameworks which were built around a collection of formal relationships and rules. Late developers is an inappropriate description for those youngsters and adults who by fate, chance or choice, did not reveal or develop their talents at school. There is a clear echo of the feelings expressed to Alec Clegg in a letter he wrote to an 'old Bradfordian' who sent him the Memorial Service Programme for Sir Henry Thirkill, former Master of Clare College, Cambridge. As he wrote -

"I suppose there must be many people of all ages from time to time say to themselves that they owe more to Henry Thirkill than to almost anyone they know. I am certainly one of these. Both my parents died in my second year at Clare and I had no idea where money would come from to see me through my course. I was given an Exhibition and Henry Thirkill lent me additional money which enabled me to finish, and did so with as little fuss as he would have made over handing me a penny stamp." (12)

The exchange of reminiscences can give the impression of the final years being a comfortable twilight. This was not the case for Alec Clegg's life was punctuated with criticism of his policy and matters such as foreign visits. A manager of two primary schools in Bingley saw Alec Clegg's primary changes as 'gimmicks' and 'crazes' which had been accompanied with the destruction of the past which had been thrown away " ... under the label of old fashioned." The substance of the criticism was that " ... children are not taught or encouraged to spell correctly, neither are they taught their multiplication tables nor in many cases allowed to learn them." Criticism which had little foundation in fact scarcely merited detailed rebuttal but if it gained public support it had to be addressed. In a memorandum Alec Clegg sent to his staff in December 1972 he described his participation in the discussions of the Bullock Committee. (13) In it he made this significant comment -

"By and large I managed to make the points I wanted to make but it wasn't till I got towards the end of the session that I realised what was worrying the Chairman. His concern is that the 'great British public' is convinced that standards generally, not just reading standards, have dropped and it surprised me that he thought this, but it is something we ought to be prepared to do battle about." Alec Clegg asked for observations, particularly on two issues. "The first is that so called progressive work in our junior and infant school lacks 'rigour' and the other is that standards are lower."

Dennis Pickles, Senior Psychologist in the West Riding, produced a very comprehensive report on the screening procedure which covered 799 primary schools. The report was reassuring not only on the general standard of reading in the county, but on identifying once more the problem areas where social deprivation and educational problems went hand in hand. As the report put it -

"The results of the survey can be considered very reassuring regarding the general standard of reading throughout the county. According to one source of information, for example, given in the manual of the Young group reading test, the average score of 28 obtained by the West Riding children at this average age of 6 years and 11 months could be considered equivalent to a reading age of 7.0 years on the Young test and 7.4 years on the Southgate Test 1."
(14)

Eighty per cent of headteachers thought the screening was valuable and should take place annually. No doubt this conclusion was reassuring but Alec Clegg was concerned on the public viewpoint of test results in some areas, for instance in a school with a large immigrant population where the results

"... were not nearly as good as the results of a neighbouring school where there was a considerable proportion of children from professional classes and hardly any immigrants."

An exchange of letters between the Chief Education Officer and an Area Adviser for Special Education dealt with information which was to be passed on to the new local authorities. Alec Clegg refers to the well known specialists in the field of psychology quoted by the adviser and inevitably concentrates on the remedies and the serious cases rather than the overall picture. As he put it, in typical Clegg fashion -

"But I am disturbed in other ways about these screening procedures. They seem to me to be aimed at detecting the people who suffer from mild catarrh in a crowd where there are many with obvious smallpox." He went on -

"... but the folk who we should have consulted first and foremost are half a dozen of our best infant heads who know far more than you or I or these great names or even than psychologists, about the likely effect of this business." Alec Clegg reduced his standpoint to a simple proposition when he wrote to the Principal Medical Officer, Simpson Smith -

"... what we need ... is a, more efficient cure rather than a finer screen."

Alec Clegg wrote to a group of infant headteachers and amongst the replies he received was one from Maltby Manor Infants School. The aim of his enquiry was to obtain opinions and ideas on teaching reading and the training of infant teachers. In her carefully worded and detailed reply the head of Maltby Manor maintained -

"... I am sure that the skill of teaching reading is one that grows greater with experience, provided that the basic under-standing of the techniques involved, the enthusiasm for the task, and the open-minded attitude is instilled in the teacher during training." Later on in her reply the flexibility of approach is referred to again.

"Students need to be told too of the importance of talking to children, getting them to talk to you, on a 'one to one' basis as well as in small groups, and as a whole class group. Too often teachers rush into teaching reading before a child can even verbalise his own thoughts.:" The sensitivity and practicality of this letter is in stark contrast to the shallow dogma of those keen to condemn progressive methods. The emphasis upon fitting approach and method to the needs of individual children is carefully described and underpins the whole approach to the teaching of reading. This passage is another illustration of the heads approach -

"Increasingly children need to be taught to listen too, whichever method of teaching reading is employed, a varying amount of listening to and imitating sounds is necessary to the process, children need games and activities to learn to descriminate one sound from another. They need too, activities geared towards visual discrimination of shapes, and apparatus which will encourage a left to right movement of the eye, not every child faced with a line of print with no previous experience of it, would naturally begin at the left, one only has to give a child a pattern of beads to thread to discover this!"

If skilled teaching, the results of thorough screening and the expertise available in Medical and Social Services could be integrated to help youngsters with special needs there was a chance that real progress could be made. Alec Clegg pursued this goal throughout the final years of the West Riding, and to portray him as a man devoted to the maintenance of a public image of perpetual innovation is very wide of the mark.

The same attention to detail characterised Alec Clegg's response to criticism by a local M.P. of his two month visit to Australia in 1970. In a letter to the Clerk to the West Riding Council he quoted the committee resolution which authorised his acceptance of a two month travelling fellowship, one month of which was taken as part of his annual leave and the remaining month to be deemed leave of absence on full salary. If the criticism contained the inference that the visit was something of a holiday funded by the West Riding, Alec Clegg responded by giving the Clerk to the Council the following complete picture of his working life from his office diary covering the years 1967 to 1970. (15) Not only does it rebut any inference that impending retirement was shading into holiday, but gives an exact picture of the time a Chief Education Officer could, and did, devote to his work.

The two men who served as deputies to Alec Clegg during his term of office, Jim Hogan and Peter Newsom, drew attention to his modesty, or reluctance to acknowledge, how thorough and time consuming his work was. As Jim Hogan put it - "Under an air of modesty there rested a record of achievement that will be hard to equal." As some have rightly said achievement is 99% perspiration and 1% inspiration.

Apart from the 146 invitations to speak in Britain in six months Alec Clegg had requests to speak on radio and television, and to provide articles for newspapers and magazines. His state of health obliged him to refuse a majority of these invitations which by their sheer number indicate the place which the West Riding and its Chief Education Officer occupied in British education. It is easy to imagine someone in Alec Clegg's position in the early seventies taking the opportunities offered to him as an educational pundit whilst he scaled down his work in the West Riding. That he did not do this is not just an indication of his declining health, it is a reminder that his style of administration wedded him to people. He was determined to ensure his staff had a secure future. This involved more, not less, work - a mix of human reallocation along with the dismantling of a large, complex organisation.

Throughout the last few years the concern for children and young people in problem families and areas increased, partly due to the impending end of the West Riding but also through the build up of evidence that social problems in this country and elsewhere were getting worse. A detailed collection of figures based on Home Office statistics was sent to Alec Clegg by the County Children's Officer in January 1971. Categories such as 'Children from thoroughly bad homes' showed a marked increase between 1959 and 1969 (1959 - 997, 1969 - 2680) and at first glance the collection confirmed the view things were getting worse. Only two out of the nine categories showed a decrease - fewer orphans in 1969 than in 1959 and fewer children received into care because their families were homeless. This final category prompted the additional comment from the County Children's Officer -

"This alas is not the position for the West Riding, but it reflects the efforts made by many authorities to ensure that families are not broken up because they are homeless." Alec Clegg always sought detailed evidence and as soon as detail was injected into this general picture it changed for the worse. In trying to assess the social problems British schools might face in the future Alec Clegg often drew upon information from the United States. Generally the picture was grim, and the account George Shield, head of Mexborough Sixth Form College, sent to Alec Clegg describing his visit to the George Washington High School, just north of Harlem, seemed to confirm this view. The school was visited by the Bullock Committee, and no doubt like George Shield they had to pass through the chain link fencing which surrounded the school and be checked by the security guards. Security guards patrolled the corridors as well as manning the gates and the place must have seemed more of a prison than a school. The school had experienced serious student riots a year or two earlier, but George Shield punctuated his letter with two shafts of sunlight. He was surprised at the friendliness of the school and he felt "... things do not seem to be so impossible as I had thought." He ended - "Altogether I came away much cheered." Cross currents of information which prompted hope, or caution, were important to Alec Clegg. They could be guides to policies that would, or would not, work.

NAVIGATING THE LAST MILE

The collection of letters and papers which cover 1970 to 1974 is a tale of agony. They cover the piece by piece dismantling of a major county, the promotion, retirement and deaths of associates and friends with all of this taking place in the unavoidably choppy waters of the day to day administration. The collection invites the maximum use of detail as the means to illustrate the agony. Yet this would be a mistake for running through all four years is a gritty determination to continue initiatives such as those in the field of social education, innovative primary teaching and the integration of services for the benefit of disadvantaged children. The four years underline Alec Clegg's commitment to educational progress despite bad health and the impending end of the West Riding. These years give indelible evidence of his " ... passionate belief in the educatability of the ordinary child." elevating ideas far above the pressing demands of four years of administrative surgery. The nature of those demands was described first in a letter to Sir Herbert Andrews, Permanent Under Secretary of State and then nine months later when he had reluctantly to refuse the Chairmanship of the Crafts Council. In the July 1970 letter he wrote -

"I really wish this were not happening. You are going, and my good colleague, Evans, our Divisional Inspector, is going, and I am not, and I don't like it one little bit."

The second letter ran -

"My difficulty is this. I was to retire within a year but the break up and disappearance of the West Riding is causing such confusion and difficulty here that it seems unlikely that I shall be relieved of my duties; indeed they are likely to become very much more vexatious and troublesome."

Alec Clegg sent a collection of amendments to 'Children in Distress' to his friend, Lord Boyle, Vice-Chancellor of Leeds University in March 1972. (16) He quoted the results of a study by the National Children's Bureau of 17,000 children along with the results of a 'rough check' on some of the youngsters dealt with in 'Children in Distress.' Half of the latter group had overcome their difficulties in the last few years and were leading reasonably normal lives. The others had " ... gone from bad to worse and some are costing the public purse more than would have been paid for the education in the most exclusive of our independent schools."

To illustrate possible avenues to relieve distress Alec Clegg turned to Educational Priority Areas where help at pre-school level was giving interesting results. In Mexborough visits to mothers offering advice on pre-school education in the widest sense showed parents were shy rather than feckless and indifferent towards school. Moreover in matters such as walking, running and getting home trained working class mothers did better than middle class ones. However once rudimentary educational training began the middle class mothers took the lead. Time and time again the importance of identifying special needs as early as possible is illustrated along with the stress on providing the services to cater for these needs.

Dealing with disadvantaged youngsters in secondary schools led to visits to the Red House in Denaby and to Minsthorpe and also to schools such as Countesthorpe in Leicestershire. Countesthorpe received a great deal of publicity and Alec Clegg was one of its stream of visitors. Like so many comprehensives in their infancy Countesthorpe had an intake very different to the one planned for the future. Eventually it would be an upper school catering for 1400 students between the ages of 14 and 18. It opened as a high school with a full range of 11 to 14 pupils who by 1972, the year of Alec Clegg's visit, provided a fourth and fifth year but no sixth form. Countesthorpe had gone aggressively for equality and for democracy seeking to get away from the long established hierarchical model of the traditional secondary school. Alec Clegg described it as "unpleasant, uninviting and sad." He was very worried for the parents and local residents saw the school as an example of the shortcomings of progressive education. He praised the community services and community newspapers but saw in so many aspects of school life a lack of quality, typified by a visit to the gymnasium. There he watched a movement group which he said "... I can only call physically illiterate." Countesthorpe was a massive plunge by staff and pupils into a new organisation and Alec Clegg saw the new headteacher facing a momentous task if there was to be genuine progress. Experiments such as Countesthorpe and Minsthorpe pointed to the need for a sustained investment of money, time and effort before the social aims of such schools could be realised. These needs were way beyond normal school budgets and extended into areas of provision provided hitherto by other services. Yet again Alec Clegg's observations and conclusions point out the need to integrate services and to reassess priorities in social provision.

Social change is best studied in decades and centuries rather than years and the recent addition to the Oxford History of Britain takes the story from 1945 up to 1990. Looking back on the post-war years the author, Kenneth O.Morgan, says Britain was a country with "... endemic social inequality." (17) It was a country where 'On these rooted distinctions of wealth and social class (masked by the apparent growing classlessness of dress and speech, especially among the young) were superimposed other more specific inequalities." Alec Clegg was fighting against this tide and aware he would be beached in 1974. (18)

In 1974 the editor of 'Education' asked Alec Clegg if he would canvas a few Chief Education Officers on their views when they left local government in March of that year. Alec Clegg centred his reply around Roman Terrace School in Mexborough. Six years of wartime dirt, peeling paint and fallen plaster made it a drab, dirty, unkempt environment. He took his Chairman, Alderman Hyman there and he told Alec Clegg to get it put right and not to wait for a committee resolution. Within a few weeks the school

291

was colourful, clean and well-equipped. Staff and pupils were at ease, appreciative and making good progress. Alec Clegg reflected on this change and wrote -

"It was at that time that it became obvious to me that attitudes, values and behaviour are at least as important as the facts that twice two are four, and there are two "m's" in accommodation." The solitary letter from Ernest Peet, Superintendent of Caretakers, to Alec Clegg drew attention to the personal element in administration. Like so many of Alec Clegg's staff he became an authority in his own right; in his range of matters associated with caretaking. Yet it was one incident in the Chief Education Officer's room at Wakefield which stuck in his mind. A young assistant drew attention to a spelling error in some work by Ernest Peet. As he advanced in the Education Service Ernest Peet observed this man's career was marked by a disposition to irritate and anger rather than win the support of his staff. In a memorandum on 'Caning, Behaviour and Delinquency in Secondary Schools' Alec Clegg listed the qualities in a head teacher which could contribute to good personal relations in a school. The qualities were "... their courtesy to children; their infinite patience, their concern for the individual and for the appearance of themselves, their staff, their children and all the things in their school; the ease of their relationships which lies behind things which promote good discipline." (19)

These qualities provide day by day ease and support for the school community along with a bank of goodwill which can be drawn on in difficult times. These are occasions when vital decisions need to be made. There are others when opportunities need to be recognised and taken. B.H. Liddell-Hart describes the collection of Letters and Papers Field Marshal Rommel made during his campaigns as objective and graphic. He was a military genius who believed in getting right forward in a battle so that he could be near to the crucial spot at the crucial time. Like Alec Clegg he knew what was going on 'at the other side of the hill', and this contributed to maximum personal impact on his troops. The final sentence of B.H. Liddell-Hart's introduction is an example of how great leaders in war or peace could go beyond the art of the possible -

"Exasperating to staff officers, he was worshipped by the fighting troops, and what he got out of them in performance was far beyond any rational calculations." (20)

One of the priorities for Alec Clegg in these final years was to ensure as many as possible of his staff got good positions in other authorities. This was largely achieved. Another aim was to ensure that innovative schools were recognised and encouraged by the new authorities for they could be oases of excellence bringing new ideas to other schools. The personal element, so important in the West Riding, migrated, and in this way lived on. A union spokesman described the winding up of the authority in these words - "Reorganisation in the West Riding has been fairly painless." A comment on the process which gave no idea of what might have been lost, salvaged or gained by the new authorities.

Alec Clegg gave the centenary lecture on Education 1870-1970 to a distinguished audience in May 1970. He ended it by expressing his anxiety about how the 1944 Act had been interpreted. In simple terms the Act laid it down that schools should "... get the best out of every child and in so doing we should raise the whole level of our people and not merely erect a ladder from the gutter to the University, as Huxley once put it." Alec Clegg's assessment of the situation in 1970 was -

"Secondary Education for all must be what adult society wills it to be and if the only challenge we can offer the young is that of material prosperity and we over value the quick who can add to it and discard the slow who cannot. The former will despise our values and the latter resent our indifference and we shall blame both for what is our failing. And there will be much bitterness and much discord in our society."

Two years later he gave the Convocation Lecture at Leeds University concentrating on attitudes, opinions and prejudices and their effects on the education service. He felt gaps in society were becoming rifts and that much more emphasis had to be put on personal happiness and less on material progress. The Schools Council was one of the main sources of curricular change. It was thought to be a major contributor to educational progress as it had concentrated on finding - "... more enlightened ways of conveying prescribed facts to our pupils." Alec Clegg described how Derek Morrell, its founder, had a very different view some years later -

"You will see at once that this is very much a turncoats' perception of the curriculum. When I was at the Schools Council I should have found it difficult to perceive as closely as I now do that the curriculum, if it exists at all, is a structure erected on a base of reciprocal personal relationships. I should have found it difficult to assert, as again I do, that in curriculum we are concerned with human beings whose feelings and aspirations are far more real and immediately important to them than the cognitive development which is the educators' stock in trade."

The attitude Alec Clegg embraced had been written with a hot poker many years ago in his late aunt's front room. It read,

> If those of fortune be bereft
> And of thine earthly store hath left
> Two loaves, sell one and with the dole
> Buy hyacinths to feed the soul.

Senior West Riding Staff who are believed to have become Chief or Deputy Chief Education Officers after the West Riding ended in 1974

Ernest Butcher, CEO Kirklees
John Crawford, CEO Birmingham
Reg Eyles, CEO Wakefield
Dudley Foulds, CEO Barnsley
John Haynes, CEO Kent
Richard Knight, CEO Bradford
Tony Lenny, CEO Haringey
Sir Peter Newsam, CEO Inner London
Ted Owens, CEO North Yorkshire

Jim Bolton, Deputy CEO Humberside
Mark Thompson, Deputy CEO Hampshire

References

1. Sir Alec Clegg - The Man, His Ideas and His Schools

1. There are no references to Sir Alec Clegg in 'Educator Extraordinary The Life and Achievment of Henry Morris', by Harry Rée. Published in 1973. There are 3 references to Sir Alec in 'Stewart Mason. The Art of Education' by Donald Jones. Published in 1977.

2. Chapter Two

1. The raising of the school leaving age and the rise in the birth rate after 1945 led to the need to provide for an additional 1 1/4 million children in West Riding schools between 1958 and 1961.

3. The Development Plan

1. Rudolph Laban An expert on movement and its connection with dance, drama and physical education who came to this country from Hitler's Germany. Diana Jordan drew many of her ideas from Laban.
   Cizak. A Viennese teacher who had worked with Basil Rocke in Vienna. He believed that all children had the ability to draw and to paint.
   Ruth Scriver. She was appointed as Basil Rocke's assistant. She taught at Bedales. As an Art Adviser in the West Riding she wanted children to have maximum freedom to express and develop their artistic skills. She deported much of the jargon which surrounded the teaching of Art.
   Herbert Read - son of a Yorkshire farmer. He was born in 1893. He went to Leeds University and served as an infantry officer in the First World War, winning a DSO and an MC.He held a variety of posts before becoming Professor of Fine Art at Edinburgh University. He had a deep and wide interest in the Arts and the Clegg Papers illustrate his contact with Alec Clegg on the part that the Arts can play in education.

2. Page 37 'The Changing Primary School' - a headteacher is quoted as saying "But in 1948 I attended a Vacation Course on the Junior School and the developments which followed this seminal course are well known in the West Riding."

4. Foundations and First Fruits

1. J.F. Wolfendein, Chairman, A.B. Clegg, R, Gould, Professor A.V.C. Jeffrey and Roy Lewis.
2. T.S. Eliot 'Notes towards the definition of Culture' - P.98
3. Letter to Alec Clegg dated 16th November 1961.
4. The 1965 Chuter Ede Lecture given at Hamilton House, Tuesday 30th March. In the Chair Michael Tippett, C.B.E.

5. The Bulge, Buildings and The Shortage of Teachers

1. Member of Manchester City Council and Education Committee, also of Central Advisory Council for Education which produced the Newsam Report in 1963
2. From the 1955 Report on Colne Valley by Mr. Andrews. Class of 19 at Grindleton Lane Ends. Report for 1955
3. Bristol, Durham, Kent, Lancashire, Manchester and Sheffield.
4. A.B. Clegg "The Education of the Professional Teacher".

6. The Comprehensive Debate - Thorough or Partisan

7. The Foundation - Infant and Junior Schools

1. Chapter 4 - "Can't we do better than this?"
See Chapter 4 - page 49
2. Tapes at Bretton Hall College.

8. Alec Clegg and the Wider World of Education

1. p.274 Lord Robbins 'Autobiography of an Economist'
2. Course 276
3. See 'Essays in Economic and Social History of South Yorkshire'. Introduction by Sidney Pollard for personal characteristics of the people of South Yorkshire.
4. Dennis Potter 'The Nigel Barton Plays' - Penguin Books

9. Newsom and the Change of Heart

1. Robert Lowe 1811-1892. His time in Australia made him distrust democracy and when he was head of the Government education department he instituted payment by results in English schools.
2. D. Ayerst - p.202 "Understanding Schools.

3.   See Courses at Woolley Hall 1952 - 1974 at the end of chapter 11.

Woolley Hall Courses 1952 - 1974

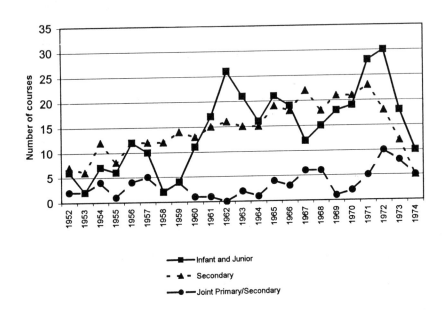

4.   W.G. Hoskins "English Landscape" Page 6
5.   The War in the Far East

10. 1960

1.   D. Birley - 'The education officer and his world' Published 1970
2.   Pages 100-101 Airedale Middle School. Mrs Pyrah's class.
3.   Times Educational Supplement 4.10.1974

11. Technology, Handicraft and Rural Studies

1.   page 34 - MAURICE COLLIS 'Stanley Spencer'
2.   L.T.C. Rolt's biography of the great Victorian engineer was published
      in 1957

12. The Excitement of Writing

1. Iona & Peter Opie 'Children's Games in Street and Playground' - P.vi
2. Yorkshire Post 12th February 1964 - William Walsh Professor of Education, Leeds University
3. 11th January 1966
4. 6th November 1963. In his letter to Miss Laski Alec Clegg referred to her review of Mrs Sybil Marshall's book 'An Experiment in Education', Cambridge University Press 1963
5. Letter to Alec Clegg dated 2nd April 1964.
6. 10th July 1964 - Ann Arden-Clarke wrote that the extract was plagiarism from Edward Ardizzone.
7. Letter to Miss Sonia Abrams, A.C.E. Cambridge, 17th July 1964.
8. p118 - Barry Hines 'A Kestrel for a Knave'
9. See Stan Barstow - introduction to 'Enjoying Writing'
10. Letter from Herbert Read - 6th January 1964
11. Yorkshire Post - 12th February 1964
12. 13th August 1963 - Alec Clegg to G.C. Allen
13. Writer of foreword to 'The Excitement of Writing'
14. 13th October 1964 - Letter from Witchford County Secondary School - Ely
15. North of England Conference Address by Robert Birley - January 1956
16. p.223 - Jewkes, Sawers and Stillerman 'The Sources of Invention'
17. They could knap flint to make scrapers. They could mould, fire and use Roman lamps. They could make the Roman surveying device, the groma, and use it to mark out sites for imaginary roads and buildings on the school field. *(Local Studies scheme at Rossington).*
18. See Chapter on Social Education

13. The Plowden Report - Education and its Social Background

1. 19th January 1965
2. Professor Tibble - Director of School of Education, Leicester University
3. Professor A J Ayer - Professor of Logic, Oxford University
4. Professor Peters - Professor of Philosophy of Education, University of London
5. Paper on 'The Aims of Education'. Working Party No.4 by Mr E Blishen
6. p.5 Evidence from A B Clegg, Education Officer West Riding County Council

7. p.396 - Plowden Report
8. p.136 - 'The Politics of Education' Edward Boyle & Anthony Crosland in conversation with Maurice Kogan
9. Paragraph 949
10. Paragraph 960
11. p 176 R. M. Titmuss. Essays on the Welfare State.
12. Department of Education and Science, 9-13 Middle Schools 1983
13. Plowden Report, Chapter 2, Paragraph 59 ... " if the IQ had been made the single criterion at nine or ten for sorting the children into sheep and goats, and if the same criterion had been used again at 19, it would have been found that a mistake had been made in 20 per cent of the cases.
14. Ken Coates and Richard Silburn. "Poverty: The forgotten Englishmen. p.146 describes Plowden recommendations as ". . . very modest steps to meet an extremely serious problem".
15. B.Megson - 'Economic deprivation in School Children'

14   Alec Clegg - Examinations and Society at Large

1. Presidential address by A.B. Clegg to the Association of Chief Education Officers New Society 11th February 1965.
2. p.14 'English for the Rejected', D. Holbrook: the danger will grow that we depreciate and devalue all those children who are not selected and who cannot pass exams: the danger will grow that we divide the whole of the next generation into successes and failures according to their academic record.
3. See page 86.
4. Report and Proposals of the Local Government Commission Proposal No.7. Proposed non-county borough of Wakefield. Public Inquiry 9th February 1965. Proof of Evidence of A. B. Clegg County Education Officer.
5. Proof of Evidence of A B Clegg to Public Inquiry 9 Feb. 1965
6. Report to Alec Clegg - May 1964
7. Report to Alec Clegg - 1965
8. Memo - 7th May 1968 - 'Waste of Human Potential in Education'
9. Jan 1968 - North of England Conference speech by A.B. Clegg
10. p.197 - 'Commitment to Welfare' R.M. Titmuss
11. Robbins Report - Appendix 2
12. See p. 110.
13. Catherine Caufield - 'Thorne Moors' - The New Yorker, February 1991

14. See Appendix ....
15. B. Jackson 'Working Class community' Page 17
16. B. Jackson 'Working Class Community' - Page 17
17. B. Jackson 'Working Class Community' - Page 177

15 Children In Distress

1. Times Educational Supplement 20.9.1974
2. p.188
3. Royal borough of Kingston-on-Thames
4. 17th October 1966. Letter from Divisional Education Officer D. Foulds on twilight children.
5. Report to the Policy and Finance Sub-Committee 10th October 1961
6. Unit at Sheffield dealing with cerebral palsy.
7. Distressed Children - Area Survey - Ripon 7th March 1967
8. A detailed study sponsored by the Department of Education and Science and the Social Science Research Council. Edited by A.H. Halsey. p.2 of Volume 1 - The Context
9. See Chapter 19
10. A recipe of one headmaster who wrote in to Alec Clegg
11. Sir Alec Clegg 'Recipe for Failure' 1972. National Children's Home Convocation Lecture

16 Social Education - Special Services

1. p.324 Y. Menuhin 'Unfinished Journey'
2. p.62. 'The Final Ten Years 1964-1974'
3. One of Alec Clegg's assistants.
4. Sick Cities' - A Penguin Special by Mitchell Gordon
5. Sick Cities' - p.220
6. See p.110 - Alec Clegg quotes this particular case to illustrate that retrieval can work.

17 Initiatives in Social Education

1. A comparison made in correspondence between Alec Clegg and a group of junior and infant Heads.
2. 'Half Way There' - Report of the British comprehensive School Reform - Caroline Benn and Brian Simon.

3. Ashton was Featherstone.
4. 'Recipe for Failure' - The Convocation Lecture for the National Children's Home 1972
5. Page 35 'The Final Ten Years' 1964 - 1974
6. Progress Report 1973 on the Red House Social Work Programmes.
7. Collection of papers on the Alternative School Experiment
8. Barry Hines 'Kes'
9. Protest and Discontent' Page 69 - Penguin Books 1970
10. See Page 52
11. September 27th 1969
12. Harriet Crawley 'Degree of Defiance' 1969
13. E.P. Thompson 'Writing by Candlelight' a term used in descriptions of Warwick University
14. Letter dated 22nd July 1969
15. West Riding Education Committee 'The Final Ten Years 1964-1974' - p.45
16. Donald Wade 'Yorkshire Survey'
17. Essays on the Welfare State' p.221

18 Social Opportunity

1. p.108 J.K. Galbraith 'The Culture of Contentment' 1992
2. p.13 - Section 10 - Conclusion, Summary & Implications, West Riding Educational Priority Area Project
3. A memorandum on 'County University Awards' - Personal file for 1956
4. County University Awards'
5. Francis Williams - Ernest Bevin
6. p.49 John Betjeman 'An Oxford University Chest'
7. Kenneth O. Morgan - 'The People's Peace' - British History 1945 - 1990

19 The West Riding - a source of educational progress

1. Coventry, London, Middlesex, Oldham and the West Riding
2. Definition of 'genocide' used in the Nuremberg Trial
3. Education Officer's visit to Australia. Report to Policy and Finance Committee 14th January 1958
4. An exchange scheme between Conisbrough Northcliffe School and Dartington School in Devon was started in 1969. The Elmgrant Trust bought The Terrace in Conisbrough which was used as a hostel.

5. Canadian Education and Research Digest - Volume 7 Number 1, March 1967
6. James D Koerner - 'The Mis-education of the American Teacher'
7. Talk given by Diana Jordan to the fourth Anglo-Norwegian Course at Woolley Hall
8. p.111 'The Excitement of Writing'
9. Douglas Dunn 'Northlight' - Memory and Imagination
10. Quotation from a lecture by Professor Bronowski to the R.I.B.A. - See also p.176.
11. See Appendix 1

20 Change Within and Without - The West Riding in the National Context

1. Sybil Marshall - 'An Experiment in Education' - Cambridge University Press 1963
2. Times Educational Supplement 29.9.74
3. 'Tales of a Rat Hunting Man' Published 1978
4. p.132
5. p.134 'Innovation & Research in Education'
6. Speakers included Dr Jean Wynn Reeves, author of 'Body and Mind in Western Thought', Pelican Books; Roger Young, sixth form master Manchester Grammar School; Mr M M Simmons, Headmaster of Kneesworth Hall (an Approved School for highly intelligent boys); Mrs Barbara Preston, Senior Science Mistress and Mr L Bradley, Headmaster of Derby School.
7. Fabian Research Series - No. 237 - January 1964
8. Young Fabian Pamphlet No.26 - September 1971. Bob Harris, Ralph Holmes, Sandra Wynn
9. The Politics of Education - Penguin 1971
10. p.30 - The Politics of Education - Penguin
11. Report of Royal Commission on Local Government - 1969
12. Report to the Policy and finance sub-Committee - 9th September 1969

21 Riding for a Fall - The end of the West Riding

1. Public Enquiry - Proposal No. 7 - Proposed non-country borough of Wakefield. Proof of Evidence of A B Clegg C.E.O. West Riding
2. Paragraph 2 - public Enquiry on Proposed non-country borough of Wakefield

3. Times Educational Supplement 2.4.71

4. See also Times Educational Supplement 19.3.71 Reports on speech at Commonwealth Institute and the Encyclopaedia Britannica Conference

5. 'This is my problem' - Article by Sir A Clegg in Local Government Review, 21st October 1972

6. This is my problem

7. Letter from W Gamble, Department of Education and Science to Miss R Scrivenor - 30th November 1972

8. Private files

9. R M Titmuss 'Essays on the Welfare State' - 'The Irresponsible Society'

10. Catherine Avant was a fellow member of the Newsom and Crowther Committees with Alec Clegg

11. By September 1970 40,931 copies sold.

12. Henry Thirkill MA KC CBE MC Fellow of Clare College 1910 - 1939; Master 1939 - 1958; Vice Chancellor of Cambridge University 1945 - 1947. Born 1886 - Died 1971.

13. 'A language for life' - Report of the Bullock committee

14. p.5 - Children with Educational and Related Difficulties in Primary Schools. Report on Screening Procedure by Dennis Pickles 19.11.1973

15. Extract from a letter to P J Butcher 23rd November 1970

16. This letter and accompanying information was sent to Lord Boyle in preparation for a speech he was to make to the NUT at Hemsworth.

17. p.514

18. In the 1970 Arthur Mellows Lecture Alec Clegg outlined how the comprehensives of the future might run. "They must be run on a three session day, seven days a week for 50 weeks in the year and the man in charge of each must dispose of a staff which will meet the needs both of the schools and the adult centre."

19. 'Caning, Behaviour and Discipline in Secondary Schools'

20. B H Liddell-Hart 'Rommel Papers' P.XXI

Notes

1. Professor Harry Rée wrote the biography of Henry Morris *Educator Extraordinary* in 1961. Harry Rée was a lifelong friend of Morris and at the time of the publication he worked for the Community Education Development Centre in Coventry.

Chapter 1

1. John Raimbach was a pupil at St Clement Danes School and he served in the navy in the Second World War. He worked in the Bank of England after the war and later became a teacher. He provided invaluable information on Sir Alec's teaching at St Clement Danes.
2. Rex Barrett was another pupil who provided details from the school magazines of the 1930s. He still works for the Old Students' Association.
3. Sir Alec's two volumes are in Lady Clegg's private collection of her husband's papers.
4. Arthur Stone. Before his death Arthur Stone lived in a flat in Leeds and much of the material is drawn from a sequence of meetings we had during 1992 and 1993.
5. Richard Titmuss. His early career was in insurance and in the late thirties and early forties he began to write books on social conditions in Britain. His study of the 'Problems in Social Policy' was published by HMSO in 1950 and soon after he entered London University as a head of department. He did not have a degree and between 1950 and his death in 1971 he was Professor of Social Administration. The last remark in the final chapter of his book on "Problems in Social Policy" - echoes of the standpoint taken by Sir Alec towards social that they would take '...time to heal and infinite patience to understand.' p.538.
6. Robert Logan - described by Harry Rée as a lifelong friend of Henry Morris was clearly enthused by Morris's ideas but he recognised that Morris had difficulty getting them established in the latter part of his career.
7. Diana Jordan. Diana Jordan was trained at Bedford College of Physical Education before the Second World War. She learned Rudolf Labans' Art of Movement and Dance at the Mary Whigman School in Leipzig and during the war she worked with Alec Clegg in Worcestershire. She was appointed to the West Riding in 1947 to encourage the teaching of Dance. As she wrote in her account of 'The introduction and Development of Movement and Dance in the West

1947 - 52.' '...a body formed of men and women PE advisors, three of whom were experienced in Movement education, and the others open minded and interested, two very enlightened Art advisors and one Inspector who through his own experience of Movement in his school and as an adviser had come to believe firmly in the creative ability of children and that Movement had a fundamental part to play in children's learning and in their personal and social development.'

Chapter 2

1. Leonard Clark - HMI. He was a poet, teacher and HMI. His book 'The Inspector Remembers' covers the years 1936 to 1970. He took part in courses held at Woolley Hall.
2. Mrs Scott, headmistress at Brodsworth Primary School was one of the head teachers interviewed by the author.
3. Murial Pyrah. Her collection of work done by primary youngsters is housed at Bretton Hall College. Sir Alec's reaction her teaching is described in 'About or Schools'. pp.14 -15.
4. Edith Sitwell, Robert Gittings and Edmund Blunden - these three are examples of the quality of those who took part in many of the courses at Woolley Hall.
5. Basil Rocke 1904 - 1966. In his tribute to Basil Rocke Sir Alec said how '...he would never lay a finger on a child's work and that what mattered to the growing child was that it should say what it had to say in its own way driven by inspiration and seen through its own eyes, and that the job of a teacher was to provide opportunity, encouragement and guidance at the right moment.'

Chapter 3

1. Richard Ollard's book 'An English Education. A perspective of Eton.' Published 1982. In the preface he seeks to explain what the book is about. His aim is to isolate those elements which he felt were persistent and of importance in the long history of the school. He refers also to the unobvious aspects of Eton in the twentieth century. A similar challenge faces anyone going through the extensive collection of Clegg Papers. Both emphasise the importance of the intangibles in education.
2. Hugh Leslie Watkinson - one of the small group of head teachers who were in charge of Mexborough Grammar School for decades rather than years.

3. Eric James, who became Lord James of Rusholme, pointed out that 10% of pupils at Manchester Grammar School in 1960 were sons of manual workers. The school drew pupils from a very wider area and he argued that neighbourhood schools could only draw pupils from a limited social strata. Selection on ability could bring a mix of youngsters from different stratas in society.

4. During one discussion I had with Arthur Stone he reflected on his pamphlet 'The story of a School', saying, 'That damned pamphlet was a shocker.' He wrote it piecemeal with the help of his staff and he did not feel it communicated fully his love of dance, movement and games. He played Hockey for Herefordshire, was a good tennis player a pianist and a fisherman.

5. Basil Rocke was sent to New Zealand in his early twenties to learn fellmongery, part of Rocke and sons family business. He returned to England in 1927 and went to Reading University School of Art for two years. From 1929 to 1931 he studied Art at Kunstegewerbeschule where he worked with Wilhelm Viola and Professor Franz Cizek. From 1932 to 1936 he taught at Bembridge School on the Isle on Wight and took part in the late thirties in the setting up of the Euston Road School of Painters. In 1946 he joined the team of advisers in the West Riding.

Chapter 4

1. Roy Lewis. Economist and associate editor of the magazine 'Future'. He went to University College, Oxford. Angus Maude, a Conservative MP when the book 'The English Middle Classes' was published. He worked as a journalist for The Times and then the Daily Mail.

2. Edith Sitwell was born in Scarborough, and sister to Sir Osbert Sitwell and Sacheverell Sitwell. Many considered her to be one of the most distinguished of women poets.

3. Kathleen Raine specialised in Biology at University. Her first book Stone and Flower was illustrated by Barbara Hepworth.
   Edmund Blunden was born in 1896 and went to Oxford University. He served in the Royal Sussex Regiment and won an M.C. His experiences in the First World War led him to write 'Undertones of War'. He wrote this in Japan where he was Professor of English Literature at Tokyo University. Apart from poetry he wrote biographies of poets and writers such as Charles Lamb and Shelley.
   Robert Gittings was born in 1911. He went to Jesus College, Cambridge. When he went to Woolley Hall he was Programme Assistant in the

Schools Department at the BBC. His first book of poems was published in 1950 and apart from poetry he was interested in archaeology, the theatre and the countryside.

Leonard Clark was born in 1905 and had his first book of poems published when he was eighteen. He edited the writings of Albert Mansbridge, the founder of the WEA. At the time of this Woolley course he was an HMI.

This group of poets provided an outstanding example of the quality of those who took part in many of the courses at Woolley Hall. In his book The Inspector Remembers' Leonard Clark wrote p133. 'I doubt if the West Riding teachers had ever experienced a course of this nature before, but their response was magnificent.'

4. At the end of the Foreword to 'The Excitement of Writing' Denys Thompson states 'This is a timely and salutary book, revolutionary in its implications for the teaching of English.'

5. Christian Schiller HMI was responsible for the country's junior schools.

Chapter 5

1. Dr Kathleen Ollerenshaw was one of the prominent education-alists who kept in touch with Sir Alec throughout his career in the West Riding. In the 1970s they were both members of the Board of the Social Sciences Research Council.

2. Geoff Edwards. When Geoff Edwards reflected on the development of Minsthorpe High School and the Carnegie Centre in 1981 he wrote - Whilst at times I have wished perhaps for some other monitoring of our growth and our effect in the community, I have nevertheless appreciated the freedom to follow a natural development rather than the pressure to follow a line.'

Chapter 6

1. The bronze cockerel made by Elizabeth Frink is a good example of West Riding policy to provide some money to new schools to buy a work, or works of art.

2. Nikolaus Pevsner praises the design of Colne Valley High School in his study of the West Riding in simple terms -'good work by the County Architect's Department.

Chapter 7

1. G.A.N. Lownes thought that many of the books written on education were duller than the subject deserved. He felt that government blue books relied too much on statistics which did not give a living picture of social progress. He added a quote from Andrew Long who said that such publications were like drunken men who used lamp posts for support not illumination.

2. Sir Alec would have nodded agreement to many of the ideas Professor A.N. Whitehead expressed in his eight Lowell Lectures delivered in 1925. His criticism of traditional educational methods was '... that they are far too much occupied with intellectual analysis and with the acquirement of formularised information.

3. This collection of films, slides and tapes is housed at Bretton Hall College.

4. Liam Hudson wen to Exeter College, Oxford where he studied Modern History, Philosophy and Psychology. He got a first class degree then he went to Cambridge and did a PhD. He became a member of the Research Centre at King's College Cambridge. He describes his interests as painting, collecting porcelain and privacy.

5. Arthur Naylor. When he was interviewed at Balby Street School he said the sincerity of the teacher was the quality that mattered. Such teachers were committed to giving children a sense of success and achievement. They were not mere classroom managers. He was critical of the National Curriculum which he felt was dull, too full and left no room for innovation.

Chapter 8

1. R. Eyles. Reg Eyles was the post-school adviser in the West Riding and he worked with Sir Alec's deputy Jim Hogan to recast the whole of the further education service. When he was an Assistant Education Officer he had a number of overseas appointments such as a two year secondment from the West Riding to help develop education in Tanzania. Also he served as a consultant to the World Bank giving advice on investment in education in Nicaragua and Ecuador. When the West Riding ended he became the Chief Education Officer for Wakefield.

2. Lord Robbins. He was a student lecturer and then a professor at London University. In the Second World War he was involved in the co-ordination of the war economy. He was an Art Administrator at the National Gallery and at the Royal Opera House.

3. Alan Bullock - born in 1914 and educated at Bradford Grammar School. Commentator on BBC radio and TV. He became the Diplomatic Correspondent on the European Service of the BBC. After the Second World War he was elected as Fellow and Tutor in Modern History at New College and then in 1952 Censor of St Catherine's College Oxford. He wrote 'Hitler. A Study in Tyranny.'
4. Dennis Potter. He went to Bell's Grammar School and then to New College Oxford. Between 1965 and 1993 twenty one of his plays appeared on television. He became one of the outstanding television playwrights of his generation. Dennis Potter died in 1994.

Chapter 9

1. David Ayerst. He won a scholarship to Christ Church College, Oxford and got a first class degree in History. He joined the staff of the Guardian and left to become a schoolmaster. He was a headmaster for three years and then became an HMI.
2. In 1973 the School Museum Service lent 35,145 items to schools, an indication of the scale of use. In 1973 Clarke Hall, a seventeenth century house and a water-powered corn mill at Worsbrough were acquired by the West Riding. These buildings were to be available for school visits.
3. In the introduction to the Newsom Report 'Half Our Future' it points out that administrative action cannot achieve the change of attitude towards those youngsters who failed to get a grammar school place. Page xiii of the report states 'It involves a change of thinking and even more a change of heart.
4. This teacher, Tom Taylor, was an Emergency Trained Teacher. He was another example of the quality of many who went through this one year scheme.

Chapter 10

1. Ray O'Connor. He had many interests ranging from rugby to the arts, especially pottery. He was very sensitive to the needs of youngsters in South Yorkshire and gave considerable support to initiatives in this part of the West Riding.
2. Christian Schiller HMI was responsible for the country's junior schools, and in Sir Alec's book 'About our Schools' he quotes Schiller's criticism of the eleven plus tests. The quotation ends with the clear condemnation - 'In my opinion the goal of a mini-mum of attainment is incompatible with continuity in the process of learning.' Sir Alec added '... that we were

reluctant to admit that tests were used as a means to check the ability of teachers.'

3. Henry Scott joined the advisory staff of the West Riding in 1957. When interviewed in November 1992 he described how much in the early years Sir Alec relied on the advice he got from Arthur Stone and Diana Jordan.

4. In the foreword to Jim Hogan's book 'Beyond the Classroom' published in 1970, Sir Alec paid tribute to his deputy and Jim Hogan's contribution to '... a wonderfully sympathetic partnership.' He describes how Jim Hogan was ' ... able to change my attitude and ideas for the better in many ways, particularly in all that con-cerned collaboration between the officialdom which we represented and voluntary endeavour in the further education field.

5. Sir Herbert Read. Born in 1893 near Kirby Moorside, Yorkshire. Sir Alec's private papers contain a number of letters from Sir Herbert Read who shared Sir Alec's view of how artistic ability could be encouraged and developed in schools. Sir Herbert Read served in the Infantry in the First World War winning a DSO and an MC. He went to Leeds University and in 1931 became Professor of Fine Arts at the University of Edinburgh. He was President of the Society for Education in Art and of the Institute of Contemporary Arts. He wrote many books on Art and in his study of 'The Life and work of Henry Moore' p.22, he wrote '... A sculptor, like a poet is born, not made, and I have already given a few indications of the presence, in Henry Moore, of an innate plastic sensibility which education might foster but could not create.'

Chapter 11

1. L.T.C. Rolt. Born in 1910 and educated at Cheltenham College. Later he served a five year engineering apprenticeship. His chief interest was the Industrial Revolution and he wrote biographies of Thomas Telford. George and Robert Stephenson as well as Isambard Kingdom Brunel.

Chapter 12

1. The writers referred to in this chapter such as Denys Thompson, Marganita Laski, Brian Jackson, Barry Hines, Herbert Read, William Walsh, David Holbrook, Richard Hoggart and Edward Blishen illustrate the range of interest provoked by the publication of 'The Excitement of Writing.'

2. An article in the Guardian, 19th November 1997, gave details of Chris Serles' career and how his radical ideas led not only to him being dismissed in Stepney but also in Sheffield from the headship of the Earl Marshal School. One of his former pupils, Alan Gilbey, still sells Stepney words in his bookshop in London.

3. It is very interesting to compare this comment from the foreword of B.H. Liddell-Hart's book with the foreword written by his wife, Lady Liddell-Hart, to her husband's 'History of the Second World War'. Lady Liddell-Hart drew attention to her husband's research on the First World War in the 1920s and 1930s. He wrote 'I came to realise how much history was handicapped because no independent and historically minded enquirer had been able to ascertain and record what the military chiefs were actually thinking at the time ... Later he wrote 'Moreover official documents often fail to reveal their real views and aims, while sometimes even drafted to conceal them.' The wealth of grassroots information in the Clegg Papers does give a writer the opportunity to appreciate the realities and qualities of a large, innovative Education Authority.

Chapter 13

1. Chapter 2 of the Plowden Report deals with 'The Children: Their Growth and Development'. Para 59 points out a major shortcoming in over-reliance on IQs for classifying youngsters for secondary schooling. It concludes - 'Thus if the IQ had been made the single criterion at nine or ten for sorting the children into sheep or goats, and if the same criterion had been used again at 19, it would have been found that a mistake had been made in 20 per cent of the cases.

2. David Medd. The views of David Medd are echoed in 'The Final Ten Years' 1964-74, p.98 where the County Architect's view is summarised as a dialogue to enable ' ... educational practice to develop in a variety of alternative ways during at least the next decade.'

David Medd drew attention to the need to discuss the design of schools with teachers. The results of such discussion not taking place were dealt with at an R.I.B.A. Conference at Cambridge in 1968 where the Strathclyde Building Performance Research Unit presented a paper entitled 'Research Approach to the Design of a Comprehensive School.' The report pointed out that - 'The lack of this kind of dialogue has painfully visible results. In a recent sample of comprehensive schools we have examined, about 40% of the space is unused at any time in spite of the fact that the school is 'full' and needs extensions to accommodate the extra children resulting from raising the leaving age.'

Chapter 14

1. In 'English for the Rejected' David Holbrook drew attention to the social risk of the exam system saying - p.14 '... the danger will grow that we depreciate and devalue all those children who are not selected and who cannot pass exams; the danger will grow that we divide the whole of the next generation into successes and failures according to their academic record.'

2. William Bunting described his visit to Wakefield in detail, how he told Sir Alec of his daughters' ability and how he beat Sir Alec's desk with his walking stick demanding that she was given a place in Thorne Grammar School. Described by Catherine Caufield in 'Thorne Moors' as Naturalist, Pamphleteer, Archivist, Rebel, Bad-tempered old sold and Inspiration' William Bunting dedicated his life to saving Thorne Moors from destruction.

Chapter 15

1. In 1966 Barbara Megson took up the post of administrative assistant in the West Riding. She went to Girton College, Cambridge and later became Head of the History Department at Totnes High School before coming to the West Riding. Her reports are detailed and are in the Clegg Papers.

2. Joe Orton, like many distressed youngsters, was an enemy of order and his plays tease audiences with the hard facts of life which many people contrive to forget.

Chapter 16

1. Many of those referred to in the second half of this book, such as J.B. Willcock, expressed deep concern on the character of social change in Britain. Social change was slow and schemes to improve the quality of life could take decades, not years, to produce positive results. Books with titles such as 'The State We're In' by Will Hutton, published in 1995, pointed out the spectacular failure of '...the conservative establishment to create the good society.' In fact a year after the book was completed Will Hutton said that social fragmentation continued. His statements on previous decades reflect the concern Sir

Alec Clegg expressed before and after he retired in 1974. One of the initiatives aimed at improving the quality of life in the South Yorkshire coalfield area was the establishment of Minsthorpe High School and Community College. In October 1997 the Principal of Minsthorpe Community College was able to present impressive details of the range of services provided to the families of South Elmsall, South Kirkby and Upton. A quarter of the local population used the College so the hopes of Barry Willcock and Sir Alec Clegg in the sixties were at last being realised.

2.   Barbara Wootton had a sense of humour which in many respects was similar to that of Sir Alec Clegg. Both could focus attention on major issues in the development of society by using unexpected, amusing comparisons. The first edition of the 'Social foundations of Wage Policy' begins with a comparison of the earnings of an elephant at Whipsnade Zoo with what Barbara Wootton earned as the Director of Studies at the University of London. Both earned £600 a year. By the time the end of the book is reached the inequalities of the wage and salary structure are very clear. It is a structure that '... bears the marks of greed and envy and of ruthless bargaining.'

Chapter 17

1.   Barry Hines - born in Hoyland Common, near Barnsley. He was trained as a Physical Education Teacher at Loughborough College. He taught in London and South Yorkshire. His book 'A Kestrel for a Knave' was a best seller.

Chapter 18

1.   Michael Young. Now Lord Young. Born in 1915. He felt that his education began when he went to Dartington Hall at the age of 14. He has been connected with the school and its founders, Dorothy and Leonard Elmhirst ever since. He studied sociology and did a PhD at the London School of Economics. He began his own research unit, the Institute of community Studies, Bethnal Green. He founded the Consumers' Association and the Advisory Centre for Education. His study 'The Rise of the Meritocracy 1870 - 2033' first published in 1958 saw a future where the intelligence ratings, exam results and qualifications would sift out the dominant class of the future. Over emphasis upon central control, uniformity and the acquisition of qualifications could produce what Michael Young termed 'the oligarchy of the future'.

Chapter 19

1. The Elmhirsts. The meetings I had with Mr A.O. Elmhirst and his wife at Houndhill, Worsbrough in 1991 were telling insights into the Dartington Trust and the initiatives which linked Conisborough Northcliffe School and Dartington Hall. Also our discussions were a regular reminder of the quality of the personal relationships Sir Alec had with a wide variety of people. 'Pom' Elmhirst expressed his deep concern about how educational policy had changed catastrophically in the 1980s with its emphasis upon central control and central dogma. During one discussion he cited instance after instance where Sir Alec resourced innovation. He underlined his view on the rampant growth of bureaucracy by quoting a prayer which was found in the office of an Indian Civil Servant in Delhi in 1921. It read:
   "O Lord grant that this day we come to no decisions
   Neither run into any kind of responsibility,
   But that all our doings may be ordered to establish
   New and quite unwarranted departments,
   For ever and ever. Amen."

2. Ernest Peet. Born in 1909 in Radcliffe, Lancashire. He went to Radcliffe Technical College and was a block cutter and engraver for 8 years. He became a caretaker and eventually the Head Caretaker and Supervisor of Cleaning Staff at Radcliffe Technical College. He was appointed Supervisor of Caretakers in the West Riding in 1948. He achieved a national reputation as a lecturer and consultant on caretaking and also as a writer of books and articles. He designed and produced new cleaning equipment for schools and many other buildings. These included tools which applied floor dressing and low cost mechanised scrubbing and polishing machines.

Chapter 20

1. When Mrs Scott was appointed Headmistress of Brodsworth Church of England School Sir Alec advised her not to follow the policy of the previous head, which was to concentrate on getting the children of richer parents grammar school places. This is an explanation of his statement 'open it or shut it.' Mrs Scott had all the old books and equipment taken away in a farm waggon to be burnt. Close relationships were built up with all the parents. The school had a firm foothold in the old rural order but it was very innovative.

2. Arthur Raistrick. Born in 1896 in Saltaire. He studied Civil Engineering, Geology and Mining at Leeds University. He gained an MSc and a PhD in Geology. Until 1956 he was a lecturer and reader in Geology at Kings College, Newcastle-on-Tyne, but his lifelong interest was in the outdoors. The offices he held such as President of the Holiday Fellowship, Vice President and later President of the Ramblers Association and member of the Yorkshire Dales National Park Planning Committee illustrate his wide range of outdoor interests.

Chapter 21

1. Nearly two decades later Kenneth. O. Morgan's book 'The Peoples Peace. British History 1945-1990' stated pp.493-4 'The attempt to achieve a national core curriculum, which widely supported as a way of improving literacy and numeracy amongst school children, was also feared as yet another turn in the ratchet of state control over local experimentation. It was also a comment on years of under-funding by international standards in the nation's schools. 'Margaret Thatcher's governments are a centrepiece of the last quarter of the twentieth century. Ian Gilmour, former member of her cabinet, 'Dancing with Dogma' published in 1992. These two comments reinforce Morgan's view on expenditure and move the discussion into the areas which characterised much of what Sir Alec had to say in the last years of the West Riding. p.213. 'Dancing with Dogma' - 'Yet even while boasting of general economic prosperity, the Thatcher government decreased the proportion of GDP spent on education from 5.3 per cent in 1980-1 to 4.9 per cent in 1988-9.' .... 'Thatcherites seemed incapable of understanding that good teachers are the key to a well-educated nation. After the strikes in the mid-eighties, the government and the Thatcher worshipping press vilified the teachers and blamed their so-called trendy teaching methods for inadequate standards in the classrooms.' The belief that education is no more than the inculcation of knowledge is not only a narrow view, but it ignores elements which, especially in poorer areas, can be fundamental to progress. A. H. Halsey in his 'Educational Priority Area Report' p.8 pointed out how government policies ... 'failed to notice that the major determinants of educational attainment were not school masters but social situations, not curriculum but motivation, not formal access to the school but support in the family and community.'

With a backcloth of statements such as these Sir Alec's forebodings about the future seem less an understandable reaction to the end of the West Riding but a well founded forecast of the future.

2. In 'Half Way There' by Caroline Benn and Brian Simon, published in 1970, Countesthorpe was described, p.356 '...as a prototype of the school of the future.' The authors advised that '...a full assessment of the significance and success of these innovations will not be possible for a few years.' A similar view could have been expressed about Minsthorpe. In 1997 the Principal, Graham Evans, was asked to speak on Minsthorpe at the Institute of Education at the University of London. He pointed out that a quarter of the people in the Minsthorpe catchment area used its facilities and that it was playing a central role in the regeneration of the area.

BIBLIOGRAPHY

Introduction
Times Educational Supplement. 20th September 1974.

Chapter 1
'Nairns London'. Penguin p.230.
Times Educational Supplement. 20th September 1974.
These two volumes are in Lady Clegg's personal collection.
Lady Clegg's personal collection.
'The Story of a School' by Arthur Stone.

Chapter 2
Raymond Williams - 'The Long Revolution'.
Much of the information in this chapter is based on the Clegg Papers which were taken to Wakefield Archives from Woolley Hall and which had not been categorised when this book was completed. Chapter 3 is based on the Clegg Papers as well.

Chapter 4
R. Lewis and A. Maude - 'The English Middle Classes'. Pelican.
T.S. Eliot - 'Notes towards the Definition of Culture.' pp.97-98.

Chapter 5
Lord Alexander. Died in 1993. Obituary 'The Guardian' 9th September 1993.
N. Pevsner - 'Buildings of England. Yorkshire. The West Riding.' p.146.

Chapter 6
N. Pevsner - 'Buildings of England. Yorkshire. The West Riding.' p.352.
Norman Dennis, Fernando Henriques and Clifford Slaughter - 'Coal is Our Life'. Tavistock Publication.

Chapter 7
G.A.N. Lowndes - 'The Silent Social Revolution'. Oxford University Press.
Thorne Scheme - see p.91.
Liam Hudson - 'Contrary Imaginations'. Pelican Books. p.136.
Herbert Read - 'Henry Moore'. Chapter 2. Early Education.

Chapter 8

Lord Robbins - 'Autobiography of an Economist'. Macmillan. p.274.
Course 276 at Woolley Hall.
Sidney Pollard and Colin Holmes - 'Essays in the Economic and Social History of South Yorkshire'. Introduction.

Chapter 9

Edward Boyle. ' Half Our Future'. Piv. HMSO.
D. Ayerst - 'Understanding Schools' p.202. Pelican.
See Courses at Woolley Hal 1952 - 1974 at the end of Chapter 11.
W. G. Hoskins - 'English Landscape'. BBC

Chapter 10

Derek Birley. 'The education officer and his world' p.3. Routledge and Kegan Paul.
See pp.100-101 for details on Mrs Pyrah's class at Airedale Middle School.
Times Educational Supplement 4/10/1974.

Chapter 11

Sir Richard Livingstone 'The Future in Education ' p.126 . Cambridge U.P.
Maurice Collis 'Stanley Spencer.' p.34 . Harvill Press. 1962.
Ten Years of Change. W.Riding Education . p.21.
Christopher Tugendhat . 'The Multinationals' Pelican 1971.

Chapter 12

Iona and Peter Opie 'Children's Games in Street and Playground' p.vi. Oxford U. P.
William Walsh, Professor of Education, Leeds University writing in the Yorkshire Post .12th February 1964.
Letter dated 11th January 1966. File in Clegg Papers - Excitement of Writing.
Letter dated 6th November 1963. File in Clegg Papers - Excitement of Writing.
Letter dated 2nd April 1964.
Letter from Ann Arden Clarke 10th July 1964.
Barry Hines 'A Kestrel For a Knave' p.118 .Penguin.
Stan Barstow, introduction to 'Enjoying writing'
Letter from Herbert Read 6th January 1964.
Yorkshire Post 12th February 1964.
Letter From Alec Clegg to G.C.Allen, 13th August 1963.

Writer of the Foreword to 'The Excitement of Writing'
Letter from Witchford County Secondary School - Ely 13th October 1964.
North of England Conference. Address by Robert Birley - January 1956.
Jewkes, Sawers and Stillerman 'The Sources of Invention' p.223.

Chapter 13
Professor Tribble - Director of the School of Education, Leicester
University.
Professor A.J.Ayer - Professor of Logic, Oxford University.
Professor Peters - Professor of Philosophy of Education, University of
London.
Paper on 'The Aims of Education' .Working Paper No. 4 by E. Blishen.
p.5 of evidence from A. B. Clegg. Education Officer of W.Riding.
p.396 The Plowden Report.
p.136 'The Politics of Education' Edward Boyle and Anthony Crosland in
conversation with Maurice Kogan.
Paragraph 949 The Plowden Report.
Paragraph 960 The Plowden Report.
p.176 R.M.Titmuss 'Essays on the Welfare State'
Department of Education and Science 9. 13 Middle Schools. 1983.
B.Megson 'Economic deprivation in School Children'

Chapter 14
Presidential address by A. B. Clegg to the Association of Chief Education
Officers New Society . 11th February 1965.
Report and Proposals of the Local Government Commission Proposal No.7.
Proposed non-county borough of Wakefield. Public Inquiry 8th February
1965.
Proof of Evidence of A. B. Clegg County Education Officer.
Proof of Evidence of A. B. Clegg to Public Inquiry 9th February 1965
Report to A. B. Clegg May 1964.
Report to A. B. Clegg 1965.
Memo. 7th May 1968. 'Waste of Human Potential in Education'
Jan 1968. Quoted by A. B. Clegg at the North of England Conference.
p.197 'Commitment to Welfare' by R. M. Titmuss.
p.198 'Commitment to Welfare' by R. M. Titmuss.
p.117 Chapter 8. as above
See Appendix giving details of the Curriculum at Rufford Comprehensive
School.
p.17 B. Jackson 'Working Class Community.'

Chapter 15

p.175. Barbara Megson 'Children in Distress'. Penguin Education Special. Royal Borough of Kingston-on-Thames.

17th October 1966. Letter from a Divisional Education officer, D.Foulds, on twilight children.

10th October 1961. Report to the Policy and Finance Sub-Committee. Unit at Sheffield dealing with cerebral palsy.

A detailed study sponsored by the Department of Education and Science Research Council. Edited by A.H.Halsey . p.2 of Volume 1. The Context. See Chapter 19. Conisborough and Dartington Hall.

Notes sent to Alec Clegg by a headteaccher.

Sir Alec Clegg 'Recipe of for Failure' 1972 National Children's Home Convocation Lecture.

Chapter 16

p.324 Y. Menuhin 'Unfinished Journey'

p.62 'The Final Ten Years 1964-1974'

One of Alec Clegg's Assistant Education Officers.

'Sick Cities' - A Penguin Special by Mitchell Gordan.

p.220 'Sick Cities'

Chapter 17

A comparison made in correspondence between Alec Clegg and a group of heads of junior and infant schools.

Half Way There' - Report on the British Comprehensive School Reform by Caroline Benn and Brian Simon. Penguin.

Ashton was Featherstone.

Recipe for Failure' - the National Children's Home Convocation Lecture 1972.

p.35 'The Final Ten Years 1964-1974'

Progress Report 1973 on the Red House Social Work Programmes.

Collection of papers on the Alternative School Experiment.

'Kes' by Barry Hines.

p.69 'Protest and Discontent' Penguin Books 1970.

27th September 1969.

'Degree of Defiance' 1969.

'Writing by Candlelight' E.P.Thompson - a term used in descriptions of Warwick University.

Letter dated 22nd July 1969.

p.45 'the Final ten Years 1964 - 1974.

'Yorkshire Survey' by Donald Wade.

p.221 'Essays on the welfare state' - Richard Titmuss.

Chapter 18

p.108 'The Culture of Contentment' - J. K. Galbraith.

p.13 - Section 10 - Conclusion, Summary and Implications, West Riding Educational Priority Area Project.

A memorandum on 'County University Awards' - a personal file. 1956.

County University Chest' - John Betjeman.

'The People's Peace' - British History 1945 - 1990. Kenneth. O. Morgan.

Chapter 19

Coventry, London, Middlesex, Oldham and the West Riding.

Definition of 'genocide' used in the Nuremberg Trial.

The Education Officer's visit to Australia. Report to the Policy and Finance Committee 14th January 1958.

Canadian Education and Research Digest - Volume 7. Number 1. March 1967.

James D Koerner - 'The Mis-education of the American Teacher'

Talk given by Diana Jordan to the fourth Anglo-Norwegian Course at Woolley Hall.

p.111 'The Excitement of Writing.'

Douglas Dunn 'Northlight' - Memory and Imagination.'

Quotation from a lecture by Professor Bronowski to the R.I.B.A.

Chapter 20

Sybil Marshall - 'An Experiment in Education.' Cambridge University Press 1963.

Times Educational Supplement 29.9.74

'Tales of a Rat Hunting Man' published 1978.

p.132. 'Innovation and Research in Education.'

p.134. 'Innovation and Research in Education.'

The speakers included Dr Jean Wynn Reeves, author of 'Body and Mind in Western Thought; Roger Young, sixth form master Manchester Grammar School;

Mr. M. M. Simmons, Headmaster of Derby School.

Fabian Research Series. No.237 - January 1964.

Young Fabian Pamphlet. No.26 September .1971.

p.30. The Politics of Education'. Penguin.

Report of Royal Commission on Local Government - 1969.

Report to the Policy and Finance Sub-committee - 9th September 1969.

Chapter 21

Public Enquiry - Proposal No.7. -Proposed non-county borough of Wakefield.

Proof of Evidence of A.B.Clegg C.E.O West Riding.

Paragraph 2 of public Enquiry on Proposed non-county borough of Wakefield.

Times Educational Supplement 2/4/71.

See also Times Educational Supplement 19/3/71. Reports on speech at the Commonwealth Institute and the Encyclopaedia Britannica Conference.

'This is my problem' - Article by Sir A.Clegg in the Local Government Review. 21st October 1972.

'This is my Problem.'

Letter from W.Gamble, Department of Education and Science to Miss R. Scrivenor - 30th November, 1972.

Private files.

R. M. Titmuss 'Essays on the Welfare State.' 'The Irresponsible Society.'

Catherine Avant was a fellow member of the Newsom and Crowther Committees.

Children in Distress' 40,931 sold by September 1970.

'A Language for Life' - Report of the Bullock Committee.

p.5. 'Children with Educational and Related Difficulties in Primary Schools Report on Screening Procedure by Dennis Pickles . 19/11/1973.

Extract from a letter to P.J.Butcher, 23rd November 1970.

This letter and accompanying information was sent to Lord Boyle in preparation for a speech he was to make N.U.T at Hemsworth.

p.514 'Caning, Behaviour and Discipline in Secondary Schools.'

p.xxi B. H. Liddell-Hart - 'The Rommel Papers.'

INDEX

325

F

G

H

331

Quotations are acknowledged as follows:

Publishers

Page

Pelican Books
7   Ian Nairn - 'Nairn's London' 1966
33   Robert Frost - Penguin Poets 'The road not taken' 1955
49 & 187   Lewis and Maude - The English Middle Classes' 1953
76   Nikolaus Pevsner - 'The Buildings of England. The West Riding'
        Penguin 1959
95   Liam Hudson - 'Contrary Imaginations' Pelican 1967
110   Dennis Potter - 'The Nigel Barton Plays' Penguin 1967
117   David Ayerst - 'Understanding Schools' Pelican 1967
169 & 229 Barry Hines - 'A Kestrel for a Knave' © Barry Hines 1968
193   Brian Jackson and Dennis Marsden - 'Education and the Working
        Class' Penguin Books
216   Mitchell Gordon - 'Sick Cities' Penguin 1966
221   Caroline Benn - 'Half Way There' Penguin 1972
221   James Jupp - 'Protest and Discontent' Penguin
271   James Jupp - 'The Politics of Education' Penguin 1971

HMSO
14   Richard Titmuss - 'Problems of Social Policy'
12 & 44   Arthurs Stone - 'The Story of a School'
77   The Newsom Report - chapter 24
104 & 112 The Crowther Report 1962 (also p276)
115   Half our Future 1963
261   Figures taken from The Plowden Report
272-3   Report of the Royal Commission on Local Government 1969
277   The Plowden Report

Cambridge University Press
141   Sir Richard Livingstone - 'The Future in Education' 1945

Oxford University Press
17   A.J.P. Taylor - 'English History 1914-1945'
89   G.A.N. Lowndes - 'The Silent Social Revolution' 1937
149   Oxford History of Technology Vol.5 p840 1958
156   Iona & Peter Opie - 'Children's Games in Street and Playground'
110   John Beteman - "An Oxford University Chest' 1979
238-9   A.H. Halsey - 'Change in British Society' 1983 - for Open University
247   Kenneth O'Morgan - 'The People's Peace'

Unwin University Books

179	R.M. Titmuss - 'Essays on the Welfare State' 1964
179	R.M. Titmuss - 'The Irresponsible Society' 1964
226	R.M. Titmuss - 'Essays on the Welfare State'
250	R.M. Titmuss - 'Essays on the Welfare State'

George Allen and Unwin

219	Barbara Wootton - 'Social Science and Social Pathology' 1959

Single Quotes

6	Harry Rée - 'Educator Extraordinary' Peter Owen, London 1973 & 1985
10	B.S. Rowntree - 'Human Needs of Labour' Longmans, Green & Co. 1937
18	R. Williams - 'The Long Revolution' Chatto and Windus
18 & 19	Leonard Clark - 'The Inspector Remembers' London 1976
24-5	The Advisory Council of Education for Scotland
40	Richard Ollard - 'An English Education' A perspective of Eton. Collins 1982
45	Sir Herbert Read - 'Education Through Art' Faber & Faber
46	Harold Massingham - 'Black Bull Guarding Apples' p28 Longmans 1965
82	Dennis, Henriques and Slaughter - 'Coalis our Life' p235 Tavistock Publications 1969
96	Clegg quote of A.N. Whitehead
97	Herbert Read - 'Bibliography of Henry Moore' Thames and Hudson 1965
105	Lord Robbins - 'Autobiography of an Economist' Macmillan 1971
118	W. Hoskins - 'The English Landscape' p6 BBC 1973
118	Arthur Raistrick - 'W. Riding of Yorkshire' Hodder & Stoughton 1970
129	Derek Birley - 'The education officer and his world' p3 Routledge & Kegan Paul 1970
133	Hansard. Maiden speech of Miss Harvie Anderson, MP for Renfrew East - ?1960
145	Maurice Collis - 'Stanley Spencer - A Biography' p34 Harvill Press 1962
154	L.T.C. Rolt - 'Isambard Kingdom Brunel' p319 Readers Union. Longmans, Green & Co. 1959
169	B.H. Liddell-Hart - 'The Letters of Private Wheeler' p9 of the foreword. Michael Joseph 1951
175	Schools Council Working Papers. WP4 Evans/Methuen International
181	Middle Schools, 9-13. 1983 Dept. of Education and Science.

189	Seebohn Report on Local Authority and Allied Personal Social Services. Rowntree Foundation 1968
191	Catherine Caulfield - 'Thorne Moors' The Sumach Press
222	N. Dennis, F. Henriques and C. Slaughter - 'Coal is Our Life' Tavistock Publications 1971
235	Donald Wade - 'Yorkshire Survey' Published by the Yorkshire Committee for Community Relations, Leeds
238	J.K. Galbraith - 'The Culture of Contentment' Sinclair Stevenson Ltd 1992
241	Eric Ashby - 'Technology and the Academics' p95 Macmillan 1963
254	J.D. Koerner - 'The Mis-education of the American Teacher'
256	Robert Nye. Quoted by Sir Alec from the New Statesman, 10th MNovember 1972 in The Excitement of Writing.
257	Douglas Dunn - 'Northlight' Memory and Imagination, Faber & Faber 1988
257	Quote from a lecture by Professor Bonowski to the RIBA also quoted on p176
271	Young Fabian Pamphlet - 'Aspects of Education' Published by the Fabian Society.
279	Gosden & Sharp - 'The Development of an Education Service. The West Riding 1889 - 1974'. Martin Robertson
293	B.H. Liddell-Hart - 'The Rommel Papers' p xxi Collins 1953

Newspapers

157	William Walsh - Yorkshire Post, 12th February 1964
161	William Walsh - Yorkshire Post, 12th February 1964
233	The Bingley Strike - Yorkshire Post, 27th September 1969
277	Times Educational Supplement, 2nd April 1971